In China's Image

Also by Rupert Hodder

MERCHANT PRINCES OF THE EAST
THE CREATION OF WEALTH IN CHINA
THE WEST PACIFIC RIM

In China's Image

Chinese Self-Perception in Western Thought

Rupert Hodder
Senior Lecturer
Department of Geography
University of Plymouth

First published in Great Britain 2000 by
MACMILLAN PRESS LTD
Houndmills, Basingstoke, Hampshire RG21 6XS and London
Companies and representatives throughout the world

A catalogue record for this book is available from the British Library.

ISBN 0–333–91795–2

First published in the United States of America 2000 by
ST. MARTIN'S PRESS, LLC,
Scholarly and Reference Division,
175 Fifth Avenue, New York, N.Y. 10010

ISBN 0–312–23357–4

Library of Congress Cataloging-in-Publication Data
Hodder, Rupert.
In China's image : Chinese self-perception in western thought / Rupert Hodder.
p. cm.
Includes bibliographical references and index.
ISBN 0–312–23357–4 (cloth)
1. China—Foreign public opinion. I. Title.

DS706 .H536   2000
306'.0951 — dc21

00–022307

This book is printed on paper suitable for recycling and made from fully managed and sustained forest sources.

10   9   8   7   6   5   4   3   2   1
09   08   07   06   05   04   03   02   01   00

Printed and bound in Great Britain by
Antony Rowe Ltd, Chippenham, Wiltshire

For Mum

Contents

Preface

This book has grown out of an article entitled 'China and the World' published in *The Pacific Review*. In this book, and in the original article, I question our perceptions of China. I argue that what is commonly understood to be 'China' is, in large part, a collage of images. These images – created and manipulated by individuals and groups within the boundaries of the Chinese state in order to pursue their own social, economic and political ambitions – have been accepted, elaborated upon, strengthened and made legitimate by European and American social scientists and by other professional commentators on China. I further argue that policies towards China, if shaped or strongly conditioned by these images, are likely to prove either inappropriate or dangerous.

It is worth saying at the outset that although this book may seem polemical (more so, perhaps, to the professional commentator on China than to the lay reader), I have not deliberately set out to make it so. I will undoubtedly be accused of grinding axes, of misunderstanding Chinese ways, and of either missing or ignoring or over-simplifying the subtle intricacies of sinological analyses. That I have chosen not to use materials written in Chinese will only confirm in the minds of some the ignobleness of my commentary on the *cognoscenti* of the Chinese world. These charges are understandable, for I am not merely questioning the details of interpretation: I am also criticising the techniques with which they are constructed and their philosophical foundations; and I am suggesting that however esoteric our sinological mantras may appear to be, they are also a very real part of the hard politics of the everyday. But it seems to me that these kinds of criticisms should be made. China is now simply too important for mystification: our understanding of, and our attitudes towards, China will affect not only how we deal with China, but also how China views itself and responds to the outside world. Moreover, the notion of an essential 'difference' which is so strongly associated with China, as indeed it is with 'the East' in general, has clear implications for the quality of every society, for it implies that we should defer to culture rather than to values held to be universal and to the interests of each individual.

And so I make no apologies, either for the criticisms which are leveled here at many of our understandings of China, or for the way in which they are phrased. These strictures, and the wider issues they raise, ought to be stated clearly and forcefully, placed into the public arena, and there subjected to open criticism and debate, rather than confined and censured by the narrower concerns of a small section of academe. I do not pretend this book to be anything more than a personal view of China; but I do hope that the reader will find this book stimulating, and perhaps be persuaded to look once again at China in a more familiar and perhaps more natural light. The Chinese, I believe, are not profoundly different from any other people; and we can, each of us, see ourselves in the other regardless of our own ethnicity or culture; the world is of our making and therefore, like us, possesses many dimensions which both hide and reveal our similarities. To some readers this may appear to be a moral, even spiritual, question; to others, our commonality of being is both logical and self-evident, and has deep political repercussions.

This book, then, is written as much for the informed lay reader, as it is for specialists and students of China. Its intention is to bring to the fore and to make plain that atmosphere of Chineseness, of exclusivity, which I believe pervades sinology. But this necessarily requires an examination (and one that is fairly detailed at times) of the way in which academic analyses are constructed. I would therefore ask those readers who are not professional social scientists, and who may intuitively be sceptical of this 'science', to bear with me, partly because these examinations might help to specify the reasons for their scepticism, but mainly because it is illuminating to see in detail how the particular methods, techniques and ideas of the social scientist are used to imbue China's images with a spurious legitimacy. A broader, more politic survey of Chinese studies, dispensing praise and judicious criticism in equal measure to imagined but convenient schools of thought, would have obeyed academic convention, pleased a few specialists, satisfied the expectations of students and their teachers, avoided charges of misrepresenting and stereotyping the complexities of the debates, and lent itself more easily to a lighter touch. It would also have left that atmosphere of Chineseness which I believe to be so potent – and the details and nuances by which that sense of exclusivity is conveyed – diluted, vague and indistinct. My claim is not that the particular interpretations of events in China selected for criticism in this book are representative of all shades of opinion concerning those events; it is that these interpretations illustrate that sense of the numinous which strongly colours many varied analyses of things Chinese.

Acknowledgements

My thanks to: Mark Blacksell, David Pinder, Mark Cleary, Richard Gibb and other members in my Department; Bob Bennett (Cambridge); Tony Binns (Sussex); Iain Stevenson; and the late Robert Steel. Without their help, advice and support, this book would not have been written. I say this, not because it is customary in the acknowledgements of a book to make these kinds of statements, but simply because it is true.

Introduction

China has always evoked a sense of mystery. Whispers of Cathay have drawn eastwards traders, priests and conquerors from Central Asia, Eurasia, India, Arabia and the Mediterranean at least since the time of Herodotus and Pythagoras. The spice of the exotic, so long as it stimulates curiosity, is always welcome. But now, as China's economic and military power strengthens, and as a desire to extend the reach of its political influence across Asia and the Pacific intensifies, an understanding of China's nature becomes of the greatest interest and importance.

The study of China has certainly been professionalised: the observations and musings of travellers, merchants, civil servants, missionaries and soldiers of the colonial era have long since been replaced by the rigorous scientific inquiries of trained social scientists. And yet there is, I believe, a tendency for this science and a love of the glamour of strangeness to feed upon each other, taking us further away from those individuals and their values, beliefs, desires, understandings, and the institutions which make up China, and placing in their stead a collage of sinological mantras that have *become* China.

This book questions these mantras, and is critical of the inviolability, integrity and purity of the 'non-western'. Doubts are thrown upon: China's historical mythography; the belief that China and Chinese culture evolved largely in isolation; the doctrine that this distinctive culture sinified any outside influences which subsequently penetrated the borders of the Empire; the image of a rational, ancient, generally stable, cohesive, passive and sophisticated moral polity with subterranean democratic elements; the faith in the inherent morality of peculiarly 'Chinese' relationships founded upon reciprocity (or *guanxi*); the belief in the Chineseness of factional politics; the belief that China's peculiarity has been moulded out of the play of aggregates and the vast

1

gyres of social, political, economic and historical forces; the assumption that there is little need to consider what occurs in other parts of the world except in so far as those events may confirm China's difference; and the presumption that such images reliably inform our policies towards China – most especially the policy of constructive engagement.[1] Fuelling trade with China and thus promoting material progress there, may succeed only in hardening a determination to defer to culture. Trade is not a causal force: it may be conducive to the secularisation and atomisation of society, and so to tolerance, the rise of humanitarianism and a concern for welfare, the rule of law, and democracy; but it does not lead to, or create, such practices or attitudes. As China's social and political elites feel more and more threatened by the permeation of trade and the initial signs of secularisation, they may choose to present with greater vigour and prejudice rapid economic success both as a confirmation of the superiority and legitimacy of culture, and as proof of the irrelevance of values, institutions and patterns of behaviour labelled as 'western'. This determination to defer to culture would be strengthened even further if China's leadership were to perceive in democratic states a strengthening reverence for culture and image (whether 'Chinese' or 'western' or both) at the expense of these democratic states' most fundamental belief – the belief that certain values, practices and institutions should be treated, not as material for negotiation, manipulation and compromise, but as if they were universal and absolute. This perception, whether or not it is grounded in fact, would have adverse implications for long-term stability in the Far East.

1
China and the Western Heartland

Introduction

It is commonly stated that China's history is that of the world's longest enduring civilisation. It is also suggested that Chinese culture, initially centred on the Yellow River, evolved largely in isolation at least until the first century BC, by which time it had become so distinctive and well-formed that subsequent external influences were altered more by Chinese culture than Chinese culture was affected by those influences. Indeed, a widely accepted canon is that Chinese civilisation was so far in advance of any other culture, both intellectually and morally, that it profoundly affected, and even initiated, the rise of modern science and technology in Europe. The image of China's history that we are presented with is that of a unique, ancient, superior culture which, over three millennia or more, emerged in isolation, absorbed virgin territory and sinified culturally weaker groups as it spread out from its point of origin, and then went on to produce ideas and inventions that were to have a profound influence upon the rest of the world.

But while the possibility that ideas, beliefs, institutions, arts, technologies, practices and values did arise independently in China cannot be ruled out, this does not equate with uniqueness or with a deterministic culture. The possibility of outside influence must also be given equal weight in any interpretation. Indeed, since Chinese civilisation emerged long after the rise of civilisations to the west and south of China, then, in view of the latitude which sinologists have allowed ideas and devices to flow from China to the rest of the world, it would seem far more likely that Chinese civilisation may have been initially stimulated, and subsequently influenced, by the western heartland – a term used here to describe a complex of civilisations stretching from North Africa to the

Indus, and from the Arabian peninsula to Central Asia and Eurasia (including western Europe).

First contacts

Recorded civilisation in China begins around 1500 BC, roughly the date attributed to inscriptions on oracle bones listing the names of the Shang Kings. Towards the end of the second millennium, the Shang Kingdom was overthrown by the founder of the next dynasty, the Zhou, which at its height encompassed the provinces of Shanxi, Henan, Shangdong and Hebei as we know them today. After the seventh century BC, permanent field cultivation gradually came to be practised, landed property was institutionalised, and the feudal system was replaced slowly by provincial governors and officers. But Imperial China was not formed until 221 BC when Shih Huang Ti, the First Emperor, abolished the feudal states and kingdoms and unified their lands under his command. After his death in 209 there was a struggle for power which left in control Liu Pang, the founder of the Han Dynasty (206 BC to 221 AD). This also marked the beginning of the maturation of Chinese civilisation and, significantly, the intensification of contacts with the outside world.

As imperial China expanded westwards, an envoy was sent to form an alliance with the Yueh Chi – a group long hostile to the Hsiung-nu (the nomadic people of central Asia and the Mongolian Steppes) who were a constant threat to China's north – and thereby to secure the Empire's western borders. The envoy stumbled upon Russian Turkestan where stood the Greek city states still populated by Greek settlers. The second-hand reports of civilisations to the west and south of China taken back to the Chinese court in the first millennium BC from these fading shadows of Alexander's empire are thought to constitute the first official knowledge in China of the western heartland. Towards the end of the first century AD, the Chinese general Pan Chao pushed further west to the shores of the Caspian Sea, and from there sent envoys to Persia and the Roman Empire. It is not known if these envoys managed to reach the Mediterranean, but half a century later embassies from Rome arrived in China, and a second mission arrived in 226 AD. Important though Pan Chao's expedition had been, his discovery had already been preceded many centuries earlier by the movement of traders, adventurers, priests and monks into China from the west.

In the five millennia before the birth of Christ, from Carthage to the Indus valley, and from the Arabian Peninsula to Asia minor, there had arisen a complex of civilisations whose histories of migration, conquest, trade and empire are entwined. This complex (the western heartland), initially centred at the confluence of the African, European, and Asian continental land masses, had gradually expanded as its focus of power shifted from Mesopotamia to the Mediterranean and then, during the first and second millennium of the Christian era, to western Europe which later came to dominate the greater part of humanity, giving shape to the world that we know today.

During the fifth and fourth millennia BC, the Sumerian civilisation emerged from the lands irrigated by the Tigris and Euphrates rivers, while further to the west, from the desert sands made fertile along the lower reaches of the Nile, there arose Egyptian civilisation. From the Arabian peninsula came the Semitic people, including the Hebrews and the Amorites who founded the cities of Damascus and Babylon. During the opening centuries of the second millennium BC Babylonian power was extended from the Persian Gulf to the borders with Syria and the mountains of Asia Minor.

A succession of empires followed, each greater than its predecessor. Babylon was destroyed and its lands seized by the Hittites – Indo-Europeans skilled in working iron who had made their way into Mesopotamia from the north. They extended the realm of their poached empire to the borders of Egypt, and drew in Anatolia, the original homeland of these invaders where it is thought the first cities arose in 8000 BC, and where composite tools with mastic handles dating back some 36,000 years have been unearthed. The Hittites were replaced by the Assyrians who absorbed Egypt to the west and Persia to the east. They, in turn, were overthrown by their Persian subjects whose empire, which stretched from Greece and North Africa to the edge of the central Asian steppes and the Indus Valley, was held together until the third century BC. In the Indus Valley, more than two thousand years earlier in the third millennium BC, the Harappan civilisation, dominated by its priests, reached its zenith only to succumb to the Indo-Europeans who moved in from the north in the opening centuries of the second millennium BC. It was also at this time that the influence of Cretan civilisation in the far west of the heartland had begun to spread across the Aegean to the Bosphores, before it, too, fell to the Indo-Europeans, some of whom settled on the Ionian peninsula, thereby sowing the seeds of Greek civilisation. As the Persian empire began to wane, the Hellenistic world began to rise. Under Alexander the Great (a pupil of Aristotle (384–322 BC)) the power of the Greeks reached from Egypt to Afghanistan and the Punjab.

Alexander brought together the new civilisation of Greece and the older civilisations of the Near East. In the first century BC the Greeks were replaced by the Romans as the dominant power in North Africa, Greece, Asia Minor, and the Near East; and it was the Romans who began to push the boundaries of the western heartland, and the centre of power, into western Europe. Yet despite the efforts of Byzantium, Charlemagne and the Crusaders, it was not until the Mongol invasions of the middle ages that the power of the Near East was finally ended.

This history of empire, conquest and repression, is also that of stimulus, of trade, and of the exchange and flow of ideas, beliefs, institutions, practices, and values. The early Sumerian documents include lists showing the ownership of goods and wealth. The pictographs which had preceded their cuneiform script were adapted and absorbed by the Egyptians into their own pictorial script; the gods of the Indo-Europeans emerged in the Pantheon of Greece and as the Vedic deities of India; and Rome adopted the Persian tradition of emperor worship – the god-ruler, the symbol to bind together diverse peoples. The Greek alphabet was adapted from the phonetic alphabet of the Phoenicians[1] whose settlements (including Carthage, the greatest of them all) were built on, and helped to protect, the trade routes which extended as far west as Cornwall and through which metal was brought into western Europe. The fragmented, self-governing Greek city states built around the Mediterranean from Cyprus to Spain and North Africa also created ideal stimuli for trade. And the philosophy, law, language, calendars, architecture, metallurgy, technology, institutions and beliefs (most especially Christianity) that Rome took from its own traditions, from Greece and from other parts of the western heartland into western Europe were key instruments in the formation and rise of the European states.

India, too, was an integral part of these exchanges at least from Neolithic times. The earliest agricultural communities in India are thought to have arisen just to the west of the Indus river in Baluchistan which forms the eastern border of the Iranian plateau that stretches to the Tigris-Euphrates plain in the west, and to the Elburz and Kopet Dagh mountains and the Oxus valley in the north. During the period 8000–5000 BC these communities developed mud-brick architecture, cultivated wheat and barley, and domesticated cattle, sheep and goats. By the end of that period trade links the Arabian south coast and Central Asia seem to have been established. The discovery of turquoise beads and humped backed trapezes at Mergarh – sited at the mouth of the Bolan Pass, one of the main routes onto the Indus Plain – suggests that links with Djeitan in Turkemenia already existed towards the end of the sixth millennium BC.[2]

By the middle of the fourth millennium, when pottery and copper tools were in greater use, other communities in the north of the Indus valley had begun to emerge. The pit dwellings of these northern sites, the form of the bone tools, the rectangular perforated stone knives, the jade beads and the practice of placing dogs in the same graves as humans are all features of the Neolithic sites of northern China. This would appear to indicate that by the end of the third millennium BC, links between the Indus valley and northern China were already established. So, too, the material culture of Assam, dating from around 2000 BC, possibly much earlier, suggests trade links with southern China.

It is possible that the trade contacts between Central Asia, Persia and Mesopotamia (and probably also Egypt and Africa) provided the stimulus for incipient urbanism in Afghanistan, in Baluchistan (the transition zone between the upland plateau and the flood plain of the Indus), and in the Indus valley itself.[3] Certainly, trading contacts appear to have intensified with the emergence of towns (many of which were ports or trading posts) from the beginning of the third millennium BC, in Afghanistan (such as Mundighak, a great caravan city, and Shortugai, a trading post further to the northeast on the southern plains of the Oxus, just beyond the high passes of the Hindu Kush); in Baluchistan (including Sutkagen Dor on the Makran coast near the modern frontier of Pakistan and Iran); and in India (including Lothal, a trading post on the Gulf of Cambay) as well as throughout the Indus Valley. By the time mature urban forms had begun to appear during the middle of the third millennium BC, trade in silver, ebony, lead, carnelian, turquoise, fuschite, lapis lazuli, copper, beads, ivory, combs, alabaster, shells, amethysts, and figurines made of copper, bronze or terra-cotta (and, it may be presumed, less durable goods such as timber) had been established with Central Asia and Afghanistan, Persia, Arabia and the Persian Gulf, Mesopotamia, South and West India, Rajasthan, and possibly Africa. Trade seems to have been conducted overland by caravan, although there is circumstantial evidence for sea trade. There is also evidence from shell, ivory and brass measurement scales dated to around 2500–2000 BC which shows that the Mohenjo-daro (in the Indus Valley) had a definite idea of decimal scale; and the system of stone weights proceeded in a series, first doubling, from 1, 2, 4, up to 64, then going to 160; then in decimal multiples of 16, 320, 640, 1600, 3200, 6400, 8000, and 128,000.[4] This system of weights and measures, together with the Harappan seals, appear to have been developed for, or became a part of, the regulation of trade.

Contacts between the Indus valley, Persia, and Central Asia proved strong and enduring. Around the beginning of the second millennium BC Indo-Aryans moved from the east of the Caspian sea into the Iranian plateau and from there spread gradually southwest and southeast into

India. The original homeland of these people is thought to have been the steppes of Eurasia which stretch from the frontiers with China to the borders of Western Europe. This vast area is also thought to have been the homeland of the wild ancestors of the horse which, it appears, was first domesticated around the Dneper and Don Basins to the north of the Black Sea during the second half of the fourth millennium.[5] Evidence of their material culture to the west of the Urals dating from around the end of the fourth millennium BC indicates that they used a range of weapons and tools made from bronze and copper. On the eastern side of the Urals in the south Cheliabinsk region is the site of the earliest known examples of horse-drawn chariots which date from around 1500 BC. The earliest spoked wheels so far discovered, however, come from Anatolia and Syria and date from around the eighteenth or seventeenth centuries BC at which time the true horse (a northern animal) were to be found in several parts of the Near East. This sequence of events, and the absence of Aryan terms in the Hittite and Assyrian manuals on chariot training, suggests that the horse-drawn chariot arose out of interaction between the people of the Asian steppes and the Middle and Near East.[6] It was not until Zhou times that the Chariot was introduced into China from the west.

Roughly coincident with the movement of the Indo-Europeans was the beginning of the bronze age in China, which had come rather late (around the eighteenth to sixteenth centuries BC). Bronze was in use around Lake Baykal (to the north of present-day Mongolia) prior to these dates and, as we have already noted, bronze tools and weapons were in use to the west of the Urals by the end of the fourth millennium; bronze was also being worked in Mundighak long before 3000 BC; and the fine bronze vessels and figurines, crafted in specialised workshops in the cities of the Indus Valley, indicate that the working of bronze was well understood in Harappan civilisation by the beginning of the third millennium BC. Iron, which is thought to have been used in West Asia by around 1300 BC, and was in common use in India by 800 BC, does not appear in China until around 600 BC, and was not commonly in use there until 500–400 BC. And while steel of high quality arrived in India probably with Alexander in fourth century BC, it was not in use in China until several centuries later.

A further consideration that is often forgotten but which may well help towards an understanding of the orientation of Chinese civilisation towards the western heartland is China's geographical and geological make-up. Northern China comprises, in part, the Xinjiang-Mongolian highland plain. This stretches from China's far western borders across the Tarim and Dzungarian Basins (which merge with the steppes of Kazakstan and south-central Russia), across the northern half of Gansu, Mongolia and Inner Mongolia (skirting the northern edges of Ningxia, Shaanxi, Shanxi and Hubei) to the Great Khingan mountains which run south from Russia to meet the Johol, Daqing, Taihang and Luliang ranges, and so form the eastern border of the Xinjiang-Mongolian highland. These ranges converge upon the Liupan mountains, part of the Tibetan plateau and highlands which border the southern edge of the Xinjiang-Mongolian highlands. On the other side of the Great Khingan-Luliang-Liupan border uplands lie the coastal and river valley lowlands which reach from Heilongjiang (in northeast China, formerly know as Manchuria) to Shanghai. Running east–west from this broad lowland strip are the two great rivers – the Huanghe (the Yellow River) and the Changjiang (or Yangtse).

The great valleys which form deep striations in the Tibetan Plateau and Highlands create the impression of a giant swirl that pours out of south-west Xinjiang, Afghanistan, Kashmir and Pakistan along China's southern borders, first southeast, then west-east parallel to the northern borders of Nepal (but perpendicular to the Nepalese valleys which run from north to south into India), and then south into Indo-China. These great river valleys include: the Indus, which originates in Tibet before flowing out through Kashmir into Pakistan; the Brahmaputra, which runs parallel along most of Tibet's southern flank before turning sharply to the south into Assam; and the Mekong and Salween, which follow the great swirl into Indochina. The sources of the Huanghe and Changjiang lie just outside the administrative boundary of Tibet, but within the Tibetan Plateau and Highlands which spill out into Yunnan, Sichuan, Qinghai and Gansu. The Huanghe cuts vast loops northwards through the Tibetan Plateau and Highlands, emerging at Lanzhou just to the west of the Liupan mountains from where it flows north, then east and then south through the mountainous edge of the Xinjiang-Mongolian highlands and out onto the coastal and river valley lowlands. The Changjiang first runs south parallel to the Mekong and Salween and then makes a sudden turn east into the Sichuan basin, from where it cuts through the Tapa, Wuling and Dalei mountains (which run southwest to converge with the great Tibetan swirl), before it too drops on to the coastal and river valley lowlands.

For reasons of practical logistics, one might expect people and ideas to have moved along these distinctive geographical and geological features since the earliest times. (The notion that the development of modern humans was multi-centred has now lost much ground to the view that all modern humans arose out of Africa in migratory waves some 100,000–200,000 years ago.) It would also seem likely, therefore, that northern China would have been oriented more strongly towards north, central and perhaps South Asia than towards either the lands and people of China's southern uplands (southeast China) which border the Changjiang valley, or the southwestern plateau which converges with the Great Tibetan swirl that flows south and southeast into Indochina.

It is perhaps significant that during the period of the Warring States (481–221 BC) the main lines of statecraft and strategies were the rival 'horizontal' and 'vertical' policies.[7] Horizontal meant an alliance from Ch'in (to the west of the Huanghe, including Shensi, Gansu and Sichuan) to the Ch'i in the east (which corresponds roughly with Shangdong and Hebei). The vertical meant from Ch'u (the middle and lower Yangtse) in the south to the Yan (around Liaoning in the north) who established their capital on the site of modern Beijing. The site was well chosen for it commands the route along the eastern side of the mountains to Manchuria (northeast China), avoiding the marshy areas near the coast; it is also close to the three main passes through the Khingan-Taihang mountain ranges to the Xinjiang-Mongolian highlands. It was along the eastern and southern uplands of the Xinjiang-Mongolian highlands that a series of border fortifications were constructed prior to the establishment of the Chinese empire. These fortifications were extended by the First Emperor (Shih Huang Ti of the Chin Dynasty) to form the Great Wall which ran just to the north of Beijing from the coast of Bohai to Xinjiang.

Beijing therefore had great strategic importance for the control of north China – a point that was not lost on either the Tang dynasty which set up the headquarters of the northern Frontier Command in Beijing, or on the Khublai Khan who fixed Beijing as the capital. Far to the west of Beijing, and more than 600km northwest of Lanzhou towards the western end of the Gansu corridor, lay Suchow, described by Cable[8] as the most important mart in the northwest, the last town in what used to be China proper, and only 15 miles from the fort of Kiayukwan, a portal of the Great Wall. Here traders from Turkestan, Tibet, Mongolia, Khotan, Kashga and Asqu and from the coastal and river valley lowlands in the east bought and sold their wares; and it was here that Benedict de Goes (on his way to Peking) arrived from Lahore, India, in 1602. It is at Suchow that the main trade routes converge:

the north trunk road leading to Lake Zaisan and passing through Hami, Kuchengtze, Urumchi, Manass and Chuguchak; the Kashgar south road trough Turfan, Qara Shar, Kucha and Asqu; and the Mongolian desert road through the Edsin Gol and Pehlingmiao to Peiping. Finally, there is the Pilgrim's foot-track across Tibet to Lhasa.[9]

These routes linked China with central and west Asia, Mongolia with Kashgar, and Manchuguo with Kuldja where the Manchurian language was still spoken. In many of the small villages of Turkestan the call to prayer was 'sounded from the minaret by a *hajji* who has taken the journey to Mecca by the Karakaran Pass and Bombay or Karachi.'[10]

Other examples of markets scattered along trade routes were the bazaars of Turfan (in what is now Xinjiang province). Here and in the surrounding settlements on the Turfan plain Grecian heads, beads and pots, and scripts (including Manichean-Syrian and Sogdian) had been found, as well as 'a great hoard of Christian manuscripts, including a complete Psalter, fragments of the Nicene Creed, portions of St. Matthew's Gospel, the legend of the finding of the Holy Cross by the Empress Helena, and numerous liturgical and Nestorian documents in the Syrian language and script.'[11]

Indeed, as early as the first century AD, when Buddhism was recognised by the Chinese court, prosperous city states (which also came under Chinese suzerainty at about this time), built on the trade between China, India and the Roman Empire, had already emerged on the watersheds of the Oxus[12] and Tarim rivers. Greek, Persian, Indian and Central Asian languages, architecture, coinage, and arts existed together in these city states, for it was through here that travellers, merchants, priests and Buddhist monks (the majority of whom were central Asians) moved back and forth between China and the western heartland along the great caravan routes. It was also at about this time that a knowledge of the relationship between mathematical properties and music may have reached China from Babylon and possibly from Greece.[13] Ideas and observations from Babylon concerning astronomy and calendar making may have also influenced the development of astronomy in China before the Birth of Christ. The discovery in the Altai region (in the far northwest where China, Mongolia, Russia and Kazakstan converge) of a Pazyryk woman dating from around the fifth century BC, buried with silk from India and embalmed in a manner very similar to that described by Herodotus, suggests that at least 500 years before the recognition of Buddhism, the routes between China, India, Central Asia and the rest of the western heartland were already well travelled. The cowrie shells, bronze artifacts, fine woolen cloth woven using techniques similar to those practised in northwest Europe, and the remains of Caucasoids unearthed in the Tarim Basin near the Tianshan mountains (to the south of the Altai region) suggests that earlier still, by about 1200 BC, there was trade with India, Persia, Central Asia, Siberia and northwest Europe, and that, as Barber and Mair believe, Europeans had already made the long journey to China.

It was also by around the first century AD that Tibet, as a people and as a state, began to emerge. The people, a mixture of Caucasoid and Mongolian nomad groups, were drawn together into a federation initially centred on the Yalong river valley (which runs parallel to the Salween, Mekong, and upper reaches of the Changjiang before joining the latter river as it turns eastwards into the Sichuan basin). The emerging state grew along the Brahmaputra which, together with its tributaries, attracts the highest concentration of settlements and population in Tibet. The movement of the capital from the Yalong valley to Lhasa on a tributary of the Brahmaputra took place during the expansion of the Tibetan empire which at its height during the seventh and eighth centuries AD encompassed Nepal, the northern end of the Gulf of Bengal, east Turkestan, Khotan on the Tarim basin, broke through at Lanzhou and pushed out north and east, threatening the Gansu corridor. By this time, too, the Gupta writing system was adopted and Buddhism was meshed with existing beliefs to create Lamaism.

South China, meanwhile, appears to have been oriented towards East, South and Southeast Asia. By about 1100 BC the Pai, a group of the Taishan people, had constructed a walled town on the site of present-day Canton which later became the capital of the southern Yueh. By the middle of the latter part of the first millennium BC, possibly much earlier, the Yueh were trading with East and Southeast Asia, including Sumatra, with Indian traders in the Indian Ocean, and with southern outposts of the Chou Dynasty. Hangzhou, at the border of the southern uplands and the Yangtse, is an old Yueh trading post that later became the capital of the southern Sung and, by the around the twelfth century AD, reputedly one of the largest and wealthiest cities in the world. Another city which borders the southern uplands and the Yangtse is Changsha, once the capital of the Ch'u. At the height of their powers, the Ch'u, another southern group, captured and ruled the more southerly states of the Chou, including lands in the Yangtse and Huaihe river valleys. As the northern Chinese expanded, however, the southerners, who had built their wealth on trade between northern China and East, South and Southeast Asia, were either absorbed by the northerners or pushed into Laos, Burma, Siam and Vietnam (or Yuenan – South Yueh). Linguistic differences and, more recently, genetic evidence, would seem to confirm this division and the respective orientation of north and south China.[14] One other interesting piece of evidence which may be relevant to the nature of this divide, is the discovery at Sanxingdui, in Sichuan province, of gold, bronze, jade, stone and pottery objects, charred animals and elephant tusks dating from around twelfth to thirteenth centuries BC on the site of an early walled city constructed before 1500 BC (and therefore contemporaneous with the Shang). There are similarities, but also significant differences, between these artifacts and those of the Shang.

It would seem likely, therefore, that many centuries before the beginning of the Chinese empire, merchants and agriculturists in China knew of, or at least had contact with, the western heartland. Indeed, the chronology of the rise of cities and civilisations, the apparently long history of trading contacts among the civilisations of northern Africa and the Mediterranean, the Middle East, most especially Persia and Mesopotamia, Central Asia, India and China, and the origins and movement of the Indo-Aryans south and east from Eurasia, strongly suggest that the western heartland stimulated the rise and development of Chinese civilisation. Eberhard suggested that ideas, devices and practices may have been brought to China by nomadic craftsmen from West Asia.[15] Sjoberg, too, observed that 'The earliest Chinese cities shared numerous traits with those in the Middle East and were considerably later in time than the latter, making it difficult to believe that at least some diffusions of urbanising influences did not occur': any extreme inventionist position, he argued, seemed dubious.[16]

Trade and China's ossification

The influence of the western heartland upon the subsequent evolution of Chinese civilisation after the first century AD and the official recognition of Buddhism appears to have been equally strong. As early as 300 AD Arab merchants had set up a counting house in Canton, by which time Arab, Persian and Indian seafarers dominated the trade routes from Africa to the Far East. Two centuries earlier, Indian merchants, followed by Brahmin priests, had begun to spread Hindu culture throughout Southeast Asia. And it was India, far more so than China, that came to have a profound influence upon Southeast Asia.[17] It was at the beginning of the fourth century AD that Tartars invaded China and held on to the north of the country for nearly three hundred years until the end of the sixth century. The arts, literature and architecture flourished and acquired new forms; external contacts with west and central Asia, India and Afghanistan intensified; and the influence of Buddhism strengthened. In the second half of the first millennium, contact and trade with the western heartland, including Syria, Byzantium and India, developed still further; Indian trade had itself become part and parcel of the Mediterranean economy by the tenth century;[18] and from the southern ports, through the medium of Arab merchants, there was traffic even with Africa.

But the most vigorous period of commercial activity and technological development in China – a period during which achievements in philosophy, literature, art, and the manufacture of porcelain also reached their height – lasted from the tenth century until the thirteenth or fourteenth centuries, a period when Arabs still thronged China's southern ports and when northern tribes invaded, conquered and ruled China. At the beginning of the tenth century, northern China was partitioned among warring dynasties, including the Khitan (Tartars from whom the word *kitai* or Cathay is derived) and the Tangut (a group related to the Tibetans), and later the Nuchen who, in 1126, seized the capital at Kaifeng, splitting China in two. They, in turn, gave way to a confederation of Mongol tribes who took north China at the beginning of the thirteenth century under the leadership of Genghiz Khan, and who then, led by the Kublai Khan, took southern China in 1279. China was not only incorporated into the Mongol Empire (which included Central Asia, Turkey, North India, most of Russia and, at its height, Poland and Hungary) but it was also ruled by subjects of Central Asia, Persia and other parts of the Empire. Even Marco Polo himself may have served as a provincial governor in China under the Mongols.

The coincidence of external contact, trade and the development of arts, crafts and technology in China is highly significant. But two other considerations may be of equal importance. The first is the attitude towards the opportunities, stimuli and trade generated by external contact. The second is the extent to which ideas, beliefs, practices, institutions, literature, arts and values are seen as worthwhile in themselves, or as symbols of, and are instrumental in, the realisation and maintenance of power. For if the predominant value is to realise and maintain control, then it is the logistics of power that will seem to override and shape all other concerns. It is with these considerations that we may begin to understand the gradual ossification of China from the thirteenth to fourteenth centuries AD onwards.

The innovations which took place in literature, the crafts, architecture and the arts during the Han Dynasty (206 BC to 220 AD) became the foundation for subsequent developments for nearly two millennia. The Dynasty was to be looked upon by following generations as a Golden Age of Chinese culture – an age that was quintessentially 'Chinese'. The Han Dynasty also marked the beginning of a long period of expansion,

growing trade and prosperity, and, from the first century AD, the strengthening of Buddhist influence. Buddhist iconography was adopted by
sculptors and artists to fit in with existing beliefs. The fitted, rounded
shapes that had often been used to represent subjects in bronze and
stone were superseded by curves that weld, rather than distort, the real
form, and imbue it with a sense of movement and life. The Buddhist
temple became the model for all Chinese temples, both Confucian and
Taoist; and the pagoda, which probably derived from the Indian *stupa*,
appeared. The practice of cutting temples from rock is a form of construction that can be traced from Tun Huang (a gateway to the trade routes
through the Gansu corridor in northern China to Kizil and Turfan)
backwards through the Hindu Kush to the Indian subcontinent. Painting, which had previously been associated with rituals, ceremonies and
social status, became more expressive and more narrative – a concept that
probably arrived with the Buddhist sutras and temple art in the first
century AD. Bamboo strips were replaced by silk and paper scrolls as the
preferred medium for written and pictorial records and for paintings. By
the Tang Dynasty the paradise scenes of the Amitabha sect were beginning to exert a strong influence on Chinese paintings. The compositions,
brightly coloured and complex, showed palace and temple compounds
teaming with mortals and immortals dancing and singing, with the
buildings in isometric plan seen from above, and the figures shown out
of scale and at eye level.[19]

Towards the end of the first millennium art, which had been dominated by narrative figures at temples, palaces and courts, began to exhibit
a growing interest in landscapes – a subject genre that probably derived
from the background and side scenes of the larger Buddhist murals.
During the tenth–thirteenth centuries, interests broadened again to
include smaller subjects, especially birds and flowers. New techniques
also evolved, most especially during the Tang and Sung (seventh to
thirteenth centuries). More emphasis was given to distance, perspective,
spatial complexity and balance. By the thirteenth century brush strokes
had acquired specific names, such as 'axe-cut' and 'dragged-dry'; inks
and colours were being used in combination; the atmospheric, soft,
almost romantic paintings of the court were contrasted with the direct,
simple, humorous style of the Ch'an Buddhists who flourished around
the great trade centre of Hangzhou.[20]

The growth in international and domestic trade, the corresponding
concentration of population in the urban centres, and, during times of
political instability and fragmentation of the tenth to twelfth centuries,
the existence of several courts (some of which developed a taste for goods

produced for export) gave a boost to the crafts, most especially ceramics. During the Tang, the colour ranges of glazes was extended to include green, blue, amber-yellow, and cream. Whitewares were produced in a variety of shapes with a body of white clay and a pale cream glaze. But the major achievement was the creation of porcelain. During the Sung, the range of ceramic products became more varied. Styles and tastes, driven by the scholar class and by the court who followed antiquarian pursuits, became quieter. The olive-green Yueh stoneware evolved into northern celadon; the blue-green misty Lung-chuan celadon also appeared and was exported widely throughout Asia and the Islamic world. The product that was to have the greatest influence on later ceramics, however, was 'Ching-pai' – a fine, white porcelain with a very pale blue glaze. Such was the quality of Chinese ceramics, and such was the growth and extent of trade, that Chinese products had an important influence upon Islamic potters. The ceramics of Persia, Mesopotamia, Syria, Egypt, North Africa and Spain reached their height during the ninth to twelfth centuries, paralleling the Sung, and were partly encouraged by the Chinese wares. But there were also advances made by Islamic potters which had a strong influence on China and Europe as early as the fourteenth century. Lustre-decorated patterns were first produced by Islamic workers in the ninth century; inspired by the whitewares of the Tang dynasty, they invented a white tin glaze to cover coloured clay, a technique that spread throughout Europe; and to the white glaze they added cobalt blue, a type of decoration that spread first to China (fourteenth century), where it became one of the principal methods of decorating porcelain, and then to Europe. Indeed, Chinese porcelain, which is thought to have been imported into Europe first during the sixteenth century, became the dominant outside influence upon European porcelain until the end of the eighteenth century.

Despite the advances that were made, however, the arts and crafts were subject to intellectualised reviews and assessments of the past and future progression which laid out rules of quality, and thus formed part of a fixed repertoire of artistic endeavour that was self-consciously Chinese. In some instances the creation of a stylised, almost clichéd repertoire had occurred many centuries earlier. Subsequent developments were merely limited variations. Most of the arts retained the decorative stigma which they had acquired by the end of the Zhou dynasty. Bronzes had already reached the peak of their artistic and technological development by this time, and the most important of these objects had become a symbol of status, for their manufacture represented control over mining, metallurgy, artisans, rites and rituals.[21] The use of the brush, ink and paper during Han times had led to a proliferation of painting styles, but these were designated by a system of aesthetic rules fixed and self-consciously applied by the literati. By the end of the Sung, the subject genre of painting and their symbolic meaning had also been set: figures; mountain landscapes (the union of man and nature); birds and flowers (decorative); bamboo (scholarly); colours (decorative); and ink (non-decorative). As Gombrich observed, there is something wonderful in the restraint of Chinese art, and yet: 'As time went on, nearly every type of brush stroke with which a stem of bamboo or a rugged rock could be painted was laid out and labelled by tradition, and so great was the general admiration for the works of the past that artists dared less and less to rely on their own inspiration. The standards of painting remained very high both in China and Japan (which adopted the Chinese conceptions) but art became more and more like a graceful and elaborate game which has lost much of its interest as so many of its moves are known'.[22] The poetry of the later dynasties also seemed to lack the freshness as well as the cohesion and logic of earlier works, particularly under the Manchus, who established more controlled and oppressive conditions for literary pursuits. Indeed, it was the non-Chinese immigrants who wrote much of the best poetry of the Yuan and Qing.

Styles and expression, then, had become stereotyped. Perhaps it was the sporadic persecution of Buddhism during the first millennium,[23] and the constant threat of invasion from the north, which had begun to sharpen a self-conscious sense of Chineseness. After the decline and fall of the Han came the fragmentation of China, and then invasion from the north by the Tartars (who held the north for 273 years from 316 AD until 589 AD) while the south was itself divided into several kingdoms. These invaders were well aware of the political value and significance of this sense of Chineseness and its symbols, and, by adopting many institutions and practices as well as dress and language, they confirmed those symbols in their importance. This stereotyping became more evident under Tang (618–906 AD) when the reunion of China achieved by the Sui in 589 AD (more than three centuries after the collapse of the Han) was consolidated. Yet, during the Tang, foreign contacts intensified and government administration, the arts, literature, and philosophy continued to evolve; and despite the antipathy often felt and shown towards Buddhists,[24] the new legitimating values of both Taoism and Buddhism began to supplement those of Confucianism during the seventh century as the state's activities expanded.[25] There was not the acute sense of Chineseness and intense stylisation which gradually crystallised following the fall of the Mongol Dynasty in 1368 and the reunification of China under the Ming (1368–1644). This new dynasty marked the end of more than 300 years of invasion and foreign rule over part or all of China. Overseas contacts did not come to an end: the court Eunuch Cheng Ho sailed to East Africa, Timor and possibly Australia. But 'Chineseness' now began to merge with xenophobia: foreigners were dangerous, untrustworthy and had to be kept out. The Ming bureaucracy became more detailed, more formalised, more clerical in its procedures, and more centralised. Always a forum for political intrigue, the bureaucracy and the court became an even more introspective arena for ruthless ambition and the exercise of terror by the military guard. In art and literature China's scholar politicians only carried on traditions begun in earlier times.

The ossification of the styles, techniques, forms and subjects that intensified after the fall of the Sung represented a consolidation of what had always been a kind of symbolic vocabulary. Originality and innovation were limited and tended to find expression within established schools of practice – variations on the past masters. This vocabulary of Chineseness, laid down by generations of politician-artists, was also the symbol for feuding cliques within the court and academies which by the second half of the sixteenth century had become an important and integral part of national politics, and which, during the remaining years of the Ming, then became more intellectually cautious and orthodox.[26] In the centuries following the Sung there were always pockets of innovation and individuality, even at court, for much depended upon personalities. Whereas it might institutionalise archaism, the court might also help to promote new ideas and bring them into the mainstream. Kang-hsi (who ruled as Emperor for 60 years from 1662 to 1722 during the early Qing Dynasty) set up workshops within the palace where he gathered expert craftsmen, artists, poets and calligraphers, including European workmen and artists. European-style paintings which, with their use of light, colour, shade, modelling and linear perspective, seemed exotic to the Chinese, became popular at court and led to the creation of a new kind of realism in Chinese painting.[27] It was also during the latter part of Kang-hsi's rule (around the second decade of the eighteenth century) that rose-pink and different whites were introduced from Europe into Chinese ceramics.

But it was under the patronage of rich merchants that artists and craftsmen found comparative freedom from a life at court which was both politically complicated and, on occasions, physically dangerous. Pottery expanded quickly in southeast China under the wing of merchants whose fortunes were made in overseas trade; potters experimented with cobalt blue and copper brought from the Islamic world, and with different glazes, and with new forms such as Grand Buddhist figurines. During the fifteenth and sixteenth centuries, too, away from Beijing, merchant families, whose fortunes were made in tea and silk in Suzhou, Yangchow and Nanjing, attracted those artists, poets, writers who managed to escape the summons of the court.

Yet, on the whole, the symbolic vocabulary of Chineseness became even more rigid and more entrenched when China again fell under northern rulers (the Manchu) for the last three centuries of its imperial history. The invaders, determined to maintain control, were well aware of the potential value of China's material culture and vigorously patronised it. Tradition became clichéd and seemed to merge with Chinoiserie. The administration of the Manchu (Qing) Dynasty was more decentralised, though it also extended more control over the economy and educational institutions. The Qing administration was also more conservative in its outlook, and its rigid adherence to Confucian doctrines won the support of the Confucian scholar class. In the academies, political independence was sacrificed for economic security, and the intellectual caution and orthodoxy carried over from the Ming was deepened still further.[28] The reaction of China's elite to the intensification of contacts with Europeans, who had reached the coast of China at the beginning of the sixteenth century, was defensive. The state would buy such technology as it thought useful, but it would not accept, at least not officially, the wider learning, the theoretical science, the experience in administration and government which the Europeans could also offer, and which were so essential to the development of a modern and materially advanced state. Even among those enthusiasts who did set themselves to learn about the new science, there were many who did no more than bend it 'into strange shapes to fit the language of their traditional thoughts'.[29] Indeed there was less technological development during these final centuries than at any other time since the Zhou. The breakdown of the imperial system brought greater stimulus but also uncertainty, doubt, and loss of confidence which, combined with a rather self-conscious belief in intellectualised progression and evolution, seemed to lead to an awkward hybrid of styles. To many it appeared as if Chinese civilisation had all but failed.

The emergence of the canon of China's isolation and superiority

To talk of China as unique, and to describe it as the world's oldest and most distinctive continuous civilisation, is to impose synthetic cultural-cum-racial wholeness upon a highly factionalised entity. This tense and uncertain society, riven by a hotchpotch of warring groups and cabals seething with envy and ambition, struggling for power, was held together by force of will, by military strength, and by the propaganda of ideas, beliefs and codes of behaviour which evolved into a highly acute sense of Chinese civilisation. From the very beginning of the Han Dynasty stylised representations, some kind of overt cultural uniformity, was imperative if the diversity of the Zhou states and the foreign groups which were absorbed by the expanding Empire were to hold together. In feudal China the nobility had been the scholars, and it was they who performed the religious rites. Art and artifacts such as the bronzes and their manufacture were but symbols of wealth and power.[30] History, too, like other forms of scholarship, merged with symbolism, mythology and totemism. Few Chinese texts predate the fifth or sixth centuries BC. Before this time the only contemporaneous records are a few bronze inscriptions, possibly some chapters of the Book of Documents, and oracle bones which reveal such matters as divinatory questions about military battles, food offerings to be made to the ancestors, and lists of Shang Kings.[31] The classics (*Songs, History, Change, Spring and Autumn Annals, Rites* and *Music* (now lost)) which were written during, or shortly before, the time of Confucius (died 479 BC), who is thought to have worked on and contributed to some of these texts, portrayed an ancient past of peace, harmony and ideal rulers.

It seemed only natural that these myths, legends, instructions and lessons (to which were later added a number of other classic texts including *Analects*, the sayings of Confucius, and *Mencius*, one of Confucius' more prominent successors) should be manipulated by subsequent generations of philosopher-politicians who vied for influence, advanced their own version of established classical views on government, and propagated their own rationalisations of the status quo. Confucianism preached loyalty, filial piety, respect for antiquity, and the old chivalric codes; the School of Law taught that only the King could bring peace, that only the workers and peasants mattered. In 124 BC the first link between Confucian doctrines and the training and selection of officials was established – a link that grew to form the very basis, not only of China's political order, but also of its social order, for the only realistic path for social advancement for most people was either to enter the military or the bureaucracy.

This official class – an exclusive, educated elite drawn from the literate gentry – had to be writers, scholars, historians, artists and poets as well as bureaucrats and politicians. At various times throughout China's imperial history, a knowledge of poetry, the Classics, essay skills, law, mathematics, the rites and ceremonies as well as a thorough knowledge of Confucian doctrine were expected of the officials. Even the strokes and visual form of the written language (which spanned mutually unintelligible dialects and thus served as a focus and means of cohesion) were transmuted into a symbol of scholarship, learning, power and exclusivity and thus into an important form of art which in later times was included as part of the entry exam of the civil service.[32] It was they, the scholar-politicians, who formalised the connection between political and social power and the symbolism of art, history, literature, philosophy and literature. It was they who determined the rules of quality and excellence, who often drove tastes and fashions. If intellectual conformity and intellectual homogeneity was demanded as the price of unity (as was so often the case, most especially during the last 500 years of imperial rule), then it is not surprising that the scholar-politicians should have been constrained within a rather narrow, stiff, symbolic vocabulary, that there was little incentive to develop ideas and critical thought, that they should have looked askance at new ideas and stimuli from the outside world, and that art, literature, philosophy, history, institutions, values, beliefs and patterns of behaviour should have become stylised representations of China and Chineseness.

Technical ideas and inventions, too, were in part an expression of curiosity, aestheticism, and creativity; and, as Qian[33] points out, great intellectuals as well as great artists did arise from time to time. Yet their achievements and even whole fields of inquiry such as astronomy and mathematics, were tied to the desire for political influence and the logistics of managing a vast agrarian state. The cosmic pretensions of China's rulers meant that the prime representative of official science was necessarily astronomy – an essential department of the central government. Agricultural methods and technology, and the procurement of new military technology and techniques, were also of concern and interest to the state, and books on medicine were often compiled under official auspices. And there was much literature almost wholly unofficial in origin, particularly in such areas of proto-science or pseudo-science as alchemy or 'geomancy'.

> But so far as technology is concerned, once the limits of direct official concern are passed, the picture is relatively barren. Thus there is no corpus of systematic works of the practical aspects of topics as mining, metal-working, paper-making, ceramic manufacture or the exploitation of water-power, despite the great accomplishments of Chinese artisans in these fields, and their great importance to the

economic functioning of the Chinese state. The broad category of concerns that nowadays we would label as 'technological' was not seen as constituting a related whole by pre-modern Chinese intellectuals, whose interest in practical matters was in general ordered according to the administrative scheme imposed by the imperial government's departmental structure. That left clear places for armaments and agriculture, but the rest of the practical arts were best left to those directly concerned with practising them or dealing in their end-products. Such men were not, on the whole, likely to learn their business from books or to write books for the instruction of others.'[34]

To emphasise the strong political associations which imbue thought on the natural world in China, Qian cites the example of Chinese explanations for earthquakes:

The dynasty of the Zhou is going to perish...When the Yang is hidden and cannot come forth, or when the Yin bars its way and it cannot rise up, then there is what we call an earthquake. Now we see that the three rivers have dried up by this shaking; it is because the Yang has lost its place and the Yin has overburdened it. When the Yang has lost its rank and finds itself (subordinate to) the Yin, the springs become closed, and when this has happened the kingdom must be lost.[35]

Against this Qian cites Needham whose summary of the Greek explanation is derived from Lones:[36]

Anaxagoras believed that earthquakes were caused by excess of water from the upper regions bursting into the under parts and hollows the earth; Democritus thought that this happened when the earth was already saturated with water, and Anaximenes suggested that the shocks were caused by masses of earth falling in cavernous places during the process of drying. Aristotle himself in the fourth century [BC] attributed the instability to the vapour generated by the drying action of the sun on the moist earth, and to difficulties met with by the vapour in escaping.[37]

The political considerations which shaped inquiry and explanation in China made the authority of *non sequitur* reasoning all the more compelling; there might be a very few remarkable men able to predict or even, through magic, influence events, but things were as they were.[38] Once the accepted political ideal or the status quo was thereby rationalised, there was no irresistible urge to question explanations on grounds of truth or logic or simple curiosity. Of Zhang Zai, Cullen remarks:

> there is really no expectation at all that we are entitled to ask for a detailed explanation of why a particular process occurs in the way that it does and in no other way. Zhang's object is served once he has shown in outline that the universe can be seen as a rational place in which basic principles operate in a universal way: it is not his task to tell us, for instance, why iron corrodes rapidly and gold not at all. Indeed, it may be asking too much of human reason to demand that it should seek for such detailed insight into the workings of the cosmos. We may point to the words of Shen Gua, a contemporary of Zhang Zai and a man with a wide interest in scientific and technical matters. Faced with the problem of why a lightening bolt had damaged metal objects while leaving wood untouched, despite the fact that wood is normally more vulnerable to fire than metal, he says: 'this is something that human abilities cannot fathom...human beings can only attain knowledge of those matters which fall within the ambit of human affairs, outside which are numberless matters whose principles would be very difficult to search out using limited human intelligence.'[39]

All that appeared to be necessary, or of practical value, to maintain power would be so used. All that appeared to be unnecessary was ignored; all that worked against the maintenance of that power would be repressed. The cosmic nature of the Chinese state, writes Gernet,

> is manifested in a whole series of terms and rituals. The emperor is the son of heaven, he rules on the strength of a Mandate of Heaven, he sacrifices to Heaven and to Earth, and he alone has the authority to do so; he is responsible for the natural and social order. China is not nation among others; it *is* civilisation, or at least regards itself as such. It is therefore necessary for the emperors to rely on literati who are specialists precisely in rites and precedents. Otherwise, the whole edifice would collapse. In the final analysis, it is such collective images and beliefs which constitute the most solid foundations of imperial power.[40]

Values, ideas (artistic and technical), beliefs, patterns of behaviour, and institutions, seen and unseen, spoken and unspoken, were formed into historical images that were in their own way highly subtle and complex as well as effective. Many sinologists would view these images as the hallmark of an advanced civilisation. There was, Needham acknowledges 'the presence of a certain amount of what one might call "propaganda" (not necessarily in a pejorative sense) in Chinese classical and historical texts – a kind of "personal equation" for which the historian has to make proper allowance. There was nothing peculiar to China in this. It is, of course, a world-wide phenomenon, notable from Josephus to Gibbon, but the sinologist has always to be on the lookout for it, for it was the *défaut* of the civilized civilian *qualité*.'[41]

Indeed, the acceptance by Europeans of such images as true representations of China and of China's superiority is itself a tradition which stretches back many centuries. The incorporation of China into the Mongol empire and the establishment of the Pax Tartarica made regular caravans into China possible once again. Marco Polo is thought to have arrived with his father in Cambulac (Peking) in 1274.[42] There he entered the service of the Khan until 1292 when he returned home via the southern seas route and Persia. He took back with him glowing accounts of the opulence, magnificence and sheer enormity of China. These accounts were later confirmed by Friar Oderic of Portendone (1324–7) who saw in China a larger version of all that was best and most desirable in Europe.[43] The images formed by Polo, Oderic and other merchants and travellers were mixed with descriptions of India and Southeast Asia which in the minds of many Europeans mingled with Tartary and China. For a long time after the fall of the Mongol empire China was perceived not so much as a distinct entity than as a shimmer which danced around the eastern seaboard and lower valleys of the Changjiang, Huaihe and Yellow River, occasionally expanding and contracting on the southeastern edge of Tartary – that vast expanse of lands which reached from north Asia to the borders with eastern Europe, India, and Persia and which included parts of modern China's northern, north western, and western territories.

Thus did the spice trade of tropical Asia which drew merchants eastwards become associated with the hazy, mystical image of Cathay. The Portuguese rounded Africa to arrive in Goa in 1510, and then in Malacca in 1511. They found in Southeast Asia and in Japan memories of Cathay's images – a place from where came all wisdom – that strengthened their own preconceptions. The Mongols had tried on two occasions to conquer Japan, and they had sent expeditions into southeast Asia to compel the payment of tributes. During the Ming dynasty Cheng Ho had led expeditions into Southeast Asia, and had pronounced Chinese suzerainty over Malacca in 1409. With renewed pressure from the north and the actions of Japanese pirates to the east, Chinese interest in the region withered. Yet the Chinese retreat from their exploits overseas was regarded by Francis Xavier as nothing less than proof that they were both wise and in possession of a strong sense of public morality. China was undoubtedly superior to all Christian states in the practice of justice and equity: to Polo's image of material opulence and size, Xavier thus added high moral stature and a love of peace.[44]

Such overt praise, acceptance and elaboration of China's images were necessary if the missionaries were to penetrate China effectively. Ricci, who lived and worked in China from 1583 until his death there in 1610, ably demonstrated the success of this policy for cultural penetration initiated in 1578 by Valignano. Missionaries were trained intensively in the language and in the study of the country to win the respect of the elite literati to whom they imparted their inchoate scientific knowledge as well as their Christianity. Following Ricci's example they lived and acted as members of the literati, chained to their own highly idealised images of the country in which they lived, prisoners of their own ambivalence.[45] Nearly a hundred years after Ricci's death, the Figurists, believing themselves to follow Ricci's plan of 'accommodation' and of giving China the benefit of the doubt, looked not only for moral and natural theology in Chinese characters, but for Christian mysteries in the Classics.[46]

If the Jesuits eulogised China, then the French Physiocrats adulated its images. In China they saw evidence, where there was little, for their own beliefs in the need for the abolition of the mercantilist restrictions, the creation of a natural agriculturally-based order, and freedom of economic choice. The French Physiocrat Quesnay (who advocated enlightened despotism) became known as the Confucius of Europe, and France itself, shortly before the Revolution (1789), became known, because of its population growth, as the China of Europe.[47] Not everyone was content to accept China's images. But many of those who found the sinophilia and the cult of Chinoiserie unpalatable formed an equally distorted caricature of China: it was a 'dormouse' and 'embalmed mummy', decrepit and incompetent.

What the missionaries, physiocrats, sinophiles and China's detractors had perhaps sensed, but had chosen to read in different ways, was the gradual ossification of China. By the time the Portuguese had arrived in China in the mid-sixteenth century when the Renaissance in Europe was already well underway, China's leaders were manipulating a highly developed and highly self-conscious sense of Chineseness to shield

China and its pillars of power from external influence. As we have already noted, the images became sharper still and the defensiveness still more acute under the alien Manchus of the Qing Dynasty who rejected foreign ideas out of hand and demanded strict observance of Confucian teaching, fearing they would otherwise be driven out by their Chinese subjects.[48]

Determined to establish diplomatic relations with China and to expand trade beyond Canton to where they were confined, the British took gifts to the Chinese court, only to find themselves being treated as barbarian tribute bearers. In the official letter to George III, the Emperor Ch'ien Lung (1736–95) wrote:

> As to your entreaty to send one of your nationals to be accredited to my Celestial Court and to be in control of your country's trade with China, this request is contrary to all usage of my dynasty and cannot possibly be entertained ... Our ceremonies and code of laws differ so completely from your own that, even if your envoy were able to acquire the rudiments of our civilization, you could not possibly transplant our manners and customs to your alien soil ... Swaying the wide world, I have but one aim in view, namely to maintain a perfect governance and to fulfil the duties of the State ... I set no value on objects strange or ingenious, and have no use for your country's manufactures.[49]

It was perhaps Lord Macartney of this British delegation to China in 1793 who managed to look beyond China's images without being contemptuous, and to perceive with accuracy what China was and what it was soon to become: 'In my researches I often perceived the ground to be hollow under a vast superstructure, and in trees of the most stately and flourishing appearance I discovered symptoms of speedy decay ... In fact the volume of the empire is now grown too ponderous and disproportionate to be easily grasped by a single hand, be it ever so capacious and strong.'[50]

Startling diverse and very telling interpretations drawn from China's stylised representations by Europeans and Americans continued to be propagated through the closing century of Manchu rule. As emigration from China to Southeast Asia gathered pace, dismissive criticism from those who saw China as a nation of degraded and incompetent coolies strengthened in intensity. China's stylised images received adulation, however, from the American missionaries in particular, who saw themselves as champions of oppressed people and who believed that any shortcomings which China may exhibit were a consequence of its exploitation by other nations.[51] Still others began to wonder – in view of Japan's industrialisation and the admiration which many felt both for the business acumen of the Overseas Chinese and, above all, for their capacity for sustained work – what might happen if China were to follow Japan's lead and successfully modernise its economy.[52] Napoleon's belief, expressed more than fifty years earlier, that China was a sleeping giant which would make the world tremble when it awoke, now appeared more prescient than anyone could have imagined.

Yet China's stylised representations were stifling the expression of creativity and aestheticism. They had made a virtue of didacticism and parochialism, and rationalised unconstrained power. Nor were they infallible. Each time an uneasy stability was achieved, China slowly gave way to ambition, corruption and greed: power and influence were the values, the criteria, by which an individual's worth was judged, and for which all was manipulated; the sophisticated bureaucracy, the ideas of philosopher and scholar politicians, ideas, arts, crafts and technology, were all subject to the desire of cliques and cabals for power. China never succeeded in replacing the manipulation of emotions, passions, relationships and images as a form of government and administration with a permanent, framework of institutions, procedures and values that were regarded as impartial and absolute in their own right. This was never achieved to any large extent because it was not thought relevant. Arbitrary power and the manipulation of relationships, of base emotions, and of stylised codes, rituals and customs remained crucial to the fulfilment of individual ambition, and to the maintenance and expansion of the Empire.

By the end of the nineteenth century China had become a sorry anachronism that crumbled easily from within. All that was now left of the Empire was its last redoubt – a fabricated sense of uniqueness and destiny which had been manufactured from a selective interpretation of centuries of migration and foreign rule. China, or large parts of it, had spent, in sum, almost a millennium under the rule of northern 'barbarians' – invaders linked with central and western Asia and the great caravans which travelled into the western heartland.

Yet the spirit of these stylised representations, and many of the representations themselves, proved enduring. Absorbed, accepted and propagated by European and American neophytes, China's images continued to evolve as the European colonial empires were disintegrating and the lines of the Cold War were being drawn. Anti-colonial sentiments were particularly strong among the intellectual elites, and many were sympathetic to the aims of communism, and more especially to the Chinese communists who appeared to adhere more closely to socialist ideals, and who seemed to provide an alternative path for economic development more worthwhile, more moral, more viable than capitalism. Perhaps there was also the belief that the marginalisation of the study of China, at least within British universities at this time, was a reflection of the pattern of colonial interests and represented yet another manifestation of colonial rulers who were, by definition, ethnocentric, narrow-minded, and could do no other but dominate 'so hatefully' their subjects. Perhaps, too, these sentiments and frustrations reinforced and, in their turn, were reinforced by, an equally powerful love of the glamour of strangeness attached to distant and exotic civilisations. For Needham, China is so utterly different:

> Chinese culture is really the only other great body of thought of equal complexity and depth to our own – at least equal, perhaps more, but certainly of equal complexity; because after all, the Indian civilization, interesting though it is, is much more a part of ourselves. Our language is Indo-European, derived from Sanskrit. Our theology embodies Indian asceticism; Zeus Pater derives from Dyaus Pithar. There is much more in common between Indian and European civilization just as there is in visible type. I often used to think when walking about the streets of Calcutta, that if the pigment was taken out of the skin of many of the people, their features would be quite similar to those of our own immediate friends and relatives in England. But Chinese civilization has the overpowering beauty of the wholly other; and only the wholly other can inspire the deepest love and the profoundest desire to learn. (GT, p. 176)

So different, that any description of it by rights requires a new vocabulary. In his defence of China against those, such as Wittfogel,[53] who would view it as a despotic state rather than a highly intelligent, organic, moral state with sophisticated democratic elements within it, Needham argued that in describing and analysing its apparatus and structures, new terms were urgently needed:

> We are dealing here with states of society so far removed from anything that the West ever knew, and in coining these new technical terms I would suggest that we might make use of Chinese forms rather than continuing to insist on using Greek and Latin roots to apply to societies that were enormously different. (GT, p. 206)

A fabulous, older, wiser and spiritual China could be extracted by sinology from travellers' tales; and the romance of Chinoiserie became professionalised. Observations, artifacts and historical texts were to be interpreted not merely according to initial beliefs about the intellectual and moral supremacy of Chinese culture; those interpretations were now to be rationalised through the medium of the scientific approach with its ritual invocations of structure and forces, and its detestation of individual human decision and thought, and of chance events. This self-conscious rigorous science of the new sinologists which, fuelled by political sentiment, could be used to construct a mystical image of a civilisation at least equal to that of 'the West'.

And so, though it may seem reasonable to suggest that on the fringe of the western heartland China received vital, though somewhat delayed, external stimulus throughout its history, and that such influences were often translated into a sense of uniqueness and exclusivity which may have washed back along the initial paths of influence as the Chinese Empire expanded, the prevailing view of traditional China is now very different. Any suggestion that the Chinese did not develop their own cities from an indigenous Neolithic base with little assistance from beyond, or that ceramics, bronzes, arts, crafts, beliefs, ideas, institutions and technologies did not either emerge independently in China or were not largely original or unique contributions, is likely to be met with incredulity and vigorous resistance. 'For close on two thousand years since the first records of the Shang dynasty', writes Fitzgerald, 'China had really no contact with any other civilized people, either by peaceful commerce or conquest. It was during this age that the Chinese civilization developed its peculiar forms, and such marked differences from any other culture: these characteristics became so much part of Chinese life and thought that when foreign influences such as Buddhism from India finally did penetrate to China, they could not really prevail against Chinese ways of thought and life: it was the foreign influences which were much more changed by China than China was by foreign influence.'[54] The northern people were successful in their military actions against China because they were, by definition, barbarians and had learned and acquired such elements of Chinese culture as were useful to them.[55] And when the end came to 'Traditional China', the trouble was seen to lie with the fact that the Qing Dynasty was alien. Whereas the true Chinese Dynasties of the Tang and Sung maintained foreign contacts as far as they could sustain them, and welcomed information from far-off countries, the Manchus of the Qing Dynasty had retreated into Confucian doctrine.

Indeed, the predominant belief today (and it is a belief that seems to be underlain with sentiments very close to those strongly expressed and acted upon by the European and American neophytes of earlier centuries) is that China not only developed independently, but that through those external contacts which did exist, the Chinese profoundly influenced the rise and development of other civilisations in the western heartland including, in particular, western Europe. This is the canon of China's relative isolation, its uniqueness, and its superiority over other civilisations.

The professionalisation of China's history

This canon has as its central pillar a voluminous study by Needham and his co-workers on *Science and Civilisation in China*. They argue that prior to the European Renaissance, science and technology in China was not only more advanced, but that most of the scientific ideas, concepts, and technological devices which they believe had a decisive effect upon Europe and the rest of the world originated in China. These ideas and technologies arrived in Europe, so it is argued, in a series of clusters. The fourth to sixth centuries AD saw the arrival of the draw loom and breast-stirrup harness in Europe; the eighth century saw the arrival of the foot stirrup; the equine collar harness and the simple trebuchet for field artillery were brought to Europe in the tenth century. In the twelfth century came the magnetic compass, the stern-post rudder, paper-making, the windmill and wheelbarrow. There then followed gunpowder, silk machines, the mechanical clock, the seg-mental arch bridge, the blast furnace for cast iron, block prints and matchable type print in the thirteenth and fourteenth centuries. The standard method for the interconversion of rotary and rectilinear motion, the helicopter top, lock-gates in canals and the ball and chain flywheel arrived in fifteenth century Europe; the kite, the equatorial mounting and coordinates, the doctrine of an infinite and empty space, the iron-chain suspension bridge, and the sailing carriage came to Europe in the sixteenth century. In the eighteenth century, China gave to Europe variolation, porcelain technology, watertight compartments at sea, and the system of civil service examinations. The clusters of transmissions from the twelfth century to the eighteenth century correspond with: the crusades and the Qara-Khitai kingdom in Xinjiang; Pax Mongolia; the arrival of the Tartar slaves in Europe; and the arrival of the Jesuit missionaries and of travellers from Portugal and other parts of Europe.

The mythographers divide the ideas and devices transmitted from China to Europe into four categories. First, there were those scientific ideas and techniques which played a decisive role in the breakthrough to modern science, 'for apart from algebra and the basic numerational and computational techniques (for example, the Indian numerals, the Indo-Chinese zero, and the Chinese decimal place value, the most ancient form of the method), China provided all the basic knowledge of magnetical phenomena. This field of study...and its effect upon the initial stage of modern science, mediated through Gilbert and Kepler, was of vital importance' (GT, p. 58).

China also occupied a 'dominant position' with regard to the second category – those technological developments which directly influenced the rise of modern science and technology before and during the Renaissance. These developments included an efficient equine harness, the technology of iron and steel, gunpowder, paper, the mechanical clock, the driving belt, the chain drive, and the standard method of converting rotary to rectilinear motion, segmental arch bridges and nautical techniques such as the stern-post rudder (ibid.).

The third category comprises 'those achievements of Asian and Chinese science which, though not genetically connected with the rise of modern science, yet deserve close attention. They may or may not be directly related to their corresponding developments in post-Renaissance modern science' (ibid.). Possibly the most outstanding of these Chinese discoveries was variolation – the first successful immunization technique. Although it had influenced the West relatively late (the end of the eighteenth century and the beginning of the nineteenth century), variolation (the forerunner of Jennerian vaccination) 'had been in use in China certainly since the beginning of the sixteenth century and, if tradition is right, since the eleventh...The origins of the whole science of immunology lie in a practice based on medieval Chinese medical thought' (ibid., p. 59).

The fourth category encompasses those 'technical inventions which only became incorporated, whether or not by re-invention, into the corpus of modern technology after the Renaissance period...[an]... example is the iron-chain suspension bridge, for while the first European description came towards the end of the sixteenth century, the first realization occurred only in the eighteenth, and in knowledge of the Chinese antecedents going back, as we now know, for more than a thousand years previously' (ibid., p. 60).

But if China was so far in advance of other civilisations at least until the fifteenth or sixteenth centuries, and if China was the source of so many ideas and devices, then why did China not develop modern science and technology (and therefore a modern industrial economy) before those achievements were realised in Europe? Indeed it was as early 1938, when Needham first began to form the idea of writing a systematic and objective treatise on science and civilisation in China, that he 'regarded the essential problem as that of why modern science had not developed in Chinese civilisation (or Indian) but only in Europe?' Sceptical of "physical-anthropological" or "racial-spiritual" explanation, he came to be convinced that the cause for the rise of modern science and technology in Europe, and in Europe only, 'was connected with the special social, intellectual and economic conditions prevailing there at the Renaissance, and can never be explained by any deficiencies either of the Chinese mind or of the Chinese intellectual and philosophical tradition' (ibid., p. 191). The historian of science must therefore look for some essential difference between the social, intellectual and economic structures of the two civilisations, between the aristocratic military feudalism of Europe from which mercantile and then industrial capitalism together with the Renaissance and the Reformation emerged, and those other kinds of feudalism (if that was really what it was) which were characteristic of medieval Asia. At any rate, 'we must have something at any rate sufficiently different from what existed in Europe to help us solve our problem' (ibid., pp. 191–2).

The guiding framework of Chinese civilisation – the institutions and moral structures which gave China its stability and perdurability – are described by the mythographers as 'bureaucratic feudalism'. Material affluence and progress were not valued for themselves. The one idea of every merchant's son was to become a scholar, to enter the imperial examination and to rise high in the bureaucracy. The accumulation of material things could give comfort, but they carried with them little prestige and they were not thought to possess any spiritual power. This was an attitude which also found an important place within socialist society, though it was now raised to a 'higher plane': party officials, whose position was quite irrelevant to the accident of his birth, despised both aristocratic and acquisitive values.

Visions of that still-to-come higher plane could be glimpsed even in traditional China. The imperial bureaucracy may have been an exploitative system (and so indeed, we are carefully reminded, was feudalism and capitalism in the west), but the non-hereditary elite opposed both aristocratic and mercantile ways of life. As such it was able both to suppress the ugly, ungainly, and despicable acquisition of material items, and to counterbalance the concentration of total power in the hands of one man or a small and privileged cabal. The Emperor might be the absolute ruler, but the scholar-bureaucrats 'constituted a wide and very powerful public opinion' who would not always obey; decisions were 'regulated by long-established precedent and convention, interpreted age after age by the Confucian exegesis of historical texts. China has always been a "one-party state", and for over two thousand years the rule was that of the Confucian party' (ibid., p. 205).

In another striking passage, the mythographers imply that while China did not possess western democracy, the Chinese did evolve their own superior form of democracy (that was later improved upon by socialism which 'undominated' justice imprisoned within the shell of China's medieval bureaucracy). It was a form that (in many dynasties at any rate) made it possible

> for a boy of whatever origin to become a great scholar (the village neighbours might club together to provide a tutor for him) and so take a high place in the official bureaucracy. Democratic, too, was the absence of hereditary positions or lordship, and democratic was, and still is, the psychological attitude of the commons within whom the four 'classes' (scholars, farmers, artisans and merchants) interchanged with considerable fluidity among one another. It explains the utter lack of *the servility so noticeable in other peoples of the eastern hemisphere.* But that particular sort of democracy associated with the rise of the merchants to power, that revolutionary democracy associated with the consciousness of technological change, that Christian, individualistic and representative democracy with all its agitating activity, which characterised the New Model Army, the Army of the Marseillaise, the Minute Men, the Floating Republic, the Dorset Martyrs, the Communards, the Sailors of Invergordon and Krontsadt, and the Motor-Cycle battalions which took the Winter Palace – that China never knew until our own day. (ibid., p. 152, italics mine)

The mythographers carefully strengthen the emotional strain running through their belief that Chinese society had (because of its sophistication and essential morality) achieved a balance between state and the individual, by drawing attention to the practice of slavery in the west. Although the dominance of clan and family obligations make it doubtful whether anyone in Chinese civilisation 'could have been called "free" in some of the western senses ... I think it seems already clear that neither in the economic nor in the political field was chattel-slavery ever a basis for the whole of society in China in the same way as it was at some times in the West' (ibid., p. 207).

The conception of wealth and the balance between state and the common man was but an expression of the most important cultural characteristic of Chinese society – the philosophy of non-intervention and of 'action-at-a-distance'. The state fulfilled its responsibility for managing a properly functioning society, but it did so almost organic-ally, with the minimum of intervention:

> leaving things alone, letting Nature take her course, profiting by going with the grain of things instead of going against it, and know-ing how not to interfere. This was the great Taoist watchword throughout the ages, the untaught doctrine, the wordless edict. It was summarised in that numinous phrase which Bertrand Russell collected from his time in China, 'production without possession, action without self-assertion, development without domination' . . . Thus, all through Chinese history, the best magistrate was he who intervened least in society's affairs, and all through history, too, the chief aim of clans and families was to settle their affairs internally without having recourse to the courts. (ibid., p. 210)

The mythographers argue that these characteristics – the conception of wealth, the constraints upon power, the absence of slavery, and the philosophy of 'action-at-a-distance' and non-interference – and the stability which they brought, profoundly influenced the evolution of Chinese science and technology:

> It seems probable that a society like this would be favourable to reflection upon the world of nature. Man should try to penetrate as far as possible into the mechanisms of the natural world and to utilise the sources of power which it contained while intervening directly as little as possible, and utilising 'action-at-a-distance'. Con-ceptions of this kind, highly intelligent, sought always to achieve effects with an economy of means, and naturally encouraged the investigation of Nature for essentially Baconian reasons. Hence such early triumphs as those of the seismograph, the casting of iron, and water power.
>
> It might thus be said that this non-interventionist conception of human activity was, to begin with, propitious for the development of natural sciences. For example, the predilection for 'action-at-a-distance' had great effects in early wave theory, the discovery of the

nature of the tides, the knowledge of relations between mineral bodies and plants, as in geo-botanical prospecting, or again in the science of magnetism. (ibid., pp. 210–11)

These qualities (the homeostasis, cybernism, organicism, intelligence, morality, non-interventionism, the stability, and the equilibrium) were the product of a society fundamentally more rational than any which could be found in Europe with its built-in instability and its restless desire for interventionism where discoveries and inventions imported from China had such an earth-shattering effect. Yet these same qualities which had characterised the social order of bureaucratic feudalism in China and which had given rise to so many fundamental discoveries and inventions there, would also ensure that those discoveries and inventions would have little effect upon that same social order. Here, then, we see China's essential difference – the answer to the 'Great Puzzle'. It is the very intelligence, the humanity, the moral sophistication and superiority of China which explains its early scientific and technical achievements, and why, though it influenced Europe, it never developed modern science. Within this paradox, lies another, deeper still, which confers upon China a supreme wisdom that is, in its severe understatement, the mark of the true sage and spiritual leader. The Chinese conception of the world may not have been 'congruent with characteristically occidental "interventionism", so natural to a people of shepherds and sea-farers; it may not have been capable of 'allowing the mercantile mentality a leading place in the civilisation, nor of fusing together the techniques of the higher artisan with the methods of mathematical and logical reasoning which the scholars had worked out'; mathematics may not have been able to come together with empirical Nature-observation and experiment to produce something fundamentally new; it may have been difficult to make experimentation philosophically respectable in China (for it demanded to much active intervention); and China may have been 'violently overtaken by the experimental growth of modern science after the Renaissance in Europe'. But such is the mythographers' faith in their own understanding of the structures of history and societies, and in their ability to fathom what might have been, that they feel at ease with this startling proclamation:

The Chinese were so much in advance of the western world . . . that we might also venture the speculation that if the social conditions had been favourable for the development of modern science, the Chinese might have pushed ahead first in the study of magnetism, passing to field physics without going through the stage of "billiard-ball" physics. Had the Renaissance been Chinese and not European, the whole sequence of discoveries would probably have been entirely different.[56]

It then seems only logical to take just one more small step:

An unexpected vista ... opens before our eyes – the possibility that while the philosophy of the fortuitous concourses of atoms, stemming from the society of European mercantile city-states was essential for the construction of modern science in its nineteenth century form; the philosophy of organism, essential for the construction of modern science *in its present and coming form*, stemmed from the bureaucratic society of ancient and medieval China ... All that our conclusion need be is that Chinese bureaucratism and the organicism which sprang from it may turn out to have been as necessary an element in the formation of the perfected world view of science, as Greek mercantilism and the atomism to which it gave birth ... The gigantic historical paradox remains that although Chinese civilization could not spontaneously produce 'modern' natural science, natural science would not perfect itself without the characteristic philosophy of Chinese civilization. (SCC2, pp. 339–40)

The science of history

This elaborate argument, however, is open to a number of fundamental criticisms. These criticisms are treated here in four sections.

(i) The mythographers claim that China was, beyond reasonable doubt, the source of ideas and technologies that played a decisive role in the breakthrough to modern science and were dominant in its subsequent development. They believe that, in case after case, they have shown 'with overwhelming probability that fundamental discoveries and inventions made in China were transmitted to Europe' (GT, p. 213). Yet it is rarely clear how, when, or if, these ideas and inventions arrived in Europe from China. The earliest periods of transmission before the twelfth century AD, the mythographers admit, are more obscure, and further research is needed to elucidate them (ibid., p. 115); how knowledge of magnetism came to the west 'remains a mystery' (ibid., p. 74); the details of the transmission of the Chinese water wheel linkage, and therefore clockwork, to Europe are still 'obscure'; whether any breath of the idea of an infinite universe reached Bruno and Gilbert, 'we do not know' (ibid., p. 85). And of cast iron, Needham states that in view of 'the long prior history of iron, and especially of iron-casting, in China, I am not disposed to entertain any belief in an independent invention in Europe; at the same time we still know little or nothing of the interme-diaries through which the knowledge and experience came' (ibid., p. 107).

Nor do they make clear the extent to which, or how, or indeed, if, any antecedent had any strong or significant influence, for modern science possessed its own 'basic originality' (ibid., p. 58). What does it mean, they ask, to be a precursor or a predecessor? 'For those who are interested in intercultural transmissions this is a vital point' (SCC4, p. xxvi). The difficulty, they argue, is that any mind is necessarily the denizen of the organic intellectual medium of its own time:

> Discoveries and inventions are no doubt organically connected with the milieu in which they arose. Similarities may be purely fortuitous. Yet to affirm the true originality of Galileo and his contemporaries is not necessarily to deny the existence of precursors, so long as that term is not taken to mean absolute priority or anticipation; and in the same way there were many Chinese precursors or predecessors who adumbrated scientific principles later acknowledged – one thinks immediately of Huttonian geology, the comet tail law, or the declination of the magnetic needle. (ibid., p. xxvii)

Nor does the influence of structures and the cultural milieu upon ideas and inventions, and of ideas and inventions upon the course of society and civilisations move beyond a moot possibility towards clear specification. Hence the marked ambiguity of the third and fourth categories of ideas and devices believed to have been transmitted from China to Europe. What, precisely, do the mythographers mean by 'those achievements of Asian and Chinese science which, though not genetically connected with the rise of modern science ... may or may not be directly related to their corresponding developments in post-Renaissance modern science' (GT, p. 58)? What is intended when first it is stated that the use of variolation in China can be dated to the eleventh century according to tradition, and then it is claimed that the 'origins of the whole science of immunology lie in a practice based on medieval Chinese medical thought' (ibid., p. 59)? What is implied by the belief that the old Chinese doctrine of infinite empty space did not exert its full effect until after Galileo's time (ibid.)? What is meant by the suggestion that the development of undulatory theory in eighteenth century physics 'immensely elaborated characteristically Chinese ideas without knowing anything of them' (ibid.)? What, exactly, is meant by those 'technical inventions of China which only became incorporated, whether or not by re-invention, into the corpus of modern technology after the Renaissance period' (ibid., p. 60)?

To all this the mythographers introduce still more ambiguity. On the one hand they acknowledge that there were ideas and technical inventions created in China which *almost certainly* had no influence upon other civilisations. The existence of the differential gear in China 'has been revealed only by modern historical research and could hardly have inspired the later mechanics of the West who fitted up again this important form of enmeshing wheel-work' (ibid.). So, too, Chinese methods of steel-making by the co-fusion process and by direct oxygenation of cast iron 'though of great seniority to the siderurgy of Europe, were not able to exert any influence upon it, if indeed they did, which is still uncertain, until long after the Renaissance' (ibid.). The seismograph as used in China from the second to seventh centuries AD was almost certainly unknown to the men who developed the seismograph in post-Renaissance Europe. Chinese biological and pathological classification systems were clearly unknown to Linneus and Sydenham. Medieval anatomy, though far more advanced than generally thought, exerted no influence on the revival and development of anatomy in Renaissance Europe.

On the other hand, however, Needham argues that:

> one must always refrain from being too positive about the absence of influence. In human intercourse there have been innumerable capillary channels which we cannot see, and especially for earlier times we should never be tempted to dogmatism in the denial of transmissions. Sometimes one wonders whether humanity ever forgets anything ... Broadly speaking, experience shows that the further one goes back in history, the more unlikely independent invention was; we cannot infer it from the conditions of modern science today, where it frequently occurs. (ibid., pp. 60–1)

But then again, this passage is preceded by doubts over the significance of attempts both to identify who it was that first thought of an idea or constructed some device, and to establish the extent of the influence which that idea or invention had had upon the course of events and the rise of modern science in Europe:

> It is not legitimate to require of every scientific or technological activity that it should have contributed to the advancement of the

European culture-area. What happened in other civilizations is entirely worth studying for its own sake. Must the history of science be written solely in terms of one continuous thread of linked influences? Is there not an ideal history of human thought and knowledge of nature, in which every effort can find its place, irrespective of what influence it received or handed on? Modern universal science and the history and philosophy of universal science will embrace all in the end. (ibid. pp. 52–3)

This passage is itself immediately preceded by the statement, bursting with intellectual hubris, that although Chinese biological and classification systems were unknown to Sydenham and Linnaeus, they are nevertheless worthy of study, 'for only by drawing up the balance-sheet in full shall we ever ascertain what each civilization contributed to human advancement' (ibid., p. 52).

In this mythography, individuals sink back into the imagined structures of society and history from which it is assumed they emerged: thought, actions, decision, choice, spontaneity, personality and argument are subsumed by the two great levellers of socialism – the forces of history and society. It is easy to understand, then, why technological devices should have had so much influence: individuals are merely convenient mediums through which civilisation and history is created, altered and structured by greater forces and variables. There is no need to consider the sea change in thought which occurred in Europe, to recognise the individuals who altered their own way of thinking about the world, who challenged existing ideas, behaviour and institutions, and who struggled against prevailing opinions and prejudices. There is no need, then, to consider the awkward possibility that China was not intellectually strong[57] because individuals saw political control and the maintenance of power as ends in themselves to which everyone, and everything, should be made subordinate.

But the mythographers' studied ambiguity does more than play to intellectual fashion or smooth the harsh appearance of their determination to fix Chinese culture as the fount of modern science and technology: it also allows considerable latitude for the operation of that organicist philosophy which they claim for China. According to their faith, the Chinese world-view depended upon a line of thought entirely different to that of the Europeans.

The harmonious co-operation of all beings arose, not from the orders of a superior authority external to themselves, but from the fact that they were all parts in a hierarchy of wholes forming a cosmic and organic pattern, and what they obeyed were the internal dictates of their own natures. (GT, p. 36)

The mythographers faithfully transfer this philosophy of intuitive contemplation, this intuitive 'sense' of the world as it truly is, to their own study, where it is used in combination with those 'world-views' which are the product of a more western frame of mind – the assumption of vast chains of cause and effect. The mythographers thus provide their analysis with considerable flexibility. What does it matter who it was that first invented some or other device or came up with some or other idea? What does it matter if the precise movements of these devices and ideas cannot be traced? The mythographers have raised themselves above personalities and therefore competing intellects. The deterministic recursive structures of Europe and China, and the transmission to Europe from China of ideas and devices responsible for the breakthrough and subsequent development of modern science: these are the realities. There is no need to ask how and why. The system exists, and Chinese culture was first. There is no need for proof, for things are as they are; all that is required is description of that reality, and brush strokes of detail. The mythographers' studied ambiguity, their occasional shift from historical chains of cause and effect to organic materialism constantly generate the hint, the suggestion, that ideas and inventions arise out of the structure and culture of China, then move through undefined, unknown and unknowable rivulets of time and space, to enter the organic intellectual structure of another civilisation. Here they infuse the subconsciousness of individuals who, as products of their own time and society, briefly serve as mediums for the transmission and perhaps elaboration of ideas and inventions which are capable of propelling whole civilisations on to an entirely different historical course.

Criticism of this mythography and its contradictions become incidental, for the logic of the mythography is only secondary. It is the sentiments, the unspoken message, and the images created which are of overriding importance, which constitute the power of suggestion and which allow the mythographers to shape to their will observations and evidence. A collage of ghostly, soft-coloured forms wait for just the right amount of fine detail to be added so that they may take on absolute clarity. For underlying these wonderful images-in-the-mist are steelhard assertions – the instrument of this detail – that make any serious questioning of the thesis of transmission from China all but impossible.

The mythographers instruct their readers that, with regard to applied science, we need hesitate little over the assumption that transmission rather than independent invention explains the appearance of similar inventions in different places:

> For example, the gaining of power from the flow and descent of water by a wheel can only have been first successfully executed once. Within a limited lapse of time thereafter the invention may have occurred once or twice independently elsewhere, but such a thing is not invented over and over again. All subsequent successes must there-fore derive from one or other of these events. (SCC4, p. xxvii)

In the next breath the mythographers lose all hesitation, for they believe that in the instances of both pure and applied sciences:

> It remains ... the task of the historian to elucidate if possible how much genetic connection there was between the precursor and the great figures which followed him ... In our work presented here to the reader he will find that we are very often quite unable to estab-lish a genetic connection ... but in general we tend to assume that when the spread of intervening centuries is large and the solution closely similar, the burden of proof must lie on those who desire to maintain independence of thought or invention. (ibid.)

The notion of transmission adopted by the mythographers is founded upon the assumption that wherever an invention or device appears first, then for all intents and purposes this place must be considered as the point of origin for all subsequent devices or variation thereon that appear elsewhere. When these assertions are brought to the fore, almost any supposition or insinuation become plausible, and the impression-istic forms can be given absolute clarity and detail.

(ii) The mythographers' notion of transmission is dependent upon, and is itself a necessary support of, attempts to push back the date of discoveries in China. To this end, the mythographers commonly draw a causal connection between, on the one hand, philosophical, religious and mystical ideas and beliefs labelled as 'Chinese' and, on the other hand, the rise of an inchoate modern science; or they suggest that the former was of direct heuristic value to the latter. In short, ideas and beliefs which are only today seen as analogous to modern science are interpreted as a direct cause of, or as a strong influence upon, the rise of modern science: the medieval led to the modern.

One example of this fusion of traditional with modern is the mythographers' study of magnetism – a discovery which they argue was of particular importance to the development of modern science. An unambiguous connection between geomancy and the discovery and application of magnetism is drawn by seizing on an analogy between magnetic fields and mystical forces.

> The term geomancy has other meanings in other civilizations, but for the Chinese it meant 'the art of adapting the residences of the living and the tombs of the dead so as to cooperate and harmonise with the local currents of the cosmic breath'. Known as the science of 'winds and waters' (*fengshui*), it did not mean merely the winds of everyday life, but rather the *chhi* or *pneuma* of the earth circulating through the veins and vessels of the earthly macrocosm. The waters too were not only the visible streams and rivers but also those passing to and fro out of sight, removing impurities, depositing minerals, and like the *chhi* affecting for good or evil the houses and families of the living, as also the descendants of those who lay in the tombs. The history of the magnetic compass is only understandable in the context of this system of ideas, for this was the matrix in which it was generated. (ibid., pp. 239–40)

The application of present-day nuances to the past, and thus the fusion of traditional with modern, is an extremely convenient device. It is not just an expression of 'chronological snobbery' (to borrow a phrase of C.S. Lewis): it also helps establish the mythographers' belief that ideas and inventions were transmitted largely in one direction from China to the rest of the world. Yet the weakness in ascribing modern-day nuances to the qualitative descriptions and mystical fantasies which medieval science in China did not move beyond is equally clear. Such analogies (which, by definition, cannot be equated with cause) can be made only when philosophical, religious and mystical ideas and beliefs are interpreted in the light of a knowledge of modern science which arose not in China but in the western heartland. To suggest that these ancient ideas and beliefs caused, or were of direct and incisive heuristic value to, the development of modern science would demand a strength of belief in the vaguest and most abstract of structures such as to constitute a faith in predestination.

(iii) A corollary of the mythographers' determination to interpret all evidence and observations in the light of their thesis that Chinese civilisation profoundly influenced the rise of Europe, is their determination to ignore or marginalise the possibility of independent invention until the weight of evidence which favours a point of origin outside China is so strong that it can no longer be overlooked. In that instance, either the possibility of independent invention in China is emphasised, and the possibility of transmission into China is marginalised; or it is claimed that the idea or invention in question had no appreciable impact on China; or it is suggested that in China the idea or device was so improved upon, or applied in such a very different way, that when it was returned, the effect which it had upon its culture of origin was far greater than it had ever had upon China. Ideas and inventions, it would seem, flowed largely in only one direction – from China to the rest of the world. The implication which nestles in both this argument, and in the connection drawn between modern science and philosophical, religious mystical ideas identified as 'Chinese', is that Chinese culture, however defined, is inherently stronger and superior to that of any other people, and that Chinese culture holds the monopoly on imagination and creativity.

There is nothing to say in the absence of incontrovertible proof that many ideas, institutions, practices, arts, crafts, technology, and the idea and practice of living in cities could not have evolved independently in China or in any other part of the world; nor does that independence necessarily mean unique or fundamentally different. Indeed, it may be that independent responses are more important than is often thought. However, it is curious that while the mythographers demand that independent invention must first be proven before it can be relied upon in subsequent interpretations of historical events, they regard as quite legitimate the *assumption* of transmission as a basis for interpretation. It is even more strange, then, that in the case of China the assumption of independent invention is implicitly accepted, for otherwise Chinese civilisation could not be established as the source of so many ideas and devices which initiated and shaped the rise of Europe. Furthermore, whilst the transmission of ideas and devices, either from China to other parts of the world, or among the civilisations of the western heartland, is accepted as a legitimate – and even the only likely – assumption which can properly be made, that assumption begins to wither away as, travelling from the western heartland, we reach the boundaries of Chinese civilisation. What is even more startling is that the mythographers tend to play down the possibility that ideas and devices which, they believe, profoundly influenced the rise of Europe may have arisen in any part of the world outside Europe other than China. The mythographers' assumptions concerning transmission, and their determination to date inventions in China as early as possible, assign to Chinese culture the monopoly on common sense, reason, creativity, and morality.

Again, however, the mythographers' studied ambiguity is brought into play with good effect, juggling, emphasising and then masking these contradictory assumptions so that the thesis may work. Thus the mythographers play up the importance of world cooperative scientific endeavour and question the importance of who discovered what and when. Yet China has always been, and remains, at least equal to the west whose destiny it shaped. For during the first fourteen centuries of the Christian Era, 'China transmitted to Europe a veritable abundance of discoveries and inventions which were often received by the West with no clear idea of where they had originated' (GT, p. 57). And then there is that qualified statement on the significance of Greek thought to the development of modern science and technology in Europe:

> There can be no doubt that in the opening phases of modern science, when mechanics, dynamics and celestial and terrestrial physics came into being in their modern form, the Greek contribution had the greatest share. Euclidean deductive geometry and Ptolemaic planetary astrology . . . were certainly the main factors in the birth of the 'new, or experimental, science' – in so far as any antecedents played a part at all, for we must not underrate its basic originality. In spite of Ptolemy and Archimedes, the occidental ancients did not, as a whole, experiment. (GT, pp. 57–8)

The vague possibility of Arab and Indian influence upon China is also left open, but the careful phraseology leads the reader away from giving serious consideration to that possibility, while all the time the mythographers leave unmentioned their hard assumptions which make the transfer of ideas from China to the rest of the world and the profound influence upon their recipients an incontestable inevitability. Thus it is acknowledged that 'Arabs (Persian and Central Asian) certainly played a role in Chinese science and technology . . . and . . . there was every opportunity for Arabic and Persian mathematical influences to enter Chinese traditions from their observatories at Maraghah and Samarkand. But whether any important effect was actually exerted, we do not know.'[58] And, as always, there is held in reserve the argument that Chinese organicism and the nature of Chinese society did not allow foreign influence, if there was any, to affect China significantly.

The possibility that China did receive some influence from the western heartland is acknowledged by the mythographers. But the dating, the innuendo, and the phraseology, are used to build up an impression of events which makes that possibility seem remote; and though left in the shadows, the presence of those steel-hard assumptions, which allow transmission from China to the West, and independent invention only in China, is always to be felt.

The way in which this impression is skilfully constructed is illustrated by the marginalisation of Greek, Arab and Indian views of the universe and their influence upon Europe and possibly China. The early conception of an infinite universe, with stars floating as bodies in an empty space, we are told, was Chinese and a very remarkable contribution at that. Their cosmological view, we are told, is 'surely as enlightened as anything that ever came out of Greece ... [it] is far more advanced (and the point is worth emphasising) than the rigid conception of Aristotle and Ptolemy, with its concentric crystalline spheres, which fettered European thought for more than a thousand years.'[59] And as the mythographers push back the date for the emergence in China of the concept of an infinite universe to the beginning of the Christian Era, they appear to turn their back on an idea which has been an important strand of Hinduism for over two millennia – the idea of a vast, immensely ancient and perhaps everlasting universe which is in constant cycles of change and which does not have the earth at its centre. The Vaiseshiva, a school of Hindu thought closely linked with Nyaya (a school of logic which taught a system of syllogistic organicism), posited that the matter of the universe is a compound of the eternal atoms of the five elements – earth, water, air, fire and space. The souls of men were involved with these atoms in such a way that they become incarnate. Jainism (fifth to sixth centuries BC), too, held that the universe contained an infinite number of souls enmeshed in a matter thought to be atomic in structure.

A further interesting comparison between 'Chinese' and 'Indian' views of the universe can be found by turning to those translations which the mythographers cite in support of their assertions concerning the originality of Chinese astronomical thought. One source for the mythographers is Chang Heng (first century AD) who argued that space must be infinite and that: 'The heavens are like a hen's egg and as round as a crossbow bullet; the earth is like the yolk of the egg, and lies above in the centre. Heaven is large and earth is small. Inside the lower part of heavens there is water. The heavens are supported by *chhi* (vapour), the earth floats on waters'. A century later, or thereabouts, Ko Hung wrote 'The sun, moon and the company of stars floating (freely) in the empty space, moving or standing still. All are condensed in vapour ...'[60]

These views are pre-empted by Hinduism which taught that the universe is vast and perhaps limitless, and shaped like an enormous egg – the egg of Brahma. The hymns of Rig Veda (completed by about 900 BC) held that the world emerged from a golden embryo, and that a primeval urge (kama) acted upon chaos and produced the universe. A belief which may have been prevalent in Indus civilisation more than a thousand years earlier still, is that the sky was circumvented by an ocean or broad river in which the stars were considered to be fishes.

The significance of the fish returns in a consideration of the transmission of the compass – another example of the way in which the mythographers skilfully play down the possibility that ideas and devices thought to have influenced the rise of Europe may have originated outside China. The Figurists do not attempt to demonstrate transmission; their intention is to impress their belief upon the mind of the reader. Evidence, such as it is, is interpreted selectively according to their initial beliefs. According to the mythographers, the first unambiguous reference to the magnetic compass in China can be dated to somewhere between the middle and late eleventh century, some 100 years before the earliest known reference to the lodestone in Europe. By fusing medieval science with modern science, the mythographers then push the date for the discovery of magnetism, polarity and the compass in China even further back in time.

These dates in themselves lead to the supposition that these discoveries were transmitted from China to Europe, and all observations are interpreted accordingly:

> Those who are acquainted with the literature on the mariner's compass in Europe are well aware of the fact that one of its earliest names was 'calamita'. While some have suggested that this was derived from the Greek word for reed . . . and referred to the small piece of reed by which the needle was assisted to float, the more generally accepted view has been that the word meant a small frog or tadpole. It is thus used, for example, by Pliny. Those who can also read Chinese are therefore liable to receive a considerable shock when they find in . . . a fourth century dictionary by Tshui Pao, the following remarks: the tadpole is also called the 'the mysterious needle' (*hsüan chen*) or the mysterious fish (*hsüan yü*), and another name for it is the 'spoon-shaped beastie' (*kho tou*). Its shape is round and it has a long tail. When it divests itself of its tail, its limbs grow out. (SCC4, p. 273)

The mythographers also cite a text dating from 1044 AD which refers to a pointer in the shape of a fish – a shape which they emphasise is described in Middle Eastern sources dating from the thirteenth century AD. The shape of the fish, they argue, 'is particularly to be noticed in connection with what we shall shortly see regarding the first beginnings of the compass as a spoon. That the floating fish-shaped iron leaf spread outside China as a technique we know from the description of Muhammad al-Awfi just 200 years later' (ibid., p. 254).

But all of this remains pure conjecture. The connection that the mythographers imply exists between tadpole (and needle) in China and Greece and the compass in Europe is innuendo. The mythographers' declaration that Muhammad al-Awfi's description provides us with the knowledge that the technique of the floating fish-shaped iron leaf spread from China to the outside world is again pure supposition: the inference that the floating compass used in the Middle East originated from China is drawn from the shape of the pointer, though as we have seen, the fish is a symbol and a word of cosmological significance that pre-dates Chinese civilisation; and the notion that Muhammad al-Awfi's description constitutes evidence of the spread of the compass from China is only valid if one first accepts the mythographers' belief that the compass originated in China. The mythographers also neglect other possible interpretations of this kind of evidence.

The mythographers note a reference from the tenth century in the Middle East which indicates a knowledge of the lodestone:

My eyes find nowhere else to look but at you,
Like what happens with the lodestone (and the pieces of iron),
Changing direction to right and left, in accordance with where you are,
Or like as in grammar adjectives and nouns must accord

(ibid., p. 248)

However, this evidence is immediately discounted and we hear no more about it:

At first sight this might be interpreted as meaning that the girl was polar and her lover the lodestone always turning to her, but it is far more likely that in the writer's thought the girl was the lodestone, the attractor, and that his eyes were like pieces of iron drawn towards it wherever it moved. Thus it is most probable that Ibn Hazm knew of attraction but not of polarity. (ibid.)

The mythographers also prefer not to follow up the mention of a compass in Tamil nautical books attributed to the fourth century, or Mukerji's[61] suggestion that an old name for the compass in India was the *maccha-yantra* (fish machine), the magnet being in the shape of a fish which floated on oil. It may also be significant that by the time the reference to the lodestone appeared in the Arab text, Indian and Arab traders dominated trade routes by sea to South China and Southeast Asia in the east, and to Africa in the west. In this connection it is also interesting to note that the mythographers believe that the first unambiguous mention of a compass being used at sea is made in a passage of text which dates from the end of the eleventh century (around the same time as the first unambiguous mention of the properties of a lodestone and of the properties of magnetic declination in China), and refers to the port of Canton. Yet in order to forestall the possible inferences which might be drawn from all this material, the mythographers quote a passage in which they claim the first use of the compass at sea is observed. Only the last two sentences are reproduced here:

> In dark weather they look at the south-pointing needle . . . They also use a line a hundred feet long with a hook at the end, which they let-down to take samples of mud from the sea-bottom; by its (appearance and) smell they can determine their whereabouts. (SCC4, p. 279)

This passage, claim the mythographers, 'is a very detailed statement of the use of the mariner's compass just about a century before its first mention in Europe. In connection with this there has been a persistent theory that the account refers to foreign (Arab) ships trading to Canton, and that it was therefore Arabs who first saw the possibilities of the Chinese geomantic compass. This is quite erroneous; it originated because of a mistranslation by Hirth and Hirth and Rockhill who thought that *chia-ling* was the name of some foreign people, the Kling [a name derived from the Kalinga or Telugu coast of the Bay of Bengal], not realising that it was a technical term for "government regulations"' (ibid., pp. 279–80).

Leaving aside wrangles over translation, the interesting point here is how the mythographers yet again use their conclusions to interpret their observations and available evidence by quietly building into their discussion their assumption that the compass originated in China (and was transmitted to the Arabs). The origin of the compass is no longer an issue; the focus of the discussion has now become whether or not it was the Arabs who first saw the possibilities offered by the Chinese compass. The mythographers' assumption, which is also their conclusion, is thereby

presented as a fact from which to continue with their attempt to demonstrate that the discovery and study of magnetism, and the invention
of the compass, first originated in China, and was from there transmitted to Europe.

(iv) The negative question – why was it that modern science and
technology did not evolve first in China – which Needham presents as
'The Great Puzzle', and which is regarded as one of the greatest problems
in the history of civilizations, is essentially rather superficial. It assumes
that it is possible to explain what did *not* happen. The Puzzle therefore
implies that it is possible to know what *might* have happened if certain
other events or conditions had been different. An associated complica-
tion with the Puzzle is the belief that comparison between China and
Europe will identify those differences which can explain why Europe
did – and why China did not – evolve modern science and technology.
The assumptions inherent in this argument are that China is fundamentally different, that those differences are capable of explaining the
economic, social, political, technical and scientific course of civilisations throughout the millennia, and that events and conditions which
did or did not occur in one part of the world are capable of explaining
events and conditions in another part of the world. It is as if the course
of civilisations is a grand experiment. The evolution of mankind, it
would seem, comprises a mainstream of cause and effect from which
various braids emerge depending upon the interaction and addition or
subtraction of particular variables. Preeminence is given to 'structure'
and historical processes: individuals, their ideas, the many dimensions
of their minds, their spontaneity, their emotions, their desires, their
actions, and their response to circumstance, opportunities and chance
events – all become residual or irrelevant 'components' in languorous
chains of cause and effect.

There is little reasoned argument to support these assertions, but in a
sense this does not matter for it becomes clear that the mythographers
have set about tasks more important than supporting the assumptions
of history and society upon which they base their study. They are continuing to institutionalise and legitimise the belief in the difference, the
uniqueness of China – a difference, a uniqueness which no longer needs
to be questioned because it bound into the assumptions from which all
analysis must proceed. The morality, humanity and rationality of Chinese society, and, fostered by this environmental milieu, the concepts
of 'action-at-a-distance' , 'waves', 'fields', 'inductance', 'resonance', and
an ever-moving cyclical universe that is more organic than mechanical,
are quite simply the determinants of mankind's future scientific and

technical development. The Chinese may have failed to develop modern science and technology, but that failure was merely a consequence of their essential cultural superiority which, via their earlier success in pure and applied science, sparked off the Renaissance in Europe and which now shapes the future. China, we must believe, was so far in advance of other civilisations, that it was one step ahead of itself. The assumptions underlying these extraordinary claims are reinforced, almost subliminally, by empty analogies between 'society' and certain natural phenomena or technical devices: Chinese civilisation was 'thermostatic' and 'organicist'; the concept of cybernetics 'could well be applied to a civilisation that had held a steady course through every weather, as if equipped with an automatic pilot, a set of feedback mechanisms, restoring the status quo after all perturbations'; China was a 'whirling grindstone', which struck off sparks – ideas and inventions – which 'ignited the tinder of the West while the stone continued on its bearings unshaken and unconsumed' (GT, p. 120).

Criticism of the superficiality underlying this grandiose voice is therefore of little consequence. The mythographers' primary concerns are those of morality and the doctrine of pride with its many shades of empathetic regret:

> '... my view is that in Chinese civilization there were factors inhibitory to the growth of modern science, while in Western Civilization, the factors were favourable. It may not be too much to say that had the environmental conditions been reversed as between Euro-America and China, all else would have been reversed too – all the great names in the heroic age of science, Galileo, Malpighi, Vesalius, Harvey, Boyle, would have been Chinese and not western names; and in order to enter today fully into the heritage of science, Westerners would have to learn the ideographic script just as the Chinese now have to learn alphabetic languages because the bulk of modern scientific literature is written in them. (ibid., pp. 152–3)

The 'West', then, is not heroic, only lucky: the other peoples of the East servile and presumably, therefore, more subject to a suffocating authoritarianism. When modern science first began to arise, individuals could make fundamental discoveries, but now individual effort must necessarily be absorbed in the efforts of teams, and, taken as a whole, there were no great men, no torches to be handed on from one generation to another; there has always been and will remain only the environment bestowing its favours randomly, but seized upon by the vanity of men and used to flatter their own small egos. That environment is now changing, and with it the fortunes of civilisations. Modern science and capitalism (which has a tendency to shift away from democracy and towards individualism and authoritarianism), the mythography reveals, are no longer compatible:

> ...as science has developed, an ever higher degree of collaboration and co-operation has become necessary... Yet this is difficult because it runs counter to the ethos of capitalist competitive civilization. Hence a paradox which only a change in the form of civilization can remove. (ibid., p. 134)

That new form of civilisation must be Chinese, or Chinese in style. Fundamentally more rational, moral and humane, traditional Chinese society (important elements of which have been incorporated within, and improved upon by socialism) not only possesses the seeds of a futuristic science which is now beginning to evolve, but also the key institutions, structures, and values of a civilisation more conducive to the evolution of that new science.

And now that the environment is changing, now that the superiority of Chinese civilisation has been revealed, now that we see that modern science cannot exist alongside capitalism, now that we see that capitalism has a tendency to shift away from democracy and towards individualism and authoritarianism, the West is finally being revealed for what is: greedy, selfish, barbarous and cruel.

What the mythographers have done – and this is vital to their message – is to create a unidimensional interpretation of China, an image that is almost Hollywoodesque. The relationship between state and science was never restrictive; and Chinese bureaucratic feudalism made highly effective the application of natural knowledge. The Chinese, 'wise before their time, worked out an organic theory of the universe which included Nature and man, church and state, and all things past, present and to come' (ibid., p. 121). China was scholarly, sophisticated, highly intelligent, organicist and humanitarian. Chinese society functioned in a learned way, the seats of power being filled by scholars, not military commanders. Modern science may have arisen in Europe, but its initial stimulus lay with China where, too, lies its future; and while modern science can provide the means to humanise, the will to do so may rest with Confucianism, Taoism, revolutionary Christianity and Marxism. This is the image of a culture which emerged from an idyllic, far-off past of dreamy Halcyon days, shaped itself into a truly modern state of world citizens enthused with the spirit of world cooperative endeavour, and has thereby created a model civilisation for the rest of mankind to follow.

To highlight this image of a culture at ease with itself and the universe, the mythographers have created its antitype – 'the West'. Europeans suffered from a schizophrenia of the soul; they were rovers, always uneasy within their boundaries, 'nervously sending out probes in all directions to see what could be got' (ibid.); they had a penchant, alas, for *Buchsenmeisterei*; they were essentially aggressive, divided, assertive, pugnacious, and subject to occasional fits of insight; they were a people who progressed by accident, in spite of themselves, and upon the back of China's achievements. The West was hateful, exploitative, interventionist, unstable and domineering; it was a hot bed of independent, slave-owning, serf-based, warring nations with a desire for things they would not or could produce.

The value of reducing the individual to insignificance while raising historical processes to a position of the utmost importance, is that it enables popular theory to work. The societies of the western heartland and China and their histories may be flattened and then pasted together into a pleasing unidimensional form. It thus allows those sinologists who are so minded to propagate their own particular beliefs as if fact, to present themselves as the discoverers of true knowledge, and to uncover the ethnocentrism and the racism of those western scholars who are not sinologists or right-thinking historians of science. It is these sinologists who become the bridge between these two very different worlds of China and 'the West'; for it is only they who are equipped to understand the cultures of both worlds, and who possess a knowledge of the causality and the inevitability of historical processes. His aim in studying science and civilisation in China with his co-workers, wrote Needham, 'was simply to try to reveal some of the causative elements in history, the underlying contradictions which make inevitable a certain historical development; to try to answer why science appears at one place and time rather than another, and why it consorts with one social system rather than another. If this task was too presumptuous for a biochemist and embryologist, the duty of a free citizen, and experiences, unexpectedly intimate, of another civilisation in another hemisphere, no less loved than his own, may serve as some excuses' (ibid., p. 153).

Conclusions: the pride and the prejudice

The power and influence of Needham's mythography lies not in its reasoning, but in its numinous atmosphere. The science of history merely provides these unspoken feelings with a more distinct shape: it is the liturgy which gives the appearance of rational form to the constant repetition of beliefs and images, transmuting them into an unquestionable authority. Subsequent analyses, bathed in that atmosphere of otherworldliness, and resounding with the chants of the liturgy, have in their turn proved extremely influential, and none more so than Elvin's[62] analysis of China's 'equilibrium trap'. With a style, phraseology, and line of reasoning strongly reminiscent of Needham's mythography, Elvin ponders over a book published in 1313 in China which describes and pictures a machine for spinning hemp thread – a machine very much like Hargreave's spinning jenny and Arkwright's spinning frame. It is natural to wonder, writes Elvin

> why it was eighteenth century England that was the scene of an industrial revolution in textile manufacture and not fourteenth century China? The sense of mystery deepens when one discovers.... that, as far as it is known, the account given of [the spinning machine] in Wang's and other books inspired no one in the centuries after its invention to attempt an imitation or improvement. Why should this have been so? (HET, pp. 137–8)

The analysis begins with an assumption that the appearance of an invention is dependent mainly upon two preconditions: 'that the inventor should have the prospect of making a profit by satisfying some particular economic need, and that a suitable stock of scientific knowledge should be available for him to draw on' (ibid., p. 138).

Upon these assumptions is placed another:

> it seems reasonable to look for the explanation of the *abandonment* of a successful invention such as the hemp spinning machine in some change in the balance of economic forces. Similarly, it seems possible to hypothesize that if the flow of new inventions as a whole comes to an end in a society, this is the consequence of (1) a change in the balance of economic forces such that possible inventions are now unprofitable, or (2) an inadequacy in the stock of scientific knowledge ... or else (3) a combination of (1) and (2). (ibid.; italics in original)

It is in the light of these assumptions that historical material is subsequently interpreted. Indeed, the assumptions, or 'the hypothesis', is not just used to interpret material – it is itself proof:

It may be noted in passing that what has already been said will serve
as an outline of a proof that in certain structural respects – possibly even
the most important structural respects, since technological advance is
the key to sustained economic progress – the traditional Chinese economy *must* have altered in some fashion between the early fourteenth
century and the early nineteenth century. (ibid.; italics in original)

The assumptions which are made are not just an interpretative device:
they are their own proof. It is now just a matter of establishing the pattern of forces, and the stock of scientific knowledge, which first induced
the invention of the hemp-spinning machine. All that then remains is
to identify those changes which prevented the next step in scientific
progress from taking place.

Elvin's analysis is, in many respects, a classic work of sinology. The
baggage of China's historical mythography is first paraded: there is no
doubt that China produced all manner of astonishing discoveries from
the Han to the Yuan, and that China was the most literate and numerate society in the world. With that most solid of intellectual foundations comes a torrent of familiar assumptions including those which
underlie Needham's 'Great Puzzle' – why was China not the first civilisation to experience an industrial revolution?

Then there is the belief – common in the study of China and, indeed,
throughout the social sciences, but rarely acknowledged and stated in
such a clear and off-hand manner – that the assumptions upon which a
study is based are their own proof. It is, for Elvin, a truth so incontrovertible, and so far above questioning or reproach, that it may be noted
'in passing'.

And then there is the play of aggregates – those vast universals – and
the intricate, subtle colourings of Chineseness, which gather in our minds,
creating an almost tangible atmosphere of the enormity that is China
and of the ancient, timeless, grandeur that is Chinese history. There,
within our mind's eye, we see open vistas, distant mountains, and the
verdure of river plains upon which lie clusters of villages and markets
forming wheels within wheels that rotate about fabulous towns and
cities. Across this immensity pass images of quiet scholars, capable
bureaucrats, remarkable artists, lofty moral philosophers, astonishing
scientists, and the great tides of peasantry. The landscape ripples with
the rhythm of the centuries; and so huge is the scale, that change is
almost imperceptible.

It is true that Elvin's analysis draws upon strands of well-used economic abstractions: the closed economic system; the direct causal link

between population increases, production output, and surplus; the drag which an increase in population exerts upon a developing economy; the creation of demand by increases in output; and the stimulation which innovation and invention receive from surplus production. And central to Elvin's analysis is the assumption that a failure to increase output above and beyond the rate of population growth, and to produce a large enough surplus quickly enough, has the effect of dampening inventiveness and scientific progress. This is so because manufacturers are starved of the supplies which prompt mechanisation as a means of processing the raw materials quickly enough; and, therefore, because not enough processed goods are made to generate further increases in demand. The more commercially developed the economy, the more unlikely it is that sufficient local surpluses will appear for long enough to stimulate inventions or the application of inventions.

But these are ideas which run against both common sense and reams of literature on other parts of the world. If it is assumed that output must rise faster than population for there to be technical progress, then how may output rise quickly enough without prior technical development regardless of the rate of population growth? If demand is generated by an increase in output, then what generates the desire or need for an increase in output? And how does an economy become highly commercialised if commercialisation, by ironing out local surpluses, makes it increasingly difficult to achieve sufficient output, sufficient demand, and thus technical progress? Moreover, if, as this closed economic system requires, an increase in population erodes surpluses, and if it is output that generates demand and stimulates technical development, then there can be no increase in population which is said to erode surpluses in the first instance. For, within this closed system, increases in population stimulate neither demand, output, surplus nor technical progress. Therefore, there can be no incentive for, nor the means to support, any increase in population over any significant period of time.

There are, then, two interesting conclusions which seem to follow. The first is that an industrial revolution was *never* possible in China; nor is it ever possible in any other closed economic system anywhere in the world, for there is no incentive for, nor means to achieve, rapid increases in output. Even if, for the sake of argument, output did spontaneously increase following the introduction of new technology from outside that closed system, the result of that increased output – stronger demand and commercalisation – would make further increases in surpluses and technical development increasingly difficult. Ironically, the

logic of this closed system dictates that progress is only possible following 'exotic stimulation'; and that constant progress requires constant
external stimulation.

The alternative conclusion is to allow oneself to be led though the
looking-glass into a world where technological and economic progress is
most likely in a backward, fragmented, economy (with low productivity
and a small, stagnant or falling population) which has formed external
links with a technically more advanced state and with areas possessing
raw materials – links though which large quantities of materials and new
technology may flow, sufficient to kick-start that backward economy
into life. What appears to be least conducive to technical and economic
progress is a large, commercially integrated economy, with highly productive workers, a large and rising population, and a highly developed
and advanced stock of scientific knowledge. Such conditions, we must
believe, make a civilisation too large and too efficient to permit an
industrial revolution.

And these are precisely the images that Elvin gives to his readers.
China's economy was huge; the performance of its 'market mechanisms' was excellent (HET, p. 162); long before the eighteenth century,
the density of China's market networks surpassed even those of eighteenth century England (ibid., p. 157); money had penetrated even the
back-country villages, and many different types of credit were in use;
there had been marked improvements in agriculture, water transport
and ferrous metallurgy; and cities were growing in numbers and size,
and some of these settlements were predominantly industrial in character
(ibid., p. 141). By the fourteenth century the Chinese already possessed
sufficient knowledge to transform textile manufacturing into an efficient and mechanised industry of mass production; their machines were
already of a technological level equivalent to that used for re-spinning
flax and for spinning silk in Europe in 1700; and none of the advances
made by Europeans up to the mid eighteenth century were out of reach
of Chinese skills in the fourteenth century (ibid., p. 148), by which time
Chinese workers were highly skilled and several times more productive
that the English workers of the mid-eighteenth century. Indeed, by the
thirteenth or fourteenth centuries Chinese society was probably the
most numerate and literate, and the most advanced technically and
scientifically, in the world.

Set against this remarkable Chinese state is the small, and 'recently
backward' (ibid., p. 172) economy of eighteenth century Britain (and
'backward', we are told, is not a word that could be applied to China).
The backwardness of eighteenth century England is highlighted by the

dramatic influx of cotton from South America, the West Indies and the Levant; and by the appearance of a particular item of technology – the spinning machine. By the eighteenth century Europe had already 'laid its hand' on a machine for respinning flax and for spinning silk; the suspicion that it was of Chinese origins is 'hard to resist'; its resemblance to the Chinese machine is 'instantly apparent'; earlier versions of the European machine 'probably resembled the Chinese model more closely, whether or not they were actually derived from it'; and as we have already noted, was not the Chinese machine very reminiscent of Hargreave's spinning jenny and Arkwright's spinning frame (ibid., pp. 146 & 137)?

In this journey through the looking-glass, which follows closely the path discovered by Needham, the significance of trade and the activities of merchants to an understanding of economic and material progress is not simply marginalised: when compared with superior technical, scientific and intellectual thought of Chinese civilisation, with the superior standards of literacy and numeracy in Chinese society, and with the assured grandeur of economic aggregates, trade and merchants appear as nothing less than a barrier to sustained economic and material progress. Supposition is stacked upon supposition until the whole monument collapses into a heap of contradiction, dogma and prejudice; upon this midden, and in the cause of China's image and its aura of plausibility, the abandonment of common sense appears quite acceptable.

Trying to explain what did *not* happen in China, and therefore to delineate what *would* have happened, is an exercise in historical fiction unless one believes in a convenient and predictable world of discrete, unidimensional variables liked together in chains of cause and effect and conditioned by mysterious historical, social and economic forces. We cannot claim with any honesty that had one or other 'variable' or 'factor' been different, that China would have developed modern science and an industrial economy in the nineteenth century or even earlier. Nor can we claim – unless we also believe in a model historical formula of development which nations either adhere to, or depart from – that what did or did not happen in Europe may help us explain what did or did not happen in China. There is no reason to fantasise about what could or should have been, for there is no reason why the choices, the decisions and actions that were taken should not have been taken.

We are left, then, with a statement that is not very startling: that the history of China is not that of Europe. If we wish to understand events in China or Europe then all we can do is to try to understand as best we can what did happen. Yet the complexity of this task, and of the events, personalities, decisions, choices, desires and chance it may reveal, and the remarkable array of questions it raises, is made obvious by even just a very quick glance of events in China. In this chapter we have suggested that the predominant concern in China, on the edge of the western heartland, remained the maintenance both of power as an end in itself and of the images upon which that power rested. Whatever China may have owed to outside stimuli, and from whatever material its stylised representations may have been constructed, trade and external contact threw ideas, beliefs, practices and institutions into sharp contrast, revealed their many dimensions and possibilities, and thus questioned and challenged those representations. The more vibrant the source of that contact, and the more intense the interaction, the greater the threat was perceived to be. China had ossified and fallen into decline not because it was an ancient, learned and passive civilisation that had been exposed to, and misunderstood by, an aggressive, immature and intolerant world. China, on the fringes of the western heartland, gradually ossified and weakened because of the supreme value which its rulers and their subjects attached to a drive for power as an end in itself, to the preservation of those images manipulated in its pursuit, and thus to the image of 'being' ancient, self-sufficient, isolated, advanced, unique, and special – qualities that were always far more apparent than real. Yet we cannot say why – that is, we cannot explain in any formal sense – the pre-eminence attached to power as an end in itself in China and to China's stylised representations; why the external stimuli upon which its representations were built should have been viewed with such caution; why institutions, values, beliefs, patterns of behaviour, and ideas, many of which may have been drawn in from the western heartland, were directed towards the realisation and maintenance of political control as an end in itself, and, for that purpose were transposed into unidimensional images.

Nor was there anything inevitable or certain about either the rise of modern science in Europe and its industrial revolution, or about the accompanying changes in the perceptions of, and attitudes towards, ideas, institutions, practices, the self, and other people. Even a very cursory glance at Europe's past makes plain the superficiality of attempts to impose a formal explanation of Europe's rise upon chance events, upon the drive and creativity of individuals, upon their personalities, and upon their perception of circumstances. Any suppositions and fantasies either about what might otherwise have been, or about the inexorable

influence wielded by ideas and devices which in analysis seem to possess deterministic and causal powers over the conduct of individuals
and their affairs, seem almost comical; and it is only in our imagination
that events and actions may form a pattern that stretches beyond the
lifetime and influence of those individuals whom we study. Perhaps
it was this very uncertainty, this play of chance and possibilities, this
multiplicity of perception and apperception, which made it more difficult for attitudes and outlook to ossify. The intense flow, interaction and
clash of institutions, values, beliefs, ideas here at the nexus of African,
Asian and European Continents, a crucible of criticism and counter-
criticism, argument and counter-argument, persecution and counter-
persecution, made it more likely that reason and an open view of the
world would prevail. Within that crucible, ideas – old and new, those
spontaneous, those drawn from antiquity, those purposeful and those
of serendipity – took on different aspects only because they were perceived as so doing; and were drawn together by a few individuals who
showed them to work and to be capable of transforming the apparently
abstract and unrelated into true and concrete advantage.

The intensity of interactions in the western heartland which made far
more evident the many dimensions and possibilities of ideas, values,
beliefs, behaviour and institutions, and which thus demanded a freer
atmosphere for thought an action, may have also heightened a sense of
being a part of something wider, something which had not evolved
from – nor was therefore dependent upon – one people or one nation.
Any number of European states could look to Greek, Roman, Indian,
Middle Eastern and Chinese influences. They were able to look to institutions, values, practices, beliefs, ideas, philosophies, technologies and
experiences *outside* themselves and *outside* a narrowly and arbitrarily
defined 'culture' or 'civilisation'. This broad, external perspective, may
have confirmed the substance and quality of that which they felt themselves to be and thereby allowed that identity to be held with greater
confidence, and with greater self-criticism. It was also this open, yet
critical, outlook which would allow the self-destructiveness of insular
and introspective thoughts, the damaging obsessions and implacable
desires, the aggression and bigotry, that would arise within or without
Europe, to be more easily revealed and challenged for what they were.

The histories of China and Europe, then, remain ultimately inexplicable, though some kind of understanding may lie in the very absence of
a numinous First Cause. The play of chance, circumstance, perception
and attitude may also help illustrate that there is no essential difference
between 'China' and 'the West'. For if there are no programmed or

deterministic forces or variables at work (structural or cultural, unique or universal), it then becomes possible to view events and actions, institutions, values, beliefs and behaviour in China or in Europe not as peculiar and explanatory devices, but as multi-dimensional expressions of our commonality of being. Whether or not particular ideas, inventions, techniques, practices or institutions were arrived at independently (for independence and spontaneity do not necessarily equate with difference and unique, nor does similarity necessarily equate with transmission), the symbolism of arts, crafts and technology, the ideals espoused by Confucius, the emphasis on the family and lineage, the nature and use of social relations in business and politics, the desire for power as an end in itself, the control and organisation of commerce by the state, the ambiguous attitudes towards trade – none of these characteristics need be considered as peculiar to China, and, if 'turned', they may reveal profound similarities to values, beliefs, institutions and behaviour in other parts of the world. It is, then, the very absence of forces, structures and patterns (historical or social, economic or political, cultural or universal) which makes the histories of China and Europe, and the fecundity of the human mind, seem all the more remarkable: that from our commonality of being such creativity and such apparent diversity should emerge.

If we wish to provide a somewhat ironic and piquant illustration of the redundancy of imagined historical or social structures, then we need only contrast the mythographers' belief that every mind is necessarily the denizen of its socio-cultural milieu, with the words of Bullock who, just at about the time Needham and his associates were constructing their elaborate view of China's history, presented, in a short and simply-worded lecture, a very different view of the world. His interest in history, he wrote:

lies less in the answers it affords than in the riddles it leaves unanswered; not in the explanations, but in the inexplicable; not in the patterns, but in the unpredictable. Let me give two last examples of what I mean. On 27th January 1756 there was born in Salzburg a child who, before he died at the age of thirty-five, was to display a genius in musical composition so rare that it is perhaps without equal. On 20th April 1889 there was born in Braunau another child who, before he died as the age of fifty-six, was to display a force of will-power and a passion for destruction so rare that these, too, are perhaps without equal. Now no explanations of which I know, biological, psychological or historical, can account for the creative genius of Mozart of the destructive genius of Hitler. Far more than any explanation which I have ever seen attempted, the facts alone of these two men's careers are a permanent source of wonder to me.

I have taken my examples from the field of biography, but they could be matched from may other fields: for instance, in the waxing and waning of religious faith, in the rise and decline of intellectual and artistic impulses – the triumph of Christianity in the Roman Empire; the monastic movements of the Middle Ages; the Renaissance and the Reformation; the scientific revolution of the seventeenth century; the spread of Rationalism in the eighteenth; the Romantic Movement, the conflict between Science and Religion, the revolt against liberalism in the nineteenth century. In every case, when we have exhausted our explanations, we are left with something unexplained and inexplicable. This, which to others represents the frustration and failure of historical study, is to me its endless fascination – an intellectual challenge constantly renewed and in the end the certainty that the vitality and variety of human life will prove too great for any of the formulas in which we seek to pin it down.[63]

However, it may be that to make such criticisms of, and thus to emphasise, the Great Puzzle, may lead our discussion away from the real significance of the Puzzle and the true design of the mythographers' work. It must be remembered that despite the grandeur which is attached to the Great Puzzle, the vast bulk of Needham's *Science and Civilisation in China* is concerned with the description and documentation of inventions and ideas in China, and crackles with the determination to date as early as possible those ideas and inventions, to fix China as their source, and to demonstrate their subsequent transmission to the rest of the world, most especially to Europe. In short, his purpose is to put Chinese civilisation first. The Puzzle, with its retinue of assumptions and sub-themes, is no more than a justification, or rationalisation, of the encyclopaedic illustration of certain beliefs. Because of the possibility (no matter how remote or contrived) that one or other device, idea or technique may have arisen in China before it did in Europe or in some other part of the world, it is concluded that China has profoundly influenced the development and rise of Europe. Yet it is not by the presentation and elaboration of proof that this belief is transformed into fact, but rather by the repetition of those beliefs and their use as a prism to interpret the past – interpretations then used as evidence in support of the initial assumptions. With the grace and style of a sophisticated political propagandist, impression and constant innuendoes and insinuations are turned either into bold statements of indisputable certainty, or into known truths that are merely awaiting final confirmation. Gilded with scholarly understatement, with the occasional recognition that China may have learnt something from other civilisations, with cautious acceptance of the possibility of independent discoveries, with the rebuke of all those writers who really should have known better, with the sticky threads of moral righteousness, and with a rich encyclopaedic fabric, the belief in China's early superiority and in its profound influence upon the modern world is now made unassailable: an icon of a new scholarly empire.

It is understandable, perhaps, why this once-iconoclastic proposition should have become today's received wisdom. Part of the answer is intellectual hubris. China was a civilisation, a culture, a phenomenon, which would have to be analysed carefully and systematically: and this was a task which requires special training, special knowledge, special concepts and analytical devices because China is special and unique. It requires a specialist, an expert, a *cognoscente* of the Chinese world, a professional in 'things Chinese'. For only a professional can act as a sound, reliable medium between the unique and very different world of China and the West. The *cognoscenti* of the Chinese world, these latter-day Figurists, might not be infallible, but they are protected by their knowledge of a place quite unlike anywhere else. Their world, their knowledge must be judged on its own terms: 'Sinologists have appreciated for more than a century the linear time – consciousness of Chinese culture, but whatever they know takes at least as long as that to become the common property of occidental intellectuals' (GT, p. 295). Indeed, at the time that *Science and Civilisation* was being put together there were few people who were privy to the truth of the 'enormous technological debt Europe owes to China during the first fourteen centuries of our era' (ibid., p. 187). What need, then, do sinologists have for other occidental intellectuals? No need, then, to consider what occurs elsewhere. The analysis of things Chinese can proceed largely without reference to literature or ideas in other parts of the world. Even objections to the mythographers' preoccupation with 'if' are outweighed by their knowledge of China:

> No doubt in true historical thinking the 'ifs' so attractive to popular thought are out of place, but I would be prepared to say that if parallel social and economic changes had been possible in Chinese society [as in European society] then some form of modern science would have arisen there. If so, it would have been, I think organic

rather than mechanical from the first, and it might well have gone a long way before receiving the great stimulus which a knowledge of Greek science and mathematics would no doubt have provided, and turning into something like the science we know today. This is of course a question of the same character as 'if Caesar had not crossed the Rubicon'... and I only state it in this categorical form in order to convey some idea of the general conclusions which a prolonged study of Chinese scientific and technological contributions has induced in the minds of my colleagues and myself. (ibid., pp. 40–1)

But then the mythographers have little time for those historians such as Crombie, de Solla Price, Gillispie, Toynbee, Watts, and Northrop[64] who do not agree with them or who stray from the straight and narrow path the mythographers have laid down. You may acknowledge the stimulus, the cross-fertilisation of civilisations, but if you do not accept the assumption of vast chains of cause and effect, and if you are sceptical of those who claim the ability to know what might otherwise have occurred, then you are branded ignorant of China. If you are content to limit yourself to an attempt to understand what did occur, and to look at the actions and achievements of individuals, and to accept that chance has a greater part in human affairs than has the social scientists' imaginings, then either you know nothing of China or you are guilty of hero worship, ethnocentrism, intellectual sterility or racism. In 1953, in a letter to J.E. Switzer, Einstein wrote:

> The development of Western science has been based on two great achievements, the invention of the formal logical system (in Euclidean geometry) by the Greek philosophers, and the discovery of the possibility of finding out causal relationships by systematic experiment (at the Renaissance). In my opinion one need not be astonished that the Chinese sages did not make these steps. The astonishing thing is that these discoveries were made at all. (cited in GT, p. 43)

Needham refuses to acknowledge the weakness of an obsession with 'if' which this letter pin-points with great clarity, and instead chooses, once again, to raise, with both condescension and didacticism, the defence that only the sinologist is competent to speak on such matters:

> It is very regrettable that this Shavian epistle with all its lightness of touch is now being pressed into service to belittle the scientific achievements of the non-European civilizations. Einstein himself

would have been the first to admit that he knew almost nothing concrete about the development of the sciences in the Chinese, Sanskrit and Arabic cultures except that *modern* science did not develop in them, and his great reputation should not be brought forward as a witness in this court. (GT, pp. 43–4)

The study of things Chinese thus takes on the serene, quiet air of impenetrable complacency which transforms 'Chinese' into much more than a mere adjective or noun. It becomes a symbol of High Intellect and High Scholarship. It is an explanation; it is a sign of difference; and it is a claim of ownership. A Chinese idea, a Chinese value, Chinese psychology, Chinese science, Chinese relationships, a Chinese family, or some act described in Chinese terms such as *guanxi* – become caught up in, and are made inseparable from, the uniqueness, the peculiarity of a culture that has been drawn away from the rest of mankind and set within the realm of the sinologist. These are things which belong to, and are to be revealed only by, the *cognoscenti* of the Chinese world.

But is this mythography more than just an expression of the politics of academe and the naive adoption of popular sentiments of the time? Is it more than just an assault on western ethnocentrism, on the western historians who talked of 'our modern culture' and 'our high civilisation' which the mythographers rail against? Is it more than just a self-conscious, romanticised attachment to something different? Is it more than just intellectual hubris or empathetic pride and prejudice? Perhaps all these criticisms miss the essential point: that the mythographers have been creating an image – their own contemporary variation of China's stylised representations. It is an image, however, of tremendous political and psychological importance to China, particularly given the support of the spurious 'science' of the social sciences. Rather like the Jesuits of old, the mythographers have written themselves into China's culture and history – partaking in the centuries-old practice of creating a *soi-disant* culture, either for their own emotional satisfaction, or for use as a political tool. Therein lies the pleasure and the danger. Those who lend themselves to aliens, warned Lawrence at the beginning of the *Seven Pillars of Wisdom*, lead a Yahoo life 'letting them take what action or reaction they please from the silent example'.

* * * * *

Events and the interpretation of the events – the truth and the myth, the prejudice and the integrity – which make up the history of a people, comprise a valuable political device and a strong emotional bulwark.

None of this is peculiar to China. Yet the extent to which China's manipulated past is accepted, elaborated upon and institutionalised by academic analysis is particularly striking. The civilisations and empires of the Western Heartland stretch back more than five thousand years. They have been the interest of generations of scholars – trained and untrained – who have been skilled necessarily in a range of disciplines, scripts and languages. To be sure, politics, ideology, and the bias and prejudice which crowd the mind of each one of us, have exerted their influence. But just as the scholarship of this complex of civilisations reflects their interaction, the external stimulus, and the cross-fertilisation, so the world of the sinologist reflects China's defensive preserves of uniqueness, difference, and superiority, where dreams and reality fuse, and where it becomes possible to shape the millennia to one's own will.

2
Deferring to Culture

Introduction

I have argued that social science – with its structures and forces proudly borne, and with the proof of interpretation made in their light – imitates China's stylised representations and the techniques of their construction. Yet, by mimicking the operation of Imperial China's scholar-politicians, the social scientist risks being mimicked in return with equal distortion. Around their ambition and desires, individuals in China's still-medieval polity construct shadowy abstractions and skeins of dry, featureless puppets. From this world, paralleled, imitated and partaken in, by the social scientist, crawl the worms of justification. Any belief or action is explained by the structures and contents of Chinese culture which retains its moral essence because it is separate from individuals; and yet these fallible individuals are themselves freed from ultimate responsibility by the structures and contents which condition and make understandable their actions, and in which they may always find just cause. To these ideas, sentiments and methods of argument each new dynasty holds as they eulogise or tear down the deeds of past generations, fabricate their own image, and there perhaps find solace.

Truth, meaning and the rites of Cathay

Holding true to this practice of China's scholar-politicians is Watson[1] who, in his determination to call upon the past in order to strengthen present-day images of Chineseness with the most venerable (and politically valuable) qualities, suggests that truth does not exist, and that the culture to which he, and the Chinese, defer is pure invention.

The Maoists' attempt to unify China through the imposition of a centrally controlled ideology led to disruption, disintegration and anomie on a massive scale: it was nothing less than a disaster. They had attempted to enforce a shift from orthopraxy to orthodoxy, from form to content. The Red Guards had set about the 'olds' – old thought, old culture, old customs, old morals – and in their place created a febrile atmosphere of public confessions and public conversions to Maoist doctrine, leaving people without a clear sense of how to act. They had run against the grain of Chinese culture and thus against something which had held China together for many centuries – the practice of fabricating Chineseness. 'What we call Chinese culture was an illusion, a façade consisting of forms and practices that had very little content' ('Rites', p. 99) – a façade which has its roots in the Confucian Annalects:

> the central theme of Confucianism is harmony in thought and action; correct ideas follow from proper behaviour. In this sense, orthopraxy is primary to, and takes precedence over, orthodoxy. At the core of Confucian notions of order is the principle of *li*...those objective prescriptions of behaviour whether involving rite, ceremony, manners or general deportment. The Confucian approach to *li* is relevant to cultural construction: following correct form ensures that one is playing the game of culture by civilized rules and, in so doing, one becomes Chinese.'[2]

The rules which permeated ancestor worship, temple organisations and the complex rites associated with birth, marriage and death flowed through the centuries and the millennia of traditional China, and have been revitalised by local villagers in the New Territories of Hong Kong from whom Watson gains his knowledge. 'My cultural instructors', wrote Watson,

> know little of the formal teaching of Confucianism or Zhuxi, but they know a great deal about *li*, or *laih* as it is pronounced in colloquial Cantonese. Villagers use the term in ordinary speech; one hears it dozens of times each day. To them it is not an abstract, philosophic concept but, rather, an ordinary, mundane idea that has concrete associations. Constant references are made to funeral *li*, wedding *li*, and the *li* of ancestral rites; the term permeates their discourse on social activities. One of the worst things to be said of someone is that she or he is 'without *li*' (*mouh laih* (*meiyou li*)), meaning oblivious to proper behaviour, impolite and uncivilized.

In the Cantonese village context, *li* (*laih*) is best translated as 'proper form', associated closely with correct performance. To perform a ritual properly, in the local view, is to follow *li*. A funeral or a wedding has a recognised form (*li*), and deviations from it cause great concern. Older people often stand on the sidelines of funerals, watching like hawks to make certain proper form is followed . . . Cantonese funeral priests are choreographers of public ritual . . . If the ritual goes wrong or is not completed in the appointed time, disaster is certain to follow, not just for the individual but for the entire community.

. . . the villagers concern for proper form (*li*) is not simply a matter of aesthetics or personal predilection. It is the glue that holds the cosmos together. Without *li* there would be chaos (*luan*), another concept that has concrete associations for most ordinary Chinese. Among rural Chinese, *luan* conjures up views of banditry, famine, and that ultimate symbol of social break down, cannibalism. Villagers in the Pearl River delta have a rich corpus of folklore focusing on mythic massacres carried out by imperial troops who intervene to reestablish order when local society collapses. The message is clear: those who depart from accepted norms of ritual and action risk the retribution of the most terrifying kind. ('Rites', pp. 99–100)

To be Chinese, then, 'meant that one played by the rules of the dominant culture and was judged to be a good performer by those who took it upon themselves to make such judgements – neighbours, local leaders or imperial officials' (ibid., pp. 86–7). The officials could not impose a uniform structure of rites. But they could promote, for instance, standardised funeral and mourning customs. Manuals detailing the accepted norms were to be found in even the smallest towns – norms to which local elites subscribed and practised, encouraged a ritual orthopraxy. It was nothing to do with beliefs or ideas. Chinese became Chinese by acting like Chinese as defined by state and villagers. The state did not to try legislate beliefs. Officials were concerned with practice. So long as beliefs were not translated into political action, or did not become ecstatic and frenzied and people did not show signs of extraordinary devotion, they were unlikely to be of immediate concern or attention of the state and its officials.

These rites were detailed and complex and they were to be strictly observed. In the case of funerals there were nine acts which are summarised by Watson:

(i) ritual wailing to announce the death, usually but not exclusively performed by women; (2) wearing hempen gard and associated symbols of mourning; (3) ritualized bathing of the corpse; (4) transfer of food, mock money, and goods to the deceased, often through the medium of fire; (5) preparation of a soul tablet in written characters (which means that the deceased must have a Chinese name); (6) use of copper and silver coins in ritualized contexts; (7) performance of high-pitched piping and percussion to mark transitions in the rites; (8) sealing the corpse in a wooden coffin; and (9) expulsion of the coffin from the community, accompanied by a formal procession. (ibid., p. 88)

These rites had to be performed in the correct sequence; the performer and the performance were either Chinese or they were not; there could be no ambiguity. Some of these acts may well be performed by non-Han peoples, writes Watson, but 'it is the package of rites, the unique combination, that makes a funeral Chinese' (ibid.). It was the overall 'structure' rather than the details of the separate acts which mattered. The bathing of the corpse and the sealing of the coffin were performed very differently from one area to the next. But the sequence, the structure, had to remain identical. Therein lay 'the genius of the Chinese approach to cultural integration: the system allowed for a high degree of variation within an overarching structural unity' (ibid., p. 89).

Behaving as a Chinese, and compelling others to behave likewise, defines 'being Chinese', or so it would seem. 'Chineseness' is not just the rules, the rites and the ritual: it is the very act of performing. 'Performing' is what Chinese people do, and they do it consciously. Indeed, Watson's intention is to shift attention 'from the passive to active mode; people at all stages of life are perceived as actors rather than reactors'. Peasants as well as officials and literati are leading actors 'in the performance that we have come to call Chinese culture' (ibid., p. 82). The villagers studied by Watson were not social automatons performing rituals which they did not understand; nor were they puppets dancing on the strings of conventions pulled by the state. And yet it is clear that this very behaviour, the act of performing, is pre-determined. It is not only the rules that are closely prescribed: the very act of performing, the desire to act, and the desire to compel others to act is what Chinese people do. Deferring to what is said to be Chinese, and thus 'being Chinese', is all that matters if one is Chinese.

The reader has been presented with the classic recursive structure of the social scientist – culture, that ever-changing entity which must be re-created by each new generation, is 'negotiated' and 'achieved' rather than preordained, immutable or passively inherited (ibid., pp. 81–2).

The rites, the rules, the form, and the very act of performing and defer-ring, establish a context to which succeeding generations build upon and change. It is a closed world in which some force is at work through the eons. Individuals act in a way that is Chinese, because that is what Chinese people do: the rites are performed as conscious actions, and change may be subtle or radical; but the salient characteristic is the act of performing, the emphasis on form. Each individual works in con-cert with every other, creating and recreating the rules; the individual's very consciousness is to act in a Chinese way and to compel others to so act. The recursive structure, the culture, is in some way ingrained or inherent.

From this circular world there is apparently no escape; and to its images every material thing, every nuance of behaviour, may be deferred. The compulsion by village, by local officials and state, the overwhelming pressure of one's peers, the shallowness of paper-thin beliefs, ideas and ideals, and sheer institutional terror, are all part of that unique culture. Deferring to a culture which is defined by those individuals who take it upon themselves to define it so; the compulsion and coercion exacted upon other individuals to adhere to that culture; and the acceptance of that culture: these are the things that Chinese people do.

Thus, the sequence of acts which is said to define a rite takes on the same fixed, didactic quality. Watson notes that each act, if viewed by itself, 'may well be practised by non-Han people'. He need not have been so hestitant for the acts he described are practised very widely in many different parts of the world. Where else, then, lies the importance of the sequence except in the claim to uniqueness? Are we to assume that sequence, or the emphasis given to sequence, marks out a trait that is inherently Chinese? If we cannot make this assumption, and if we cannot assume that the *particular* rite of the funeral and its underlying structure by itself defines Chineseness, then we must assume that the sequence of the rite imparts a sense of 'being Chinese' because it is seen to relate to a much wider structure that must underlie other rites and patterns of behaviour which together impart 'Chineseness'. In short, each conscious or unconscious action and every nuance of behaviour – for it to be 'Chinese' – must take its proper place within a vast overarch-ing structure or nested hierarchy of structures. Individuals create and sustain this structure, and they move within its dictates, because to create, fabricate and adhere to Chineseness, to adhere to and to compel others to be Chinese, is what Chinese people do.

We are being presented with a *fait accompli* – a world that has always been, and in which every act has its rightful place within the whole. It is also a world that, perhaps significantly, parallels the views of Needham, who wrote:

> The key word in Chinese thought is Order and above all Pattern (and, if I may whisper it for the first time, Organism)...Things behaved in particular ways not necessarily because of prior actions or impulsion of other things, but because their position in the ever-moving cyclical universe was such that they were endowed with intrinsic natures which made that behaviour inevitable for them... They were thus parts in existential dependence upon the whole world-organism. And they reacted upon one another not so much by mechanical impulsion or causation as by a kind of mysterious resonance.[3]

Perhaps there also exist in Watson's analysis strains of Northrop's[4] interpretation of Chinese thought and philosophy, for does not a world in which everything has its place need only to be observed and contemplated?

Do these similarities not suggest that a Chinese conception of the universe reflected in Chinese polity, society and economy? If so, would this not betray something deeply cultural and philosophical at work? And does not Watson's unspoken recognition of this undercurrent of cultural consciousness demonstrate his intimate knowledge of Chineseness – a knowledge imparted to him by his 'cultural instructors', a knowledge that penetrates not just the literati, but the everyday, the mundane, the 'ordinary' Chinese. The diversity in expression of funerals which '*outsiders* might perceive to be chaotic local diversity' ('Rites', p. 91, my italics) Watson is able to reveal as but part of the cultural system – a system 'so flexible that those who called themselves Chinese could participate in a unified, centrally organised culture while at the same time celebrating their local or regional distinctiveness' (ibid.).

The analyst, and the Chinese, are left with nowhere to go but to accept and to contemplate what is said to be. Doctrine is no fault when the desire is to propagate image; and when there is held to be no truth, what else is left but uncompromising declarations of opinion? That there is no truth we may be sure:

> The set of cultural attributes that makes one Chinese appears to have little to do with beliefs, attitudes, or a shared creed. There was never a unified religious hierarchy or church in China charged with the responsibility of dispensing truth, as in Christendom. The notion of

truth, in fact, may very well be culture-bound concept that only has meaning in Western discourse. The closest parallel to the Western church hierarchy in China was the imperial bureaucracy, but Chinese officials were relatively few in number and preoccupied with good governance, not religious beliefs. (ibid., p. 86)

A belief in the importance of expedient absolutes which none should manipulate, above which no group or individual might set themselves above, or below which another may be condemned, is a fashionable European foible: to denigrate form and to dwell on internal beliefs, declares Watson, 'is obviously a Eurocentric view of culture and national identity' (ibid., p. 99). The village mentality, the pressure to conform, the fabrication of Chineseness, and the unrestrained manipulation of values, beliefs, institutions for political gain and personal ambition, are eulogised as orthopraxy – a legitimate practice which the present state may call upon in its cultural re-formation.

But how the gyres of dogma sing with irony! The use of 'in fact' in between 'The notion of truth' and 'may very well be a culture-based concept' makes plain the smallness of the argument, and the power of its arrogance. 'There is no truth but mine'. Watson knows the truth: and the truth is that truth is a cultural whim; and that to criticise a deferment to culture – and so to question a line of thinking which legitimises the subjugation of individuals, their values, beliefs, institutions and actions to the personal intrigues of those who define the culture and its rules – is a Eurocentric tradition. Like the officers of the Chinese state, the Jesuits, and American missionaries, Watson knows that the truth of 'being Chinese' is to defer, always, to culture.

He knows the truth that deference to culture held China together, and made it so very different from Europe or South Asia. There are other explanations of China's unity and difference which are, of course, 'correct' (ibid., p. 81). 'One cannot conceive of "China", or the abstraction we call Chinese culture, without a common script, a centralised state, and a complex hierarchy of central places. Other factors, such as a standardised education system might be added to the equation, but these are basically derivatives of the first two components' (ibid.).

But although these 'factors' – the common script, the autocratic power, the elaborate hierarchies of commercial centres and marketing communities, and standardised education – were crucial to the generation and maintenance of a unified cultural tradition, they were not in themselves sufficient (ibid., p. 98). It was orthopraxy, the 'form' of Chineseness which permitted the creation of an integrated culture in late imperial

China, and which allowed the Chinese to know that they were 'Chinese'.

All these explanations are no longer possibilities or ideas or inter-pretations: they are, *of course*, correct. They *are* right, they *are* the truth. How could it be otherwise? The script, the philosophy, the bureaucracy, the hierarchy of central places, the education, and, above all, the image, and the act of constructing that image, *are* China.

The implication that the very emphasis on orthopraxy, and that the enclosed circular existence which Chinese people are required to live, *are* peculiarly Chinese (far more than the symbols and rites which create the details of the façade) is confirmed by comparison. China was 'so very different' from South Asia and Europe:

Unlike China, the Indian subcontinent does not have a standardised set of rites to mark important life crises. Even if one restricts the analysis to the Hindu population, the contrast with China is striking. In funerary ritual, for instance, Hindu performances do not follow a standard set of acts that distinguishes this tradition from other ethnic or religious traditions. There is, in other words, no elementary structure of Hindu rites; various communities ... perform funerals in different ways and there are more differences than similarities. The same, apparently, is true of marriage rites.

Thus it is not orthopraxy that holds Hindu India together as a uni-fied culture. What, then, of orthodoxy? Here too there are serious questions, given that the subcontinent has not had a standardised set of religious beliefs nor a uniform creed ...

Louis Dumont and his followers have proposed that the unity of Indian society is to be found in the realm of ideas and values, specif-ically those relating to the ideology of pollution, purity and social hierarchy ... Dumont and David Pocock argued that the unity of India is evident in 'the existence of castes from one end of the coun-try to the other, and nowhere else.' Furthermore, 'the very existence, and influence, of the higher, sanskritic, civilization demonstrates without question the unity of India'. F.G. Bailey replied that it was not, in his view, the task of sociologists and anthropologists 'to make sense of the "flagrant contradictions in popular thought" by abstracting out consistent elements' in search of an underlying struc-ture of unity, as Dumont and Pocock had advocated. Thus for Bailey, and a host of other critics, the ideology of caste is not the universal glue that holds Indian society together. Viewing this debate from the perspective of China, we are left with the conclusion that India may have had the formal apparatus of a modern state, but it lacks the essential ingredients of a unified culture. (ibid., pp. 97–8)

The point from which comparison starts is the *fait accompli* presented by Watson – the emphasis on form and orthopraxy, the vast superstructure which *is* China and in which every act derives its Chineseness by virtue of its position within the whole. There is nowhere else for the analyst to go. No argument that Hindu India was held together by orthopraxy, and no evidence in support of that argument, could be constructed unless it was first assumed that there was some vast Indian structure in which every act had its rightful place in relation to every other act, and that each action derived its 'Indianness' from its position in the whole. Moreover, in the case of India, Watson determines that scholarly disagreement and uncertainty about the nature or existence of orthodoxy in India is sufficient reason to conclude that orthodoxy was not the glue that held India together. And since there was no orthopraxy, and disputes among scholars throw doubt upon the role of orthodoxy, then we may conclude that while India 'may have had the formal apparatus of a modern state, it lacks the essential ingredients of a unified culture.'

Not only are different assumptions made for India and China, but different lines of reasoning are required to establish the existence and significance of orthodoxy. First, in the case of India, a dispute among scholars over the significance of orthodoxy is sufficient to remove it as a consideration in attempts to understand the cohesion of India. That test of scholarly agreement or dispute is not applied to the study of China, and yet clearly it could be. We noted in the previous chapter that Needham viewed a certain amount of propaganda as the '*défaut* of the civilised civilian *qualité*', the hallmark of any civilised society; but that Chinese society was, in Needham's view, supremely moral. The sentiment is also strong in Lau's view of the traditional Chinese family which lived by a clear set of fixed rules, principles, values, ethics and relationships, but which, under the corrupting influence of British colonialism, became distrustful, manipulative and individualistic.[5] Even so, modern Chinese, at least overseas, are still indoctrinated by following well-defined rules for behaviour whereas westerners, perhaps because they are more individualistic, must look to others for their behavioural guidelines. Then again, others would argue that it is the westerner who operates according to well-defined moral principles and abstractions; and it is Chinese who are dependent upon context and relationships.[6]

Second, in the case of Hindu India, it is argued that since there was no standardised set of religious beliefs or uniform creed there could have been no orthodoxy. Yet of Christian Europe we are told that its history 'is very largely a history of changing beliefs or, more precisely, a history of fragmentation resulting from disagreements over correct belief. This is, of course, a simplistic view of the Reformation and its aftermath, but in general there seems always to have been a heavy premium on correct belief in European society and relatively less concern with ritual form. This is a matter of emphasis: obviously orthopraxy played a important role in the spread and maintenance of Christianity. None the less, there is a clear contrast between the Chinese system of religion, which stressed ritual form to the near exclusion of standardised belief, and the European religious system, which emphasised both (at different times), with heavy emphasis on truth and the eradication of heresy' ('Rites', p. 96). In the case of Christian Europe, then, tension, conflict, and fragmentation of beliefs is an expression of the significance of orthodoxy. In the case of Hindu India, however, the absence of standardised beliefs indicates the absence of orthodoxy.

Watson is able to apply the notion of orthodoxy and orthopraxy at will because the distinction is arbitrary. How far is belief ever genuine? When can we say that belief has no justificatory or ulterior purpose, or that in practice there is no belief? Was a desire for power in the Chinese Imperial empire and to that end the manipulation of China's images – 'the most solid foundations of imperial power' – any less intense within the Catholic Church and the Holy Roman Empire? Yet can we say there was no genuine belief in Taoism, Confucian, Buddhism, Islam or Christianity? Do not the rituals of the Catholic Church, the incantations, the incense, the dress, the grandeur of its buildings, the music, and the repetitions of faith, all work to intensify and to focus beliefs, ideas and emotions? Nor is Judaism less a faith for the individual whether he holds that to be a Jew he must behave like a Jew by following the rules for living prescribed in the Torah and the Talmud; or whether he simply believes himself to be a Jew, believes the central truths of God's transcendent unity and his revelation 'which requires of man to do justly, love mercy and walk humbly with thy God', and chooses not to follow what he may regard as the harsh uncompromising codes of the orthodox.

Where lies the distinction, then, between the right practice and its propagation, and the right beliefs and their propagation? Suharto's performance of his many roles (such as loving father, prayer leader, and simple-farmer-made-good), and thus his embodiment of national unity; the constant repetition of, and compulsory instruction in *pancasila* (the principles of God, humanitarianism, nationalism, popular sovereignty and social justice) in schools and the civil service; the repetition of the notion that Indonesia is a family in which disputes arise but which cannot tolerate divisive opposition; and the idea of an Indonesian form of democracy untroubled by 'western values': all comprised attempts to construct a culture for a nation that is highly fragmented, and to legitimise and preserve Suharto's rule. The similarities with China's orthopraxy are striking. But, as in China, is there no point at which the images created by such practices become sincerely held beliefs? The power and effectiveness of the propaganda lies in the simplicity and naiveté of these correct practices. The roles that seem like caricatures, the obvious and disingenuous maxims which demonstrate a willingness to defer to the culture, and the declaration of tolerance and putative universals which are both taken to be attributes of that culture, are effective precisely because they appear so anodyne, so normal, and so acceptable, that all manner of hopes, desires, beliefs, values, gods, and actions (provided they do not challenge the status quo) may be attached to those images. So 'everyday' are these images that they become a reflection of the individual; and the distinction between practice and belief soon dissolves.

The ambiguity between practice and belief is also true in our everyday contact with other people even where there is no concern to demonstrate an adherence to culture, faith or political views. Ritualised behaviour helps release the mind from the need to constantly re-think and re-work actions and responses; it makes it easier to avoid embarrassment and giving offense to others; it is a ready-made demonstration of respect and of a willingness not to disrupt; and it hides what one individual may feel another will regard as a fault or weakness. Indeed, is it not upon this more subtle and instinctive redirection and turning of expressions, intonation of behaviour, voice and language that the more obvious declarations of faith, and of political and cultural loyalties, are built?

For Watson, culture and cultural unity are not just shallow unidimensional images hiding a seething mass of tensions and conflicts; Watson presents culture and cultural unity as a structural fact. He thereby demands that individuals cannot engage in acts or hold beliefs or have ideas without participating in the creation of that fact. Cultural abstractions become the only reality: actions, thoughts, beliefs, and institutions created by individuals are but the stuff of dreams to be shaped by that reality. For Watson there is no truth: beliefs and values are quivering ephemera. Yet he knows and defines what is China and what it is to be

Chinese; he knows the intimate detail of these images. He, like the literati, the imperial officials, the local elite, the older villagers and priests, the American missionaries, Jesuits, and many present-day sinologists, takes it upon himself to define and to map out the culture to which others must defer if they are to be Chinese and if they are to understand correctly China and things Chinese. His science, his knowledge, are at one with the rites of Cathay.

Culture and democracy

Wilson,[7] too, knows Chinese culture, and sees in China's past an essential morality that is now working to re-shape Chinese society. Cultural meanings in China, argues Wilson, are shifting away from a stress on particularistic obligations and towards an emphasis on universal rights, creating a society that is, unlike 'the West', characterised by communitarianism and care.

The term cultural meanings refers to the recursive structures of the social scientist:

> The rules that coordinate exchange are independent of any individual yet come into being as the consequence of interactions among people. Because of this link to individuals the cultural meanings embedded in rules have structure in the same sense that an individual's reasoning does (for they are rooted in a comprehensive explanatory framework), but that structure need not correspond with that of any given person. As individuals interact, they interpret the meaning of behavioural rules. From this process of discourse there emerges the possibility (albeit often retarded by conservative influences) of a transformation of explanatory frameworks at both individual and social levels. ('Change', pp. 105–6)

These cultural meanings can be typed structurally. The criteria for this typology are 'inclusivity' and 'abstractness'. For example, particularistic, face-to-face rules that govern patron–client relations are inclusive; property rules embedded in general laws of contract are 'abstract'. Culture may also coordinate behaviour, and may therefore be typed, according to its 'content'.

> Content differs from structure in that it is the idiosyncratic agglomeration of beliefs and expectations that characterise a society in any given period and frame the ways people are expected to orient

themselves one to another. Content is interwoven with particular moral and ethical precepts that justify social stratification in a way that sustains solidarity. Cultural meanings, therefore, partake of two characteristics. They have content that defines appropriate orientations toward others through specific injunctions and structure that reveals the sophistication of underlying explanations of social reality. (ibid., p. 106)

In any particular society, argues Wilson, it is possible to ascertain dominant patterns of cultural meanings (that is, dominant patterns about how individuals treat and view each other, and how they interpret and explain this interaction) which appear related 'to the ways that care and autonomy are differentially stressed as social ideals. When care as an ideal is emphasised, role relationships are infused with concern, human feeling and responsibility; the stress is on the community and solidarity. When autonomy as an ideal is emphasised, role relationships are founded on justice considerations, contract and the right of the individuals to be free from interference. Western psychologists have tended to favour autonomy as the end point of preference in human development, but love of humanity is certainly just as reasonable. And, indeed, historically most societies have tended to favour communitarian values over those associated with individualism' (ibid.).

Turning to the specific instance of China, it is argued that, as in all societies, 'traditional Chinese conceptions of reciprocity were delimited by particularistic criteria, yet care, human feeling and responsibility were articulated in universal terms that were developmentally advanced' (ibid., p. 107). These terms were advanced because as cultural meanings become 'structurally more sophisticated', the concept of reciprocity (which helps in all societies to regulate exchange, by answering who is entitled to what and in what manner) 'becomes largely neutral with regard to situational and particularistic criteria' (ibid.). In other words, reciprocity is 'increasingly legitimised by abstract criteria that hold equally in all instances regardless of which side of a relationship is referenced' (ibid.). Not only was China developmentally advanced but, unlike many cultures,

the Chinese developed a set of concepts that defined desirable behaviour independent of the context of any particular instance of exchange. Such virtues as *ren* (human heartedness), *yi* (righteousness), *zhong*(conscientiousness), *shu* (altruism), and *li* (propriety) were not restricted in their application to a particular social stratum (as was the code of chivalry in Europe), although it was assumed that the *junzi* (gentlemen) was the true bearer of these qualities.

These non-differential virtues, which were at the centre of Chinese moral life, were, however, interwoven with differential ones such as *xiao* (filial piety), which established the process by which the moral order was made realizable, especially for those considered natural inferiors . . . In fulfilling *xiao*, emphasis was placed on particular status obligations; meeting these was then presumed to reveal the non-differential virtues that define a moral being. By carrying out particular duties, a person ideally exhibited qualities that served to harmonize the groups of which that person was a member, from the family up though society as a whole and also backward through preceding generations, knitting together in a total moral community both the living and the dead. (ibid.)

Following Unger and Lyons,[8] Wilson takes up the argument that these cultural meanings and changes in cultural meanings are best 'empirically validated' by examining laws that 'adjudicate relations among individuals' ('Change', p. 108). In other words, law is taken to be a direct reflection of cultural meaning and of changes in that meaning.

By 'law', is meant 'authoritative rule.' At another level it means

the processes and institutions that carry out and enforce these rules with the avowed function of settling disputes and imposing punishments. Law accomplishes these functions by defining what obligations are owed among broad classifications of persons (classes, guilds, families, and so on) and among different roles (parents and children, for example, or husbands and wives). It acts like a kind of rationing board that tells people what they can and cannot do by setting forth their rights and duties in respect to one another; it confers benefits and takes them away and enforces its own rulings. Law articulates cultural meanings in that it serves ideally as the enforcer of community standards. At the same time it is a framework for discourse about the structural adequacy of cultural meanings. As law evolves, structured and content changes in cultural conceptions of rights and duties are revealed. (ibid., p. 109)

Law also has different forms. It may be customary,

defining long-held expectations of obligations. Or it may be regulatory, establishing and enforcing explicit rules. The way in which law is administered also affects the ways obligations are defined. Procedural law imposes conditions on the processes by which obligations are determined. Substantive law governs the outcome of decisions regarding obligations. Here the moral ends of community life are directly articulated as criteria that are to regulate conduct. (ibid.)

Wilson then returns to the case of China where, we are told, 'law developed very early':

Chinese rules of law, unlike those in much of the ancient world, were not tightly intertwined with religious norms. Nor did there develop a Chinese legal profession distinct from policy makers, like the *juris prudentes* (those wise in law) of ancient Rome. There was also no third estate as in Europe or strong ecclesiastical body to promote the idea of law as universal principles of divine will which govern the adjudicating of interests independently of role and status. Instead, from very early on, bureaucratic law was paramount, while there were rules of process, they existed in an intellectual framework that stressed knowable virtue and definable obligations ...

... ancient Chinese law ... developed in its bureaucratic form with little dichotomy between commands and law and with greater or lesser degrees of particularity as rulers themselves required. For ordinary people the cardinal virtue was absolute obedience. These laws were supplemented by injunctions regarding *li* (propriety) which established the etiquette required in interactions among people of different status. The legal conception of reciprocity depended on a clear definition of status and the precise articulation of particular forms of obligations as rules of conduct. Both bureaucratic law and the rules of propriety, which became part of law as it became Confucianised, were structured in accordance with this vision.

Thus, in determining culpability, the law tended to emphasise dereliction of obligations as required by *li* above the actual nature of the transgression. (ibid., pp. 109–10)

For instance, a woman who injured or killed her father-in-law as he tried to rape her could be sentenced to death unless the Emperor decided otherwise; sons who divided family property while their parents or grandparents were still alive, could be transported; a son who attempted to conceal the murder of his father by his mother might be punished with a hundred lashes, but he would be permitted to conceal the murder of his mother by his father.

The reader is then led back to the general – this time the notion of 'rights', the study of which is extensive and complex

> and beset with multiple definitions and too often infused with polemical assertions. Suffice it to say here that rights as such – entitlements that inhere in persons – is largely a modern construct. As an underpinning of definitions of reciprocity, the idea of rights represents a major structural shift in cultural meanings. Whereas reciprocity as a series of obligations focuses on rules of conduct constrained by status definitions, rights are both analytically more abstract and more inclusive in that they define reciprocity in terms of entitlements that are universally shared. They are, thus, a more sophisticated way to conceptualize reciprocity than emphasizing obligation alone. Obligations, of course, do not vanish, but in their dyadic relationship to rights, they too are structurally transformed: into duties that, like rights, are not constrained by status rules. (ibid., p. 112)

Two categories of rights are identified: those that are positive (permitting a person to participate in social life and to have a fair share of social rewards) and those that are negative (protecting a person from undue interference from others, especially from authority). 'To the degree that societies adhere in their ideals more to one type of right than the other, they betray a major bias in the content of their cultural meanings. A disposition toward positive or negative rights derives from the linkage of these rights with the ethics of care or autonomy. The ethic of care, because it promotes concern for the welfare of others, underlies a dedication to positive rights. The ethic of autonomy, by its promotion of privacy and individualism, underlies negative rights' (ibid., pp. 112–13).

With the notion of structure, content and rights (which together make up a sense of cultural meaning) established, and their relationship with 'law' delineated, Wilson then argues that a major shift in cultural meaning is revealed by 'a shift away from a historical content in which the ethic of care was realized by fulfilling differential obligations depending upon status and toward an emphasis on care by honoring equally held rights' (ibid., p. 113).

The argument draws on a number of studies in support:

> Chu found, for example, that of eighteen traditional Chinese values, respondents still felt positively, in descending order, about loyalty to the state, benevolent father and filial son, submission to authority,

harmony, and tolerance and deference, whereas they felt negatively, in ascending order, about chastity of women, glory to ancestors, house full of sons and grandsons, pleasing superiors, and treating men and women differently. Various comparative studies make clear, however, that this shift is taking place firmly within a persistent communitarian orientation. Fritz Gaenslen, for instance, shows that the Chinese, in comparison to the Americans, put far more emphasis on the public realm and on the importance of upholding the social order and its values. George Dominio, in a study of children from Guangzhou and Phoenix, found that the most common response for American children is individualism (getting the greatest reward for oneself), followed by competition (getting a greater reward than the other child), whereas for Chinese children the most common response is equality (an equal division of rewards), followed by group enhancement (getting the greatest joint reward). These responses point clearly to content differences between the two societies along the dimensions of the ethic of autonomy/negative rights for Americans and the ethic of care/positive rights for Chinese. (ibid., pp. 113–14)

The recent history of this transition, however, has been far from smooth. The first 30 years of communist rule emphasised status in class relations and citizen obligations; officials sought maximum leeway for their own instrumental rationality; the leader was a patriarchal figure. And from 1958 until 1978 rights were disregarded: there were no explicit guarantees against torture or degrading treatment; arrest and detention, though carried out in accordance with the law, could be arbitrary and unreasonable; there was no equality before the law. Rights were seen as benefits granted by society – privileges that are subordinate to definitions and modifications of the law. Nor does the communist party have any intention of giving away its power over the legal system that defines those rights.[9]

In China, then, there has been an extraordinary emphasis (by comparison to any modern Chinese society) on obligation. Now, however 'obligation' is being directed unambiguously towards the Party and the State. 'Into this obligation-centred political environment', writes Wilson:

a conception of rights has begun to intrude. In 1979 political and civil rights were restored to landlords and rich peasants . . . Equality for all citizens was recognised in the 1982 constitution, which also included a provision (Article 38) that the personal dignity of citizens is inviolable. There has been too a heightened emphasis on law that is at least partly in accordance with the conception of the rule of law as a restraint on evil power and as a resource to be harnessed in the service of society. However frail this rule still is in China, it is undeniable that there has been a great increase in the number of law institutes and law students, of statements about educating the Chinese public about the nation's laws and legal system, and injunctions to cadres to subject themselves to the limits of law and to recognise that they have no special entitlement to ride roughshod over legal requirements. Lawyers, however, are still enjoined to . . . 'protect the interests of the state and collective as well as the lawful rights and interests of citizens'. ('Change', p. 115)

Nowhere is this new conception of reciprocity more apparent than in family relations. Marriage laws, for instance, still reflect older conceptions of obligations, but now with equal emphasis on all parties. Parents have a duty to raise children properly, while children are legally responsible to heed the demands of the parents for support (ibid., p. 116). But these changes in cultural meanings also have important political implications:

> the Chinese people today overwhelmingly endorse, above all other propositions, the greatness of China's heritage. Yet when they express pride in this tradition, they do so from a world view now removed from the central value of that tradition. An understanding of the particular obligations associated with status is no longer the pillar of interpersonal relations, and the result is a profound change in how the Chinese see themselves. The world is no longer a succession of nested 'middle kingdoms', each 'kingdom' demanding deference and the performance of appropriate duties from those of lower status. China's national identity remains collectivist, to be sure, linked in this manner with its past, but composed now of beings who, in some areas of their lives, are being challenged to see themselves as equals with the right to advance equal claims. (ibid., pp. 117–18)

The actions of the dissidents, and the reactions of those in authority demonstrate this clearly. New ideas and political change had in traditional China been voiced with great trepidation with every effort being made to appear worthless, powerless and insignificant; there was no pretence at claiming 'rights'. In pre-reform China there was only obsequious deference and phrases to highlight obligations expected of inferiors. The students of 1989 were firm in their demands: a free press; strong measures against corruption, including the publication of the private assets of China's leaders; better funding of education; freedom to migrate; an affirmation of democracy; legal guarantees covering the rights of citizens, including the right to demonstrate and to argue with, and to criticise, the government without fear of retribution, for they believed that 'relations among people and between people and government must be based on a recognition of a right to equal treatment' (ibid., p. 121). True, these demands included 'negative' rights, such as press freedom and the right to demonstrate, but they did not exalt individualism as such, 'being framed, rather, as policy changes that would benefit society' (ibid.). The students remained loyal and committed to the state, and they retained their deep sense of communitarianism.

The reactions of those in authority also reveal a shift in perceptions of rights and obligations. China's leaders did not immediately brand the students rightists and counterrevolutionaries, nor did they have them seized humiliated and punished immediately. 'Granted that serious factional infighting was also taking place among the leaders, with party secretary general Zhao Ziyang increasingly moving to support the student demonstrators for his own political ends. A debate about rights was talking the place within the government itself as well as between the government and the students' (ibid., p. 122). And then there was Li Peng's statement that 'The Chinese government attaches great importance to the question of human rights. Since the end of the Cultural revolution the basic rights of the citizens have been guaranteed. We continue to make improvements in this regard' (ibid.). The government stressed that mourning for Hu (whose death in 1989 was followed the political campaign for political reform organised by the students), should be kept orderly. 'Rights were not ignored', argues Wilson, 'but they were defined in the context of acceptable activity'. Even when martial law was finally declared 'the government was at pains to justify its actions as complying with the law and its provisions regarding rights' (ibid.). The country, stated Peng Zhen (chairman of the National People's Congress), is to be led by the working class, not the bourgeoisie; and promoting bourgeoisie liberalisation runs counter to the interests of both the People and the Party. The constitution permits demonstrations, the government said; but it stressed that in the exercise of freedoms and rights citizens may not infringe upon the interests of state, society or collectives, or upon the lawful freedoms and rights of other citizens; it pointed out that the criminal law provides that nobody may use any means he wishes to disturb the social order or the people's daily life. Thus, the decision of the State Council to impose martial law is some parts of Beijing was entirely lawful, necessary and proper (ibid., p. 123).

The government's appeal to the law in order to help justify its suppression of the students in Tian'anmen strikes Wilson as 'ironic' (ibid.), though he also sees more 'primitive motives' at work, for did not Deng Xiaoping speak to military commanders noting that student activity had developed from turmoil into 'counter-revolutionary rebellion'?

And yet profound change had taken place:

> in the context of China's historical development, the autocratic words must be placed side-by-side with the emphasis by the government on legality, however self-servingly the legal cloak has been used. For to talk of law and rights at all, to feel a need to justify actions by these criteria, is to reveal a profound shift in cultural meanings. It is also, in the end, likely to be the basis for the transformation of the absolutist political system ... [into] ... a new sense of national identity, based on equality of persons combined with communitarian ideals. (ibid., pp. 123–4)

Wilson's analysis exhibits two classic hall marks of the contemporary social scientist. The first is the presentation of a world of highly abstract forces and structures which comprise and hold together institutions, values, beliefs and patterns of behaviour. Individuals are separated from the 'culture' which they created; and yet inexorably and often unconsciously they also reinterpret and remold that culture, and by doing so reshape themselves and succeeding generations. The second is the organisation of these forces and structures and assumptions into a internally consistent theoretical framework which is then used to interpret observations.

Cultural meanings comprise structure and content – the rules and explanations, the beliefs and expectations of social interaction, which shape, and are in turn shaped by, individuals. As these cultural meanings are interpreted and reinterpreted by each succeeding generation, they may shift or develop from particularism towards a universalism that is dominated by either care or autonomy. These cultural meanings and their evolution find direct expression in the law – a connection which allows Wilson to empirically validate the theory. His theory is his conclusion, for observations are interpreted in its light, and provide it with the proof of its validity.

The authority and power which science gives the creator of this conceptual framework is enormous. If he knows the law, then he also knows the society's cultural meanings and their transformations; if he knows the cultural meanings and the sweep of society, then he also knows the law. The authority of his vision is felt in his language – 'empirically validate', 'evidence', 'data', 'adjudicate', 'injunction', 'structure' – with its legalistic and scientific tinge. It is with this authority that he proclaims rights to be complex, polemical, and full of assertions; they are fuzzy, uncertain and unclear, in sharp contrast to the clarity of law and cultural meanings which his theory allows him. It is with authority that he states rights are a modern conception, the product of the structures, contents and transitions which his theory reveals. It is with authority that we may assume 'the West' has the monopoly of autonomy and selfishness. It is on his authority that we may ignore Christian and Judaic scriptures, the writings of Locke, and how, as trade evolved and society became atomized, relationships became distanced from the conduct of trade, and emotions came to be seen as something good and proper in their own right; and how these writings and changes in perceptions, and the rise of humanitarianism, came of age during the industrial revolution.

Wilson's judgement is pure; his recognition of Chinese culture's morality demonstrates the perceptivity and morality of his science. Chinese traditional culture was infused with altruism, righteousness, warmheartedness, propriety; it was a moral community that stretched beyond the grave into past generations; it was a culture developmentally advanced, and quite unlike that of traditional Europe's; it was a culture in which 'the law developed early'. And since the law developed early (and since it is, by definition, an enforcer of community standards and a clear expression of cultural meanings), then we may safely assume that China must have been one of the first true cultures. Is it not inevitable, then, that the moral essence sensed by Needham and, before him, the American missionaries and, before them, the Jesuits, should now be flowering into an almost holy union of universalism and communitarianism, a state beyond anything to be found in China's ubiquitous antitype – 'the West'? 'Western' psychology, we are told, favours autonomy. 'But is not love of humanity just as reasonable?' declares Wilson, his words shaking with piety. Rights in China are 'positive', an adjective which emphasises the nature of those rights: care, communitarianism, the right to participate in social life, to a fair share of rewards, harmony, loyalty, benevolence, tolerance, equality of rewards, and group enhancement – words that ring in the mind like silver bells. The 'West', however, has an obsession with rights that are described as 'negative': privacy, freedom from interference, autonomy, individualism (or, in other words, 'getting the greater reward for oneself'), competition ('getting a greater reward than others') – words that are hard, officious, dark. It is 'the West' – a cold, private, selfish, private, autonomous society – which is set against the warm, loving, communitarian society of the Chinese.

Wilson, in a wonderful exhibition of the marriage of science and sinology, confuses the coldness of his scientific and legalistic words and the steady rhythm of fashionable sentimentality, with intellectual detachment and compassion. Individuals are transformed into notional beings that drift in and out of theory, graced with whatever noble characteristics, or bearing whatever faults, he chooses to dispense. Individuals, groups, even whole societies, are relieved of responsibility: all is structure and discourse. Law, it is argued, supported the conventions of a culture which allowed a son to conceal a murder committed by his father, but would have a women executed for killing her attacker. Are law and culture so intimately related here that injustice is merely a consequence of ill-judged interpretation by the participants of 'discourse' in a state that was essentially moral? 'The rules that coordinate exchange are independent of people; the structure need not correspond with that of any given person; discourse produces transformation', argues Wilson. This is a formula which allows evil to be done while the structure retains its morality; and because the individual who participate in discourse are conditioned by structure and content, they too are exculpated.

Or do these cases from traditional China suggest that justice is conditioned by culture? Did those who appealed to the Emperor feel that they had been done some injustice, or were they simply trying to preserve their lives? Does a sense of injustice attributed to others in another culture mean very little in the face of that culture? Is the sense that laws were unjust merely contextual, a symbol of ethnocentricity?

In either reading of these events and Wilson's arguments, what freedom does Wilson give to the play of politics, to the imposition of laws which derive their authority from culture, and to the presentation of Chineseness as justification! To what extremes of political repression and ruthlessness may the virtues of communitarianism and warmheartedness be turned? Still more poignant is Wilson's interpretation of China's present-day leaders and students whose actions and responses, which have been conferred by him with the morality that *is* China, are taken as proof of the validity of his model and his judgement. The students are at the vanguard of China's cultural transformation and moral advance towards and communitarianism, for they do not exalt individualism, they are committed to state, to the People, and to society. China's leaders, though still conditioned by that ancient mix of particularism, inclusivity, and communitarianism, have begun to sow the seeds of a new morality. The very fact that they feel the need to justify their actions according to the law indicates, to Wilson, that a profound transformation in taking place. Ill-judged interpretations by those participating in the discourse may produce bloody events, but the theory explains; the morality of the structure and the content remain untainted; and China moves towards the greater good.

The essential morality of China and Chinese culture, the presence of its antithesis (the West), and the use of recursive structures and occasional moral relativism to justify action, to alleviate responsibility and to confer moral heroism where it seems fitting, are but an imitation of China's own stylised representations and the techniques of their construction. Yet by deferring to culture, and to its transformation, Wilson, as but a representative of an attitude pervasive in the study of China, denies precisely that which is necessary to realise the equality of persons and the rule of law and democracy. For if we defer to culture, then that culture must be defined: its values, its institutions, its patterns of behaviour and conventions must be specified. It is the culture which defines the people, which determines what is and what is not acceptable, and decides what should and should not be. It is from this culture that law emerges, and it is in the law that culture finds expression. It is this culture which reinforces, and is in turn reinforced by, the law. By deferring to culture, we are appealing to an abstraction which is separate from, but which is also a product of the interaction of individuals, and to which individuals must logically be subordinate if they are to belong to that culture. The culture and its people must therefore separate themselves from, and be distinct from the rest of humanity. The culture is ultimate: it stands above the individual; and those individuals who do not adhere to the definition of the culture and its precepts which infuse every nuance of daily life, must therefore lie outside that culture and may be treated as beings of a different order. Deferring to culture implies that the opportunities, benefits, rights and duties of individuals may be defined, conferred and removed as the culture's representatives determine. Deferring to culture implies enforcement and the threat to exclude. All institutions, beliefs, values, conventions, patterns of behaviour and sentiments – including notions of democracy, rights, law, elements of democratic institutions and procedures which are regarded as but a expression and product of culture and cultural change – may be manipulated, for judgements can only be made by reference to what is said to be The Culture. The lives of the vast majority are thus dependent upon the benevolence and balanced judgement, or otherwise, of those who are privileged to define, to interpret, to enforce, and to exclude.

This line of thinking is implicit in Wilson's very concept of the law. It is not primarily about describing the duties and limits of the power of officials, about protecting the individual from the whims and fiats of officials; it is not concerned to protecting the majority from the minority, nor the individual from the mass. It is not about protecting rights which are held to require no special conferment by the state. It is not even about the decisions, actions and responsibilities of individuals and groups. The law emerges from culture.The law, for Wilson, is a plaything – a reflection of complex recursive structures and contents. It is about punishment; it is about defining, enforcing what is said to be the culture.

Democratic elements?

Whereas both Watson and Wilson see in Imperial China what can only be described as a higher morality, and in Maoism a disasterous break with the past, Schram, writing in 1985, saw in Mao's complex, and often paradoxical, ideas and practices a dramatic sea-change in thought that will help transform China into a more progressive state. Before 1949, Mao had spoken of a united China within which Manchus, Mongols, Muslims and Tibetans could decide their own statutes, and of a federal China that would embrace Mongolian, Mohammedan and Tibetan republics. After 1949, however, circumstances changed, and 'there was no longer any hesitation in proclaiming the rigorously unitary nature of the new People's Republic'.[10] Indeed, not only was the unitary nature of the Chinese state affirmed, but China entered Tibet, there suppressed a rebellion, and asserted control over the Tibetan people. Other striking elements to this 'paradox' soon became apparent. Mao saw government as an 'educative process'. If the scattered and unsystematic ideas of the masses were to be translated into effective action, they should first be 'concentrated', systematised and explained by the leadership before being returned to the People who would then adopt those ideas as their own. And yet Mao's thought was also marked by an insistence on the need for firm leadership by a political elite. Centralism was, in the last analysis, of prime importance. Then again, however, Mao apparently questioned the need for any locus of authority during the initial stages of the Cultural Revolution. And throughout his life, while he cocked a snook at the Party bureaucracy, Mao argued that the Party should necessarily permeate, guide and coordinate state administration and government at all levels. The explanations for these contradictions are extremely revealing, but less so of Mao than of those who stand in China's image.

Strategic and tactical considerations – political, military and administrative – were of great importance in the new Revolution. There was among Mao and his comrades 'an overriding desire to avoid the disintegration of the national polity and the consequent subjection or extinction of the Chinese people' ('Decentralisation', p. 81). The prospect of commanding and coordinating an entity as large, as diverse and as complex as China seemed to indicate (at least during the 1920s and 1930s) a level of self-determination or even federalism, which was duly offered to Manchus, Muslims and Tibetans. The experience of guerrilla warfare had also made plain the advantages of dispersing political, military and economic units while maintaining tight, clear and centralised command. The possibility of future wars, concern that rigid centralisation might rob subordinates of purpose, initiative and drive, and the logistics of managing the procurement, transport, distribution and production of goods and materials in this vast administratively organised state all seemed to demand that centralisation be married with dispersion and self-sufficiency.

Underlying these strategic and tactical considerations were more important, and more fundamental, reasons for the paradox. There was in particular, argues Schram, a strong democratic theme which ran through the thought of Mao and of others in the communist Party and the state organs. The evolution of this theme, they believed, should be allowed expression within the limits determined by the perceived overriding need for centralised control. Mao's belief that 'correct' leadership stemmed from the masses, from whom ideas should be taken and systematised, marked 'a very great rupture' with traditional Chinese thought. The Annalects taught that 'people may be made to follow a path of action, but they may not be made to understand it'. Mao's views, believes Schram, were more progressive; he attempted to break down old prejudices; he shifted emphasis away from the local official (who, in Imperial China, paid for his wide powers with ultimate responsibility to which he was held accountable by central government) and towards the People. The notion that Mao's reign was Stalinist or could be characterised as despotic, repressive, or hatefully totalitarian, is thus biased and simplistic; and any belief that attempts at genuine reform in China have been snuffed out is too one-sided.

But what exactly is meant by these democratic elements? Schram acknowledges 'the obvious fact that decentralisation or devolution of certain decision-making functions cannot in itself be equated with democracy'; we also learn that there were many Chinese in responsible positions who believed that 'socialist democracy remains still in large measure to be invented' (ibid., pp. 124 & 116). And yet we are told that Mao 'consistently . . . regarded centralised leadership as in the last analysis even more important than democracy' (ibid., p. 85). Were these undefined democratic elements therefore present? The answer would seem to be 'yes', for Mao 'treated democracy and centralisation as two indissolubly-linked aspects of the the political process, one of which could not be promoted without reference to the other' (ibid., p. 114). In Mao's thinking these democratic elements existed in a complex dialectical relationship with centralisation. Within an essential centralised framework there had to be an 'appropriate degree of local power'. Mao's speech on the 'Ten Great Relationships' given to the Politburo on 25 April 1956, believes Schram,

> is unquestionably one of his half dozen most important utterances after 1949, and one of the two or three most authoritative statements of his administrative philosophy. Section v, on the relationship between the centre and the localities, must be interpreted in the context of the speech as a whole, which tended above all to argue that the one-sided and doctrinaire pursuit of any policy goal was self-defeating. Thus, if you really wanted to develop heavy industry, you must not neglect light industry and agriculture, and in order to build up new industrial centres in the hinterland, it was necessary to make proper use of the existing industry in the coastal areas. Reasoning in a similarly dialectical fashion, Mao said . . . "The relationship between the centre and the localities is also . . . a contradiction. In order to resolve this contradiction, what we now need to consider is how to arouse the enthusiasm of the localities by allowing them to run more projects under the unified plan of the Centre.
>
> As things look now, I think that we need a further extension of local power. At present, it is too limited, and this is not favourable to building socialism". (ibid., pp. 99–100)

The trick, then, was to realise the 'appropriate degree of local power'. This effort to achieve balanced 'democratic centralism' was, in Mao's view, inextricably linked to the issue of dual versus vertical control (ibid., p. 101). The central ministries should exert direct control over large-scale and other important enterprises; but in other cases the central authorities should confer with provincial and sub-provincial authorities before reaching a decision, and control should be exercised through the established hierarchy. And the key to balanced democratic centralism was, in Mao's view, to recognise the coordinating role of the Party at all levels, both central and local. Mao goes on to explain, that when decisions were pronounced and directives issued, there 'must first be a phase in which Party members enter into contact with those who are not Party members or government organs, enterprises, cooperatives, people's organisations, and cultural and educational organs, discuss and study things with them, and revise those parts [of higher level directives] which are inappropriate [to the particular conditions]; only then, after they have been approved by everybody, are they applied' (ibid., p. 102).

The 'main' or 'great' power concentrated in collective bodies such as the central committee and local party committees was simply used to oppose dispersionism. Following Schurmann and Harding,[11] Schram argues that in this way the centralisation of general policy impulses and decentralisation of specific policy impulses was 'a unity of true opposites'.

But then what of the initial stages of the Cultural Revolution when Mao called into question the need for a locus of power which was not immanent in society itself? ('Decentralisation', p. 85). This was partly an extension of his administrative philosophy and his approach to revolution, believes Schram. Part of the explanation, however, may be attributed to arguments within the Party over changes in the class and nature of state power. Throughout the 1950s Mao had believed that the People's dictatorship (the democratic state of the People) was under threat from enemy classes – the surviving privileged strata of the old society; and he had repeatedly, if obliquely, attacked 'the working style' of the Party and its cadres. In 1962 he turned more forcefully and directly on what he believed to be a new bourgeoisie element. In Mao's view, the central state authorities were working hand-in-glove with the Party at regional levels, their intention being to lead China down the capitalist road. Faced with opposition to his views within the central administration and the Party at both central and regional levels, Mao was 'obliged momentarily to jettison the axioms of centralised authority and of obedience to the majority... [and]... when the Red Guards burst upon the scene, Mao gave it as his view that "we should let disorder reign for a few months... even if there are no provincial Party committees, it doesn't matter; aren't their still district and *xian* [county] committees?"' (ibid., p. 110). Mao had not ceased to believe in the need for effective leadership, argues Schram, but he did see the provinces as one of the main bastions of Party power and he was prepared to swamp the Party if that was the only way to purify it (ibid.).

Mao stepped back from near anarchy in 1967 and moved against the communes and in favour of the Party: 'Heads' were always needed; and over the next few years efforts were made to draw the Party together once more. The Party constitution of 1969 declared that 'party committees at all levels shall set up their working bodies or dispatch their representative organs in accordance with the principles of integrated leadership, close ties with the masses, and simple and effective structure.' The revised constitution of 1973 formally legitimised the Party's tightening grip: 'state organs, the PLA and the militia, labour unions, poor and lower-middle peasant associations, women's federations, the Communist Youth League, the Red Guards, and the Little Red Guards and other revolutionary mass organisations must all accept the integrated leadership of the Party' (cited in 'Decentralisation', pp. 111–12). If there had been any doubt, the Party was no longer to be considered parallel to the organisational hierarchies of industry, agriculture, commerce, culture, education, army or government. It was the Party which now led and to which all else was subordinate.

But as the Party once again built up a coherent organisational structure, reaffirmed its internal hierarchy, and reasserted its authority, the irreconcilable contradictions which lay deep within Mao's approach to revolution (and which had found expression in the dialectical unity of democratic centralism) became more personal and more intense, and brought about still more instability. Mao attached supreme importance to central power, to the state, and to the Party; and yet he was anti-elitist, intent on encouraging initiatives from below, and perceived authority as a personal attribute rather than the prerogative of an organisation. And during the last decade of his life, he set himself up as the guarantor of the People's right to rebel against Party and bureaucracy. Exercising personal authority likened to the first Qin Emperor, Mao 'promoted something very much like anarchy, and at the same time continued to assume his own absolute right to direct events' ('Decentralisation', p. 114).

Democracy and centralism were replaced by two different concepts – rebellion and personal loyalty to the great leader:

> No doubt Mao Zedong saw these tendencies as bound together in a dialectical unity, like democracy and centralism, which he had not in principle repudiated. Nevertheless, he allowed a situation to develop in which the 'heads', of which he had himself acknowledged the

necessity, at all levels of society and economy, could not in fact function as heads because, though they were held accountable, they had no power to take decisions. The alliance of the leader and the masses took the form, on the national level, of an un-structured plebiscitary democracy, sadly reminiscent of earlier examples. At lower levels, it produced a mixture of arbitrary rule by *ad hoc* committees, military control, apathy and confusion. This, too, is part of Mao's objective legacy to the Chinese people. (ibid., pp. 114–15)

With Deng's succession came yet another reaffirmation of China's democratic elements. Writes Schram:

The most authoritative document defining the reasons why a more democratic system is needed, the means by which it can be promoted, and the frontiers which cannot be transgressed, remains Deng Xiaoping's speech of 18 August 1980 to an enlarged session of the Politburo. The goal, forcefully proclaimed, is 'to reform and perfect, in a practical way, the Party and state systems, and to ensure, on the basis of these systems, the democratization of economic management, and the democratization of the life of society as a whole'.

Concretely, this means, in the political domain, 'to develop in full measure people's democracy, and to ensure that the people as a whole truly enjoy the power to supervise (*guanli*) the state in a variety of effective ways, and especially to supervise political power at the basic level, as well as all enterprises and undertakings'. (ibid., p. 117)

If we take this authoritative document at face value, as Schram appears to suggest that we should, then it is difficult to see from these statements what frontiers are left to transgress: Deng appears to be suggesting nothing less than full democracy for China. Schram then goes on to observe that Deng blames the fact that such rights have not, during the previous three decades, been 'adequately guaranteed to the people' upon over-centralisation, the confusion of the functions between Party and state, and on the excessive powers enjoyed by individuals leaders including, in particular, Mao Zedong.

This phenomenon, in turn, is of course explained by the fact that 'What the old China has left to us is rather a tradition of feudal autocracy than a tradition of democracy and the rule of law'. But Deng also adds that, in addition to the 'tradition of feudal despotism (*fengjian zhuanzhizhuyi*) in Chinese history,' this phenomenon also reflected the 'tradition of concentrating power to a high degree in the hands of individual leaders in the work of parties in various countries in the days of the Communist International'. These influences, Deng argues, led to a bad system, and when the system is bad, even great figures may be encouraged in evil-doing rather than restrained by it:

'When Stalin gravely disrupted the socialist legal system, Comrade Mao Zedong said that this kind of thing could not have happened in Western countries such as England, France and the United states. But although he himself recognised this point, because the problem of the system had not really been solved ..., there none the less came about the ten years of calamity of the cultural revolution.'

It is hardly necessary to remark that this comment of Mao's, and Deng's evocation of it, do not imply in the case of either man a feeling that perhaps, in some respects, the capitalist system is superior. (ibid., pp. 117–18)

Unified leadership there had to be, but if the economy was to be successful, then decentralisation of government and economic management was also essential. This required a distinction between the Party and the state to be maintained; and this in turn required the rule of law. An editorial in the People's daily went even further:

A fundamental task of the socialist revolution is gradually to establish a highly democratic socialist political system ... It is necessary ... gradually to realise direct democracy for the people (*renmin de zhijie minzhu*) at the grass roots of political power and communist life and, in particular, to stress democratic management by the working masses in urban and rural enterprises over the affairs of their establishments. (ibid., p. 119)

China does not just need democracy – it needs 'high-level' democracy. Indeed, Schram would have us believe that the signs, though ambiguous, are encouraging, for there do appear to be 'processes ... under way which may yet lead to greater degrees of decentralisation, and greater freedom of choice for the citizens' (ibid., p. 125).

Schram acknowledges that the most basic factor in the matrix out of which this orientation emerged was unquestionably the logic of the economic reforms; and that the hope for democracy depends in large measure upon the progress of democracy within the Party itself, and thus upon the success of those who countenance democratic reform in securing the acceptance of their ideas by the central Party organs them-selves (ibid., pp. 123–5). It is also true that the authority of the Party and its internal hierarchy has again been reaffirmed: 'the constitution of December 1982 once again defines the People's Republic of China as a "unitary multinational state", and asserts that "all the national auto-nomous areas are inalienable parts of the People's Republic of China." People's congresses at *xian* [county] level and above once again have the power to annul "inappropriate resolutions" of their counterparts at the next lower level, and local people's governments are, once again, responsible both to the people's congress at the same level, and to gov-ernment at the next higher level. And all local governments are, once again, "administrative organs of state under the unified leadership of, and subordinate to, the State Council"' (ibid., p. 121). It is the Party, then, which retains the power to rule on all senior appointments to the state and Party hierarchies; it is the Party which lays down basic policy guidelines; it is in the Party and the centre that ultimate power remains.

But Schram does identify a trend – however broad and ill-defined it may be – towards greater political and intellectual pluralism.[12] The Party, despite its ultimately supreme role, is being discouraged from meddling in the day-to-day running of affairs of state. To that end the importance of socialist legality has continually been emphasised and a more wide-ranging debate on the role of law in the political system has developed 'centred in particular around the question of the rule of law versus arbitrary personal rule' ('Decentralisation', pp. 120–1). Indeed, the fact that the Party is not above the law 'is now explicitly proclaimed in the Statutes of the Party itself, as adopted at the Twelfth Congress in September 1982' (ibid., p. 121).

There has also been an attempt to separate, in practice, legislative and executive powers:

> A key device for achieving this is the very considerable increase in the power of the Standing Committee of the National People's Con-gress, and the provision for the establishment of standing commit-tees in all peoples congresses at *xian* level and above. This provision is complemented, at local as at the national level, by the stipulation that no member of such a standing committee shall hold 'any post in any of the administrative, judicial, or procuratorial organs of the state.' Plainly, the intention is that these standing committees... will be able to supervise the executive far more effectively than the unwieldy, and infrequently-convened, plenary sessions of the peo-ples' congresses at various levels can possibly do.

Nevertheless, of greater weight, presumably, than this system of checks and balances in determining the relations between central and local power in the future will be the expansion of the functions of the lower-level bodies. The scope of action of local people's governments is spelled out in rather wide ranging terms...It could be argued that all this is implied by the 1954 formulation 'administer their respective areas', but the new language does appear to have been chosen to convey the message that these are active and significant organs. (ibid., pp. 121–2)

The gradual separation of Party from the government and administration of the state has been accompanied by measures designed to allow ordinary villagers and urban residents more say in government. Residents' committees and villagers' committees have been set up to deal with such matters as public security and public health. Intended as mass organisations of self-management, these committees also transmit opinions, demands and suggestions to the people's government. The introduction of direct and comparatively free elections to lower level people's congresses have been of particular symbolic importance, however, particularly given the continued emphasis on devolving decision-making power to cadres at the lower ends of the Party hierarchy.

Although plainly aware of the importance of image in China's polity, however, Schram opts not for simplicity, but for intellectual complexity. His purpose, or so it would seem, is to trace China's images, to present that outline as an analysis of China as it is, and thus to bring consistency and credibility to rationalisation. Democracy is used as a word to convey a sentiment that few would disagree with; but its meaning, which is never allowed to crystallise, shifts with circumstance and the details of the argument. Schram acknowledges that China did not achieve democracy, but its presence, its weight, is always to be felt.

Schram's scepticism of the more romantic, sentimental and spiritual assessments of Mao and of China's mercurial political life (such as the notion that Mao, a sage leader, who had no interest in power, saw no place for coercion, was concerned only to allow the People to liberate themselves, to run things in their own spontaneous way, and to decide for themselves what they should study and learn) is used to enhance the sense of Schram's own balance and objectivity. His presentation of the Cultural Revolution as something of an aberration – a sad period during which progressive, democratic centralism was at some point replaced, or transmuted, into the Qin cult – is used to similar effect. The notion that China possessed any democratic elements to be extinguished in the first place, that the values and beliefs which lay at the core of Mao's being represented a true break with China's past, seem plausible when set against the arbitrary personal rule which brought China to near anarchy. Even the suggestion that in Deng's view the aim of reform, at least in part, was nothing less than to democratise 'the life of society as a whole', and that Deng's statement of his view represents one of the most authoritative documents defining the reasons why a more democratic system is required, now seems entirely reasonable; and thus Schram's argument that China does seem to be moving towards democracy, seems both sensible and logical.

But it is Schram's own understanding which gives China's democratic image its weight and presence. There is something colloquial and very intimate about his knowledge. Mao was avuncular, paternal, irascible, irrepressible and always poking fun at authority; and yet he was also guided by intricate thoughts and complex ideas about Revolution. He was both a committed revolutionary who saw the need for leadership; and yet he was also racked with a determination to sweep away self-interested elites and to give the People more power and control over their own lives. The last few years of his life were also his saddest. Mao had already begun to take to extremes his own approach to Revolution when his acolytes, seeing him ageing and ill, corrupted for their own purposes the values and ideas by which he had always lived, turning democracy and centralism into rebellion, mobocracy and the cult of personal loyalty. Schram sees not in black and white, but in subtle shades of colour; his judgement is untainted by the prejudice of simple right and wrong or by misinformed preconceptions about Oriental despotism or the romantic eastern sage. It is Schram who is able to identify the progressive and democratic elements in a state that is first Chinese and second communist. It is he who understands the contradictions within the personality of the leader, for it is Schram who knows how to enter the leader's mind and how to empathise and sympathise with his foibles and failures. Again and again Schram treats his reader to the *correct* interpretation of Mao's thought and actions. It is Schram who knows the true meaning of such exotic terms as *daquan*, *xiaoquan* and *yiyuan hua*, for they are far more than just slogans or coded maxims – they are windows into the soul of Mao.

Schram exhibits the knowledge of the insider. There is no need to clarify or harden the meaning of democracy, democratic elements or the quality of democracy. By virtue of his knowledge and his understanding, China's images need only be traced; and dialectics of democratic centralism and the mass-line need only be accepted by Schram as indicative of the struggle within China's democratic elements, and of the need for central control. His authority is enough to mark China out from a repressive and hatefully totalitarian regime: *tout comprendre c'est tout pardonner*.

Schram's analysis has about it the air of a skilled but contrived rationalisation of China's stylised representations. He acknowledges the obvious fact that the decentralisation of decision-making cannot itself be equated with democracy. But to suggest or imply that such 'elements' confer the quality of democracy to a state that is otherwise non-democratic, transforms multi-dimensional institutions, values, practices and beliefs into unidimensional causal entities. Democracy and its associated sentiments become no more than a unidimensional image, a plaything, which helps mask or legitimise the manipulation and redirection of institutions, values and beliefs and practices in order to give credibility to the status quo. It could, and, indeed, it often is, argued that China is already more advanced democratically because it is socialist, and has bound into its constitution all manner of democratic elements.

In Schram's analysis, 'democracy' becomes an indistinct but strong presence which impregnates individuals, institutions and procedures with the quality of reason, balance and morality; the flat, unidimensional, causal and universal properties of democratic elements which are thought to exist as an empirical fact quite separate from the individual, endow the concept of those elements with a legitimacy which leaves it open to manipulation; and an explicit deferment to culture allows that manipulation respectability. As Schram points out, Deng believed that the excessive powers enjoyed by individual leaders, and most especially by Mao himself, owed something to the days of the Communist International when power was concentrated in the hands of the leaders of individuals of parties in various countries; but it was also to be explained by the fact that old China had left the communist leadership with 'a tradition of feudal aristocracy rather than a tradition of democracy and the rule of law'. If there is the implication here that democracy and the rule of law is a-cultural (as the lengthy discussions in China on the role of law, and the apparent movement towards democracy identified by Schram would seem to bear out), then there is also the implication that something cultural – and even something akin to the notion of oriental despotism – is at work, corrupting even the greatest of men. This ambiguity is strengthened by Schram who – immediately following Deng's comment about the stability of 'the systems' in England, France and the United States, and their ability to resist the pernicious influence of one man – is quick to point out, even though he believes it hardly necessary to do so, that neither Mao nor Deng felt that in some respects capitalism was superior.

Schram's statement, bristling with empathetic defensiveness, could be taken to imply either that China need not model itself on Western capitalism because democracy and the rule of law is a-cultural; or that there is every reason to think that China will develop its own form of democracy and its own legal concepts. It was perhaps this latter position which Deng held, for another of his stated beliefs is that the human rights and democracy of 'the West', and those of China, are two different things.[13] Entwining arguments and sentiments which gleam with the colours of both positivism and postmodernism provides ample room for maoeuvre – to twist and turn with whatever rationalisation appears necessary in the construction of China's sylised representations.

And the simplicity of what Mao was about is not to be considered. Mao, like his supporters and competitors, would throw and keep open as many opportunities as possible. Power was to be multi-stranded, though bunched at the top in his hands; institutions and procedures, ideas and beliefs, as they bent to his will, were merely a means to an end. If opposition within the establishment became too strong, then the rules of the game would simply change: he would denounce, then circumvent the establishment, its hierarchy, its institutions, and its procedures, and play directly to the people through the mob; he would chop and change, confuse, and take opportunity where it came. This made for unpredictability, confusion, uncertainty and instability; and thereby created highly fluid circumstances in which nothing seemed fixed or absolute except personal ambition and survival, and in which the multi-dimensionality of values, beliefs, institutions and individuals became apparent and could be turned more easily to advantage. Those whose thought followed channels laid down by others, whose minds followed the lines of procedures and institutions, whose thinking needed some external framework, whose horizons seemed more limited by the circumstances created by others, and who therefore seemed less imaginative and more staid in thought and action, became Mao's to shape and manipulate with contempt. Emotions, relationships, ambitions, fear, beliefs, values, policies, and the dry, anodyne slogans of Marxism were but tools to be adapted or disposed of as seemed fit. The world of Mao and his supporters and opponents, was reality; the world created for, and which surrounded, those whom they governed was made up of flat, bland images to be unfurled like a painted canvas, the back-drop against which China's mercurial leaders stood like wooden figurines. With that knowledge of what was reality and what was imagery, and with a sense of the ease with which they could manipulate others, came arrogance and contempt. This was, and remains, a raw, undiluted, earthy polity comprised of individuals and loose factions who have no respect for institutional, procedural, legal or individual probity. This is a polity which marks no great rupture from the past, nor contains within it cultural structures, universal forces or other imaginings which, some believe, will lead to a more democratic, communitarian and caring state.

Revolution or reconfiguration?

Once released from the sentiments of China's stylised representations and the ornate intellectualisms of social science, China's recent past appears far less refined. Although imperial China had crumbled and the communists had set about eradicating the remnants of its past, the new regime which emerged in 1949 after more than thirty years of internecine war and political struggle was but a reconfiguration of the dimensions of China's old polity. The energy and power of this new regime came not from above, but from below, from the everyday relationships that surrounded each individual. Strength lay not in the visible institutions and defined procedures, but in the village mentality, in the prejudice of petty, narrow minds, in the everyday concern for social power and status, to which end relationships, emotions, values, beliefs and images were manipulated. Friendship, loyalty, trust and altruism were not recognised or treated as values or emotions in their own right. There was in consequence no satisfying stricture against perfidy; institutions, values and beliefs were not treated as if absolute; and the absence of such absolutes implied acceptance of envy, suspicion, bitterness and resentments and other base emotions – all instruments of the politic individual. Where so much depended upon the complex play and manipulation of emotions and relationships, the individuals' fear that each was subject to the whimsical judgement of another bred an obsessive desire for conformity and for the expression of sameness. There, in the ordinary, unremarkable, and mundane life of the everyday, lay the surest foundations for totalitarianism and the most intolerant extremes.

Into this mire of emotion which surrounded him and upon which he rested, the leader could reach and shape according to his will. He did not merely represent or espouse laudable ideals: he embodied them. To the leader, the individual was either loyal or disloyal; with the leader the individual would or would not identify directly. For only he, the leader, was anti-establishment and a true revolutionary. The beliefs and values that the leader did not hold, the institutions he ignored, the behaviour or actions in which he did not participate, constituted the establishment. All that was suspect, errant or hostile need not be specified nor that judgement explained, for such judgements were defined by what he was not. His personality, whims and actions were the touchstone of the acceptable and unacceptable. His very being legitimised and sanctified the vent given to envy, jealousy, frustration, petty disputes, and long-standing grudges against the denunciated or those who, it was decided upon some or other whim, did not seem to fit in and should therefore be held up for ridicule.

The roughly-hewn intellectual framework which gave shape and direction to the instinctive political thought and action of the leader and the Party was militaristic. Ideas, intentions, ideology and philosophy were, as Meissner[14] argues, expressed in a lexicon of coded terms pregnant with allusions to military strategy and tactics. Victory after years of guerrilla warfare against the nationalists and the Japanese had been far more a military achievement than a political one. The highest offices of the Party, Administration and Government would not be reached without the favour and respect of the military. And without them, control over a state the size and diversity of China and its transformation into a world power would not be possible.

The most striking characteristic about the phrases, maxims and explanations wielded by the Party, government and bureaucracy, however, was their banality. The vague, bland, almost soporific quality of the wording, suffocated by ambiguity and emptied of life, pounded against the senses like dull, thudding waves. Their purpose was to transmit not clear intent or understanding, military or otherwise, but *non-sequitur* rationalisations; they were but symbols of guile, intrigue and *courtiserie*. China was the servant of its leaders' ambitions and sense of history and of their place within it. These ambitions were not abstract ideals of statehood, nor were they collective: they were personal and individualistic. The battles amongst China's new rulers were fought by proxy through the manipulation of relationships with individuals and groups at all levels and through the façade of institutions and policies which these networks of relationships threw up. But in the prosecution of these struggles millions would die; and the leaders who worked those faceless marionettes, and who lost the struggle, would themselves also suffer political or physical death.

The village mentality and totalitarianism

The village mentality infected every sphere and nuance of daily life, for it was not so much imposed from above as encouraged to rise from below. What better way to unleash and then harness the emotions and petty tensions generated, than by providing easily defined targets against whom hatred and violence could be turned? The individual need demonstrate loyalty only by public expressions of anger and violence against symbolic criminals, by pouring vitriol upon the denunciated, and by garish displays of ecstatic joy and fawning towards the righteous in authority. While the PLA set about eradicating its enemies, the Party, concerned to consolidate its rule, increased its membership by recruiting the young; but it claimed to be a broad church that would incorporate non-communist parties; Party cadres were moved into every community; and People's courts were set up in rural areas. Here the People were classified by the People into landlords, rich peasants, middle peasants, poor peasants, and landless labourers. The landlords were judged and sentenced; hundreds of thousands were executed.

Xenophobia, transformed into an exalted creed by the Korean War, anointed the village mentality with the religiosity of national security. Any long-standing dislike, disagreement or grudge, any errant behaviour or view, was justification enough to level charges against another individual. The greater the spite, the more intense the paranoia, the more petty the disagreement, the more reasonable it seemed. In this atmosphere of fear and steely self-confidence, the movement of the PLA into Tibet, the centuries-old weakness on China's western flank, and into Matsu, threatening Taiwan, were righteous and imperative actions which needed no further justification; and the centralisation of bureaucracy, government, commerce and industry needed no explanation.

The good effect which centralised state control seemed initially to have upon China's economy during the 1950s was illusory. Performance was being measured from an extremely low base, for little of the country's industrial capacity had been in use: peace and some degree of organisation, whatever its nature, would allow the Chinese labourers to practise the valuable skills they had learnt as workers for the Japanese war-machine, particularly in Shanghai, Manchuria, Canton, Hankow and Tianjin, and to produce immediate results. More importantly, the Soviet Union made available credit and technical help, and opened itself as a market for any goods that China might care to produce. But the political significance of the centralisation of control over industry and commerce in Beijing was considerable. The industrial labourers in the cities were favoured: they had job security, comparably high wages, and housing supplied at nominal rates; and strict controls over the movement of population from rural areas to the city protected them from competition. They became a conservative bloc, ready to support those who rewarded them and upon whom they depended.

While his opponents, men like Liu Shao-ch'i and Deng Xiaoping, built up a centralised bureaucracy, emphasised heavy industry, secured influence over industrial workers, and turned to the Soviet Union for help in their efforts to strengthen the economy and the armed forces, Mao set about creating an atmosphere of righteous morality in which his opponents' strategies would seem out of place, and in which control was exercised more flexibly through his own personality rather than through a rigid bureaucracy that would only frustrate his desires. The campaigns used by his opponents to tighten discipline over cadres, to remove those who seemed to oppose their wishes, were gradually turned in Mao's favour. Selfishness, material gain and disloyalty were deemed to be the ultimate sin; morality was defined by community, spiritual rewards, loyalty, and self-reliance. Anything which did not originate from Mao or did not fit the moral context he created was improper. Mao looked not to industrial workers, but to the youth, to students and to the peasants. The control and criticism of intellectuals which had begun in 1950 intensified. The young were to be his; there was to be no thought, no virtue or sentiment but his; they were to have no heroes, no doyen but him; acolytes were to have no master but him. There was to be no culture save that which he defined.

First, Mao encouraged the intellectuals to say what they felt, to criticise both government and Party and even Communism itself; there was to be a hundred schools of thought, and a hundred flowers were to bloom. Then he launched the Anti-Rightist campaign against those who spoke out. The campaign merged with the continuing rectification campaign in which every organisation had to set aside time to weed out improper, impure thoughts; and both campaigns merged with an attack on bureaucracy and centralisation. The cadre member was to become an activist; and administrative controls were to be loosened.

At the same time, Mao pushed for rapid collectivisation and the mobilisation of large numbers of people into enterprises that would require little capital. This was not a matter for debate: it was to be. It was all a question of loyalty or treachery. The new units, the communes, would supply the materials the state needed, but would otherwise be self-sufficient and self-reliant; they would develop and apply 'walking-on-two-legs' technology; they would embody all-round development of agriculture, education and industry. They were to be no less capable of bringing about rapid, though dispersed, industrialisation. All energies, all resources would be channeled into the backyard furnaces for iron and steel. This was to be China's Great Leap Forward: China would surpass the Soviet Union as a communist power; and China's economy would surpass that of Great Britain within fifteen years. People were to work in constant shifts, and machinery was to be pushed without regard to its limits. As an economic policy, it was a flight of pure fancy. But it all made good sense as far as Mao's political ambitions were concerned. Mao did not need a complex centralised bureaucracy, for Mao had no need of anything that would only frustrate his ambitions.

For all Mao's emphasis on the dispersal of power, the question with which he and others in the leadership were especially concerned, was the way in which power was concentrated. The tension between the centralisation and decentralisation of power, between the dictates of policies from above and the mass-line (integration of the People's views into policy) was only apparent. Centralisation was a palpable hierarchy of institutions and procedures – the visible route through which power was focused upon the leadership. But decentralisation – the concentration of relationships in the hands of the leadership directly, without having to pass through contending factions within the bureaucracy – brought the leader true power and security. Institutions comprised individuals; the procedures were the actions those individuals performed. This frippery would be permitted just so long as it served the purpose of the leader. If, however, the leader could not satisfy his will, if competition became too intense, and if his position was threatened, then that ornate hierarchy would be circumvented, undercut or dissolved, and the webs of personal relationships, left floating without direction, would be quickly gathered into his hands, new groups of individuals which answered to him would be formed, and he would play to the People directly.

To some extent Mao was favoured by the organisational arrangement of the economy – a monolithic or unitary system in which the production, procurement and distribution of goods and materials was centrally controlled. The logistics of managing and running this huge administrative labyrinth demanded the fragmentation of the economy into areal and functional divisions. Hierarchical and compartmentalised economic units were often required to practise self-sufficiency: the state could not plan for, nor physically handle, the procurement and distribution of every item in a country the size and complexity of China. With its position fixed in the whole, each unit was dependent upon the hierarchy and upon the state system of procurement and distribution to the extent that producers had little choice but to subordinate their decisions to those of the authorities, and every individual was constantly reminded of their own dependence upon the great, paternalistic state. Control over the procurement and distribution of goods thus provided the central authorities with a vital means of political and social as well as economic control. When the formal institutions and procedures were by-passed and began to fray and dissolve, leaving exposed the personalistic webs upon which they had always rested, and when factionalism and personal interest became unrestrained and open, economic units found themselves cut adrift and made still more dependent upon the favours of those with influence. Collectivisation meant the establishment of still larger units less dependent upon a centralised bureaucracy, into which Mao could tap directly. Decentralisation was also necessary for China's break with the Soviet Union without whose support China's planners would have to abandon rapid modernisation of industry and of the military – strategies which Mao had attacked at every turn.

But the organisational arrangements of the economy also worked against him. Self-sufficiency and administrative fragmentation combined with centralised control over production and procurement and distribution – the 'cellular' and 'integrative' characteristics of the economy – had obvious implications for efficiency. More importantly, these characteristics were symptomatic of the key problems with a unitary economy – the necessity for balance. If more and more production activities come under central control, the centre inevitably becomes responsible for the allocation of goods and materials if production is to take place and if needs and desires are to be met. And as the government takes on more responsibilities, its decisions regarding one unit cannot but have implications for another, whether it effects its orders through command, by direct expropriation, or by manipulating such tools as profit margins, tax or interest rates. But if the decisions made are based upon inaccurate information, or if orders are not synchronized or are delayed, or if orders are wilfully corrupted or disobeyed or cannot for whatever other reason be fulfilled, or if it is necessary to increase output or the quality of an item produced by one sector (which therefore requires greater amounts of materials, energy, transport, technical knowledge, information and tools and skilled personnel), then imbalances – shortages and surpluses – will be created in the rest of economy, adversely affecting the production and supply of goods elsewhere. The logic of the system required imbalance (as goods and material are shifted to favoured units and sectors) if progress was to be achieved. The favouring of urban industrial workers and the determined push to modernise heavy industry

and to increase its output, which had been made possible by the support of the USSR, had also required that the rest of the population
should have their living standards suppressed. Yet the reality of our
world and the extreme complexity of the administrative arrangements
made it very difficult in practice to sustain balance, let alone to control
imbalances necessary for material progress. Inefficiency, the shortages,
and the surpluses, did not explain economic stagnation and deteriora-
tion; they were merely indicative of the workings of a unitary economy.

Even as collectivisation was underway, Mao felt himself being
marginalised. He was replaced by Liu Shao-ch'i as chairman of the government in 1958. Mao had not lost his bite: when Peng Te-huai, the
Defence Minister, who had earlier criticised Mao's policies for communes, argued that ties with the Soviet Union should be strenghtened,
Mao had him removed from office for anti-Party activities. Shortly
thereafter Peng disappeared. But Mao's opponents were now being
aided by the logic of the economy which they, and Mao, had helped to
create, and which Mao had contravened, strengthening their hand
against his. Sudden collectivisation and the dispersal of heavy industry
into every commune and 'backyard', the punishing treatment of both
workers and machinery, the idealisation of 'walking-on-two-legs' technology, the weakening and then, in 1960, the withdrawal of Soviet
support and markets, combined to exhaust and demoralise peasants
and industrial workers alike, to ruin machinery, to waste raw materials
and to set in motion huge imbalances. Materials and human energies
were turned away from the production of food and towards small-scale
heavy industry by localized cells of workers and peasants with no
thought about how they would supply their other material needs or
whether others could do so. Aggravated by the lack of attention given
to the coordination of production, procurement and distribution, and
with no independent trade networks to fall back on, imbalances led to
severe famine. In South China, order broke down and people flooded
into Hong Kong.

Despite the return to more orthodox policies as the authorities sought
to restore balance, and once again permitted the operation of free markets and private trade networks, it was not until 1962 that China began
to recover from the Great Leap Forward. But although Liu Shao-ch'i and
Deng Xiaoping now seemed to have the upper hand, the problems
which Mao's actions had brought, and the pragmatic solutions which
his opponents had implemented, were turned by Mao to his advantage.
He now set about the destruction of Party and government bureaucracies, and cut away the body from its head. By gathering personal

relationships into his hands, and by setting up extremist revolutionary bodies of school and university students – the Red Guards and Revolutionary Rebels – he circumvented and undermined Party and government bureaucracies, and played directly to the mass and its village mentality, allowing himself to be presented as the embodiment of ideas, morals and principles with which 'the People' should identify. Yet all the while he kept the army (with its own contending factions) behind him. Mao renewed his propaganda and indoctrination campaigns: the party and the army had been demoralised by the failure of the GLF, but now the righteousness of equality, self-sacrifice and revolutionary purity, which helped to legitimise the imbalances set off by the GLF, became their clarion call; and the strategies which had been used to rescue China from the economic disaster wrought by Mao became the foil to his socialist education campaign – an attack on all forms of revision and on excessive bureaucracy. Peng Te-huai, who desired technological modernisation and links with the Soviet Union, had been removed by Mao in 1959 and replaced by Lin Biao who, like Mao, believed in guerrilla warfare conducted with armaments of a rough and ready technological standard. The people were enjoined to learn from the PLA's political commissars who paralleled the chains of command of the Party and government, confusing political and economic communications still further. Propaganda cadres declared that power originated from 'learning the thought of Mao'; and youths were to carry knowledge, educations, skills and experience from the urban areas to the countryside.

When in 1965 Deng Xiaoping called for better relations with the Soviet Union and for rapid modernisation, the idea was denounced by the Mayor of Peking (who also commanded the Peking garrison), P'eng Chen, whom Mao had made chairman of a group to supervise the intensification of ideological training – a group which had included Wu Leng-hsi (the editor of the People's Daily), Lu Ting-yi (the head of the Party's propaganda bureau), Chou Yang (a specialist dealing with intellectuals), and K'ang Sheng.[15] Mao then began his struggle to wipe out bourgeoisie ideology in all forms of activity – academic, education, journalism, art, literature. High officials in Beijing were denounced, heads of universities were purged; the bulk of Party professionals, including Liu Shao-ch'i and Deng Xiaoping became targets; and Mao even turned on P'eng Chen and accused him of organising a coup.

The sentiments, the attacks, the soaring ambition, the atmosphere of bile, hatred and self-righteousness, and the appeals to 'the People' were given expressive focus in the Red Guard and Revolutionary Rebels whose most active members were the sons and daughters of lower-order cadres who now saw, and took, the opportunity to better their station. They attacked 'old' ideas, 'old' values, 'old' customs, 'old' history, and anyone in authority – teachers, administrators, Party bureaucrats and high party officials; museums and art objects in private houses; and anything to do with traditional China or traditional culture labelled 'bourgeoisie' were vandalised. Old scores and grudges, personal frustrations and bitter emotion could now be given righteous vent and, at the merest whim, could be directed legitimately at anyone who did not seem to fit.

With the logistical support of the PLA, the Red Guard travelled the country, took over the railways, poured into Beijing to adulate Mao, and disrupted the factories. In their turn, the factory workers, who constituted the conservative bloc through which Mao's opponents hit back, initiated strikes, moved to take control of the railways, and, in order to aggravate inflation, spent factories' treasuries on consumer items. By 1967, Mao had achieved what he had set out to achieve – a state of chaos. China was now on the brink of anarchy.

This turmoil and confusion had been created on Mao's terms; now he would bring order on his terms. Initially the Revolutionary Rebels and Red Guards formed an alliance with both the PLA and the Revolutionary Cadres – bureaucrats now remolded as Maoist supporters. This 'triple alliance' formed the basis of the Revolutionary Committees. In the provinces, disputes among factions of the Red Guard, revolutionary rebels and cadres required the Army to step in and to assert order. Mao was beginning to distance himself from the youths: they had served to mask the influence of the army, but now the mask was no longer needed. The Regional commanders of the PLA broke up the Red Guards and sent 20 million youths from the cities into the countryside. By September 1968, the Revolutionary Committees, now run by the army, had replaced the Party organisations. With the army left in control and under his leadership Mao turned his attention to the re-construction of Party and bureaucracy according to his will. Liu Shao-ch'i was expelled from the Party; the Central Secretariat of the Party was eliminated, leaving Deng Xiaoping, its Secretary-General, without office. Zhou Enlai, seeing which way the wind was blowing, had associated himself with Mao several years earlier, and now took charge of the details of re-construction. Mao wanted Party and bureaucracy staffed by younger people and by the army: more than a third of the Nineth Party Congress were army officers; and 123 of the 279 members of the Central committee were from the military.[16] Following the army model, regional, provincial and sub-provincial governmental units were given considerable autonomy; but the lines of power and authority emanating from each unit were focused directly upon Mao rather than being diffused and filtered through a complex bureaucratic hierarchy in which opposition and blocs could be established easily and surreptitiously. For Mao, decentralisation meant direct, unfettered, personal rule.

It is true that, despite the proxy wars, the Communist Party had in many respects managed to provide a better life for the vast majority in China. But the cost had been enormous. The unleashing of the village mentality, the emotions that were aroused by memories of the hardships suffered before 1949, and the pressure to exhibit hatred, bile or unparalleled joy as demonstrations of loyalty, gave legitimacy and righteousness to intense feelings and extreme actions. Hundreds of thousands of people had been executed immediately after the Communist Party took command. The logic of the new economy took the lives of more than 20 million; and another million or so had died in the excesses and violence of the Cultural Revolution.

Reform or succession?

By the time Mao died in 1976, China's economy had been far outpaced by the achievements of many countries in East and Southeast Asia. Indeed, it was partly the examples of their success and of China's poverty which helped to discredit socialism wherever it was practised. Sustained and rapid material progress was now more than ever a strategic necessity for China and for the survival of the Party. The goals remained the same – the maintenance of unity and power, and the construction of a strong and powerful state with global status and reach – and they seemed to remain, for the leadership, as intensely personal as ever. But the means would have to change. The prevailing strategic and political dictates – the pillars of state control – would have to be re-examined, rejected, replaced, redirected, or temporarily subordinated to the demands of trade; and China would have to open itself to the very nations which it had ultimately held responsible for more than a century of humiliation.

Now again in command, Deng Xiaoping would have the final word in his long-running battle with the Maoists. He began to modernise China and bring about greater prosperity by drawing a distinction between state administrative organs and economic units, by devolving economic decisions to individuals and enterprises, by loosening administrative control over the procurement and distribution of goods, and by turning partially to the market and to foreign investment. The maze of visible, gimcrack institutions and procedures of the revolutionary, centralised state would, in consequence, gradually fall away or dissolve into personalistic networks; the surviving economic concerns of the state and collectives would fall into the hands of the political elite; the concepts and values with which his old enemies had built and legitimised their power would also seem moribund; and the material interests of the urban population, and the rural communities (where the decentralisation of economic power first began) would be associated with Deng. Yet all the while, his control over the army would be strengthened.

His ambition was clear: to secure power and to make China a more worthy vehicle upon which to impress his will and legacy. But there was no intention to transform China into a classical market economy, and the only Grand Design was that which the passage of time might allow an observer to impose upon uncertain struggles and chance events. Whatever seemed to work in the judgement of the moment would be acted upon; the more indistinct the network of relationships and workings of power, the better, for this would allow the leader greater opportunity for movement, and leave others guessing. China would be held together far less by planning, bureaucracy and procedure than by a common desire, and a shared need, for material progress; and by the common understanding that the interests of merchants (whether or not they also held political, bureaucratic or military office) were ultimately subservient to, and dependent upon, Deng's largesse.

This was a continuation of war by proxy; but now bureaucrat, politician, soldier and commoner would see in their leader their own material well-being. The dissolution of the institutions, procedures and values of the Revolutionary state, the haze of personal relationships, and the strengthening of Deng's control over the army, would make it difficult, if not impossible, for either revolutionary messiah or democratic hero to move against him. And if they should try, the army, whose entrepreneurial activities would help fund its modernisation and their leaders' material comfort, could be relied upon to act quickly and ruthlessly.

Yet there must be doubts over whether this reliance on informal personal relationships, and the institutions which rest upon those relationships, can provide the necessary stability, cohesion and predictability in a country as large and as diverse as China, or do so without appearing to threaten and challenge the rule of the Party. These questions are likely to be sharpened by the weakening economies of East and Southeast Asia, by the intensification of competition which may follow, and by the circulation of debt and loans within China itself.

Beijing may have good reason to worry that its people, most especially at the fringes of the Chinese state, will look more to the outside world, to Northeast Asia, to Central Asia and to Southeast Asia, as they come to view the very concept of 'China' and 'Chineseness' as a dead weight upon their personal interests. The practice of trade, and contact with other views and practices, may encourage changes in perception, the expansion of ideas and the opening of minds, bringing accepted beliefs, values, and concepts of worth into question, and forcing self-reflection and criticism. Greater flexibility and multi-dimensionality in thought combined with the need to organise in defence of personal interest and ambition as the state withdraws its responsibilities over welfare, and as the political elites prosper, seem ideal circumstances in which associations of merchants, thrown up by, and resting upon networks of personal relationships, will continue to expand in their scope, size and influence. Rather than align themselves with Beijing, private traders may well continue to develop inherently unstable alliances with members of the provincial and sub-provincial administrations, for both merchants and China's bureaucrat-politicians share the same goals – the realisation of material progress, and their professional and physical survival.

Logic would therefore seem to demand that the state relinquish most of its control over both state and collective enterprises, for without such change, China might well shatter into a kaleidoscope of merchant-bureaucratic empires, loyal only to themselves and oriented more towards the outside world than to Beijing. And with privatisation may come the operation of private and independent banks, the creation of private insurance schemes for welfare, unemployment, pensions and health, and, in order to provide a stable and predictable framework around which this increasingly atomised economy and society may operate, the establishment of strong and impartial legal institutions and procedures for the conduct of business. China may even find that, in the interests of prosperity and stability, political action must not only be constrained by a concern with material well-being and the economy, but that the polity must also undergo fundamental and, to many both inside and outside China, unthinkable reform including the setting up of a truly independent judiciary and a democracy without which the tensions and conflicts of interests currently building up in China may prove extremely difficult to defuse peacefully. International and domestic trade, then, may stimulate greater awareness of the many dimensions of individuals, their values, beliefs and ideas, and so bring opportunities for greater pluralism and tolerance as well as for material progress.

Paradoxical though it may seem, Party and government may come to believe that their own survival, and the stability and coherence of China, depends upon the adoption of expedient absolutes which so many commentators, often with disdain, have labelled 'western'.

On the other hand, China's leadership, in common with many observers outside China, may see in democracy either the secession of Tibet, the acceptance of Taiwan's self-determination, and the subsequent break up of China, or the descent of Chinese civilisation into chaos and internicine conflict. China's leaders might conclude, therefore, that they have nothing to lose, and everything to gain, by holding on to power by whatever means available and at whatever the cost. Some within China's *apparat* may look to Maoist teachings and techniques. But China's merchant and political elites may find comfort in the argument that although today's national and international regulatory and legal frameworks for the conduct of commerce bring greater predictability and stability (and widen markets), those frameworks are not in any direct sense responsible for commercial success. Nor are personal networks made redundant. Decisions made informally among individuals who know each other well and who may intuitively know and understand what the other is thinking or may do in given circumstances, is crucial for quick and effective action. Personalistic networks may also be worked effectively to political advantage in China, for they may serve to bind as well as to divide. The skeins of *guanxi* which span industries, administrative departments and ministries, bolstering the material and fiscal power of provincial and sub-provincial levels might form the net into which the residual state enterprises might fall, resulting in the *de facto* privatisation of huge entities under the control and ownership of provincial merchant-bureaucrats or favoured representatives of political factions within central government oriented towards the international economy.

There is, then, always the possibility that the problems which China now faces will continue to be met with 'culture', by which I mean that China's stylised representations – though they are still turned and directed towards economic, social, but ultimately political, ends – will be reshaped into forms that are more obviously traditional forms, and layered with even thinner socialistic veneers. Beliefs, values, institutions, patterns of behaviour and relationships based on reciprocal exchange, will be presented as something peculiarly and uniquely Chinese, and thus wielded as a justification or rationalisation for decision and action, and as a focus of loyalty and cohesion – images to which all must be subservient if they are to demonstrate their loyalty, and therefore 'to belong'.

Conclusions

However interesting may be our speculations about the way in which China's leaders will pursue their ambitions and deal with the problems they face, of far greater importance is the fact that the outside world does not know what will happen, nor how much will turn on circumstance and chance events, the ambitions of individuals, and Machiavellian scheming; and the fact that trade gurantees neither the rise of a civil society nor a democratic state. And yet it is today almost a demand of sinology that we should look upon a cloud of seething ambition, uncertainty, opportunity, and image-play, and define therein, with the aid of some theoretical artifice, ornate patterns of events; perceptivity and observations which owe nothing to China's stylised representations are nevertheless made subservient to them; and China's polity, even its official lexicon, is often taken at something close to its face value. The aim, or so it would seem, is to insist that the play emotion in the pursuit of power and the fulfilment of ambition has grown around some imagined structure of intellectual argument and explanation; for in China's Byzantine *courtiserie*, the manipulation of reason is reasonable; and consistency is regarded as the hobgoblin of foolish minds. The analyst twists and turns with every contradictory idea, policy or statement and with each of their unpredictable reversals, to create the most convoluted rationalisations. Thus are the images of China's old polity – first reconfigured as 'revolution', and then as 'readjustment' – now being aided in their re-formation.

3
Reciprocity and Factions

Introduction

I have argued that sinology has contrived to imitate the centuries-old game that is the polity of the medieval state: to define the culture and to defer to that culture; to turn it in support of personal ambition and, by its favours, to rationalise those ambitions. By deferring to culture and, in this way, by setting individuals within a discursive relationship with the imagined structures of culture, individuals are at once relieved of responsibility, while the structures (now distanced from the evils of individual action) retain an essential morality. In providing these satisfying, rounded analyses of China's polity, our latter-day Figurists help to confirm the flattering image which each newly-emerging ruling faction presents of itself, and the imperfections which they heap upon their predecessors and successors. Whereas Wilson's study confirms the moral righteousness of the new reformers because they look back to the pre-revolutionary and quintessentially 'Chinese' culture which Mao had done his best to destroy, Schram portrays Mao as a progressive visionary who set China upon a course towards greater political and intellectual pluralism.

For Solinger, too, there is a purity about the revolution, but also a scent of betrayal about the reforms. The intellectual arguments put forward by Mao, Stalin, Lenin and Marx, and the traditional Chinese values with which those arguments fitted so nicely, were viewed and treated as ideas and moral codes in their own right. The Chinese were not motivated by politics for its own sake: their intent was pure; their disputes were about values, beliefs and noble ideals; they desired to create a virtuous and moral society – a society which must therefore abandon capitalism. The debate over the state's handling and control of commodities revolved around the issue of class and the nature of the rural popula-tion. Debates such as these were not coded rationalisations of power plays. At stake was not political ambition, but varying analyses of class composition, differing views about the flaws in existing policy and the rectification of those flaws, and discussions about class, the promotion of activism, the protection of the peasants, the production of useful and suitable goods for soldiers, peasants and workers, and the efficacy of 'money-centred' market strategies compared with plan, order, hierarchy, self-sufficiency and organisation. These were the dominant concerns of China's leaders. Conflicts were about far more than just power. They were about values – socialist values, about different aspects of socialism. Conflicts were about a leadership and a people moving beyond capital-ism, and arguing as they did so, for they were breaking new ground and there were bound to be imperfections. The Chinese had also been impatient in their rush to construct a new moral entity:

> In a vision that would have pleased many Confucian scholars, Marx predicted that a regulated, planned economy would one day be the vehicle for the distribution of necessities, thereby replacing the mar-ket, money, and the commodities that money purchases. What he did not foresee, however, was that still poor socialist states, enticed by his teachings, would rush to install the trappings of a non-market, non-monetised economy ... before Marx's prerequisite of plenty could render trade truly obsolete.[1]

And so trade has continued to exist in China, and the 'style' of trade shares features – such as the omnipresence of competition, the force of supply and demand, and loopholes in the system encouraging profit-seeking – with business under capitalism. Yet there is something better about Chinese commerce: money is not its only medium (CBS, p. 31); competition does not take place within the public sector; it is not uncontrolled; it is limited by the state plan; and it also motivates cadres to push the private merchant from the scene. The force of supply and demand takes place within the restrictions of the plan, and the choice to rely on this force is never made without prior debate. As for profit-seeking, this is linked to scarcity and underdevelopment and often arouses 'more ideologically based ire than corruption does in bourgeois contexts' (ibid., p. 301).

There is an intimacy about Solinger's knowledge, something of which she is a part, more so than other scholars. 'Most previous scholars,[2] as well as the bulk of journalistic work', charges Solinger, 'have cast their interpretation of policy conflict in the format offered by the Chinese themselves ... one of a battle between "two roads" – one "left" and one "right", one ideological, one pragmatic, or one radical and the other moderate'. A format that 'misses many of the finer issues over which arguments have raged, even as it fails to account for alliances some-times struck among proponents of opposing lines' (CBS, p. 61). Their approaches, which oversimplify 'the most basic options among which Chinese politicians choose by presenting only two' are 'popular' modes of analysing that prove especially inadequate in any attempt to under-stand the Great Leap Forward (ibid., pp. 61 & 101). Authors such as Perkins, Shue and Bernstein[3] use words like 'state' and 'party' and 'regime' as if there is some kind of elite consensus. Her approach, she asserts, is more sensitive in recognising different views. It uncovers the reality and detail of what occurs; it reveals the nature and root of the conflict and the middle ground between permissiveness and prohibition; and, 'by analysing more closely the social bases, ideological foundations and power considerations that are attached to each line', her approach 'illu-minates the causes and forms of opposition that limit liberal options over time' (CBS, p. 61). Indeed, her analysis is nothing less than a revela-tion, a statement of what she knows China and Chinese culture to be: 'I grasp how it works', she declares (ibid., p. ix). It is Solinger who has 'found a framework to explain the forces that shape [socialist com-merce]' (ibid.), who has 'identified a cyclical process in Chinese com-mercial policy', who has 'presented this pattern analytically in terms of a conflict among three lines' (bureaucrat, radical and marketeer). And it is this 'pivotal finding of a three line struggle' which has 'formed the foundation for a range of insights into policy making in this one party state' (ibid., p. 297). Her investigation, then, has 'uncovered a sequence to the conflict'; it has 'shown that the dominant strategy, at which the system has come to rest, is the bureaucratic one'; and 'it has revealed that not just cyclical but also secular change, involving some learning, has occurred, from the perspective of the Chinese elite' (ibid., p. 298).

The image of China's polity which Solinger builds up is certainly one of great sophistication and subtlety. It is the image of a state in which morality is inherent in its history and its culture. Chinese philosophical thought has always been hostile to the market and to profit, and Marx's vision would have pleased Confucian scholars. The ambivalence among Chinese towards the marketplace and trade is a 'traditional' idea; goods have 'traditionally' served as a kind of currency; in the countryside indi-viduals are predisposed by 'historical habit' towards subsistence agricul-ture and exchange in goods; and Chinese people 'traditionally' rely on *guanxi* or personal connections – a 'tradition' which facilitated trading and which under socialism was preferred over the exchange of money (ibid., pp. 16, 17, 55). It is the image of a state that is committed to socialist values rather than to money, a highly moral state in which checks and balances mitigate social injustice, in which competition and prices are subject to restraint, and in which the legitimacy of the market is subject to debate before it is allowed to operate. China is not perfect: corruption there is and always has been; and yet corruption may be understood as a mechanistic product of technological underdevelopment; and in China corruption attracts more criticism than it would in a capitalist state. Solinger also gently rebukes China's rush towards socialism; and she chides those western and Chinese scholars who have compared the imagined perfection of the market with the realities of socialism, and who have consequently focused on the inefficiencies of the plan, its inability to match supply and demand, and the stockpiles and the queuing, while ignoring the inequities, immorality, and practical difficulties of the market. But despite the questionable decisions to move too quickly first towards socialism and now towards the market, Solinger also knows how China works, she knows its essential strengths and goodness, and she knows in particular that technological underdevelopment will make it difficult, if not impossible, for the market to work properly in China. She foresees China's likely mistakes, but she also knows that China's morality, its culture, its values, and its organisational abilities may provide the superstructure around which a more humane market could be fashioned.

Good and bad *guanxi*

Pye delivers a less idealistic understanding of China's political factions in China and the *guanxi* (or reciprocal relationships) which comprise those factions. He argues that the capacity of human beings 'to act in terms of willpower and commitment of purpose'[4] is something that makes the social sciences inherently different from the physical sciences. While 'the payoffs from correctly knowing the purpose of those being studied are so great that we are always tempted to believe that we in fact know what they are' ('Factions', p. 40), it is extremely difficult to judge motives. And this makes it difficult to determine the motive for public acts and thus to define the bases of any particular relationship. Pye sees *guanxi* as a pragmatic and utilitarian phenomenon free of the affected emotional gilding often ascribed to the term. There are rules to its working, but these are 'nuanced and subtle, for they accord to the particular situation', and they do not follow precise or constant formulations (ibid., p. 35).

In the same way that trust, based on non-legal sanctions, is of crucial importance to trade in a society that has no well-developed and well-enforced civil code,[5] so *guanxi* acts as a substitute for institutions:

> the functions which legal norms perform in administration and which interests serve for politics in most political systems have been largely met in China by the extraordinary powers of *guanxi*. This substitution has been possible because for most Chinese the structuring of human relationships has such a vivid quality as to be a very substantial part of physical reality. In practice, *guanxi* in action has thus structured authority and given order and form to Chinese governance and to what passes as both administrative and politics. It has been particularism in the service of generalised institution-building – which helps explain why Chinese public life can be so orderly without being institutionalised. ('Factions', p. 43)

China's polity, such as it is, therefore exhibits no clear institutional pattern nor any clear distinction between 'formal' and 'informal' politics, or between administration and politics. It has no strong legal foundation; policies are symbols of highly personal struggles; and the only constraints upon individuals are the 'realties of power relationships'. Chinese administration, then, is politics of a peculiar and very personal nature.

> In operational terms the Chinese concept of administration entails a structure of authority which is governed by human relationships that extends from the 'leading figure' to his deputies and on down a chain of status relationships. Superiors and subordinates fit together, not by a book of rules but by the more deeply ingrained rules of proper human relationships. Authority lies not in an objectified body of laws and moral codes, but in subjective understandings of the meaning of leadership, superior-subordinate relationships, and the rewards of showing deference to higher status and in return accepting command over inferiors. In a system of rule by men, not by laws, successful governance requires skill in reading character, building and maintaining personal relationships, and meticulously performing one's expected role. (ibid., p. 39)

These features of Chinese politics are deeply rooted in history:

Didn't we all learn in our first classes in Chinese politics that China follows the tradition of rule by men and not by laws? In imperial China there was, however, a strong sense of moral order and there were powerful constraints based on rules of ritualised Confucian behaviour. Thus, while traditional Chinese culture did not instil in officials and citizens a sense of awe for the majesty of law, it did have a body of moral precepts and rules of correct conduct which provided the mystique of legitimacy.

Thus, with respect to traditional China it might be said that there was a distinction between formal and informal according to whether or not actions adhered to the established moral norms of the Confucian order or responded to private considerations. The Confucian moral order was in a sense the functional equivalent of the legal systems of the West. In both cases there were accepted differences between proper and improper conduct.

In today's China there is neither a legal system nor a moral order that has been adequately internalised so as to govern the behaviour of officials. It is true that Chinese political rhetoric is still highly moralistic, but today hypocrisy rests lightly on most officials. Indeed, one should not put much weight on the distinction between what the Chinese leaders pretend their system to be and what it is actually like. Surely we all know by now that in the succession process, when the talk is of 'harmonious collective leadership' it means that the struggle for power has in fact became more intense. And certainly we know that pronouncements about 'consensus' at the top are really a Chinese way of putting a gloss on authoritarianism. (ibid., pp. 37–8)

There is something of a contradiction here between today's officials in whom neither a legal system nor a moral order has been internalised, and the historically (and so deeply) ingrained rules of proper human relationships which still influence present-day Chinese administration and government. But the image which is being fashioned is one that we have seen many times before. In the tradition of China's scholar-politicians, Pye constructs a golden past, a Confucian moral order, according to which government, administration and the people lived, and against which today's unruly and hypocritical reprobates may be set; and yet the influence of that golden past is still felt today in Chinese administration where 'superiors and subordinates fit together, not by a book of rules but by the more deeply ingrained rules of proper human relationships.' For historical and cultural reasons, too, there is not, and never has been, an open declaration and expression of interests. Confucian

ethics determined that to advance one's own self-interest is fundamentally shameful and thus, with inevitable logic, that merchants should be
treated with contempt, and that legitimate channels through which
interests could be directed were not required. The interests of different
parts of China were therefore never allowed to surface. Rural China
and urban China, rice-growing south China and wheat-growing north
China, coastal China and interior China, were all supposed to have the
same interests which benevolent rulers would take care of without any
prompting from society; and private interests had to be pursued by the
stealthy use of personal connections. This aspect of traditional Chinese
culture was 'reinforced by the imperatives of ideological conformity
basic to Maoism. Interests can only be advanced surreptitiously and
hence the current paradox that those who are doing best as entrepreneurs are happy with their indirect methods of influence and are
against any movement toward more open politics. They proclaim the
ideal of "political stability", which is only another way of praising
authoritarian rule' (ibid., p. 43).

In traditional and contemporary Chinese culture, individual interests
and groups are not supposed to exist; and so neither are factions – a term
used to denigrate opponents. That 'cultural taboo' is encased within
another – the taboo against giving any legitimacy to *guanxi*:

> The need to pretend that factions do not exist, or that they are only
> the mischief of bad officials, is fundamentally related to the pro-
> found ambivalence that Chinese have about *guanxi*. They know that
> they have to use it, but they also have a deep sense of shame over
> that need. The tradition of denying legitimacy to all forms of *guanxi*
> has meant that the Chinese have never been able to discriminate
> between its honourable and dishonourable forms . . .
>
> A historical reason why the Chinese have not been able to acknow-
> ledge any honourable forms of *guanxi* is that China never experi-
> enced the loyalty traditions of feudalism which Europe and Japan
> had with the personal bonding of lord and knight, of *daimyo* and
> *samurai*, with all their emotionally charged pledges of fealty, allegi-
> ance and undying fidelity. Instead of the European and Japanese
> traditions of heroically carrying the colours of one's master and of
> boldly defending his interests, the Chinese had a bureaucratic tradi-
> tion in which there were supposed to be no personal loyalties among
> superiors and subordinates.
>
> The feudal traditions of Europe and Japan also implanted in those
> cultures an idealistic and heroic dimension to personal loyalty

relationships which is generally lacking in the Chinese concept of *guanxi*. Instead, in China *guanxi* has always had a strongly utilitarian and pragmatic rationale. That is why it was more heavily masked during the ideological era of Maoism and less hidden with Deng Xiaoping's more pragmatic politics. (ibid., pp. 45–6)

The paradox created by Chinese culture – that of hostility towards *guanxi* and factionalism, the very heart of China's polity – has, in Pye's view, left traditional (and modern) China without any true politics.

The consequence of this pretence that private interests are shameful and illegitimate has been that China has never developed a genuine political process. The very essence of politics is the contending of competing interests, and when interests cannot be acknowledged openly there can be no true politics. For as Bernard Crick, in the spirit of Aristotle, has eloquently argued, 'politics is a great and civilising human activity', precisely because it is an activity through which contending interests are conciliated, differences are expressed and reconciled, and the survival of the whole community is protected ...

This Chinese tradition of denying the legitimacy of interests also helps to explain the historic failure of China to develop a strong civil society and why, for all the impressive economic development under the reforms, China still lags in the emergence of interest groups that might be expected to form with the greater differentiation of the economy and society. The establishment of various federations and associations presumably to look after the interests of labour, women and the like have tended to be creatures of the supposedly benevolent state and not challengers of the state. The potential for interest articulation, and hence of real politics, has thus been stifled by a political culture that has made it more natural for China to move towards forms of state corporatism. (ibid., pp. 41–2)

Nevertheless, it is within this same culture and historical tradition which has shaped China's polity, that Pye sees features that could bring cohesion, stability, and perhaps the inchoate structure of representative politics to China. The decline in reliance on ideology, the decentralisation of the entire system, and the loosening of discipline has produced different patterns of factional activity. It was not just a case of reformists being opposed by leftists or conservatives. With growing social unrest, and with so much unhappiness in the cities, no faction has been willing to criticise, to give voice to dissent: 'The divisions among the cadres thus became less about strategic differences over the making of a "New China" and more about tactical differences in preserving their collective position as China's ruling elite. For some, preserving the system has meant the advantages of decentralisation, but for others the importance of the centre has remained paramount, for it is only the centre that can pass on subsidies to failing industries and tighten or loosen the money supply' (ibid., p. 48). At the same time, *guanxi* (still unprotected by any sense of honour and dishonour, and its practice now surrounded by an ethos that promotes material wealth) has come to be exploited shamelessly for personal material gain: 'what in other societies would be called "corruption" abounds in China' (ibid., p. 49).

However, the decline in ideology and the rise of corruption may themselves mark the start of profound change in the polity of China: the absence of ideology and the strengthening of corrupt behaviour may not only bring greater stability, but may also constitute the inchoate structures of representative, competitive politics. The personal interests of the sons and daughters, believes Pye, will ensure strong commitment to the Communist party and the preservation of its power; and most Chinese believe that stability is all-important, and that liberation can wait. 'History may prove them right. Indeed, those who hold to "neo-authoritarian" views insist that corruption need not be a sign of political decay and the death knell of a regime. After all, throughout history, tolerance of corruption has often given strength to the position of rulers and thus served as a source of legitimacy. This has been the case especially when a population has become cynical and lacks any compelling basis for defining and justifying morality' (ibid., p. 50). China would not be the first country in which personal connections institutionalised power relations, provided for stability, and held the polity together. 'It is not just that the cadres will band together to preserve their collective interests, but the people at large may also find it not unnatural that their leaders should have their bonding relationships, and therefore the elite's claim to status and personal authority will be enough to justify its right to rule the country' (ibid., p. 53).

Guanxi also facilitates the liberalisation of the economy: more business licenses and more banquets, more bribes, more people in each other's debt, and more income. These 'bonding' relationships between merchants and officials also help to strengthen both the Party and the state, for it is in their authority that the merchants nestle.

These links established between merchants and officials also provide the motive and means through which local interests may be articulated.

The geographical pattern of growth in China's economy, argues Pye, cannot be understood :

> without an appreciation of the role that personal ties have played in investment decisions. The dramatic contrast between the dynamic-ally developing coastal areas and the sluggish interior regions cannot be understood in terms of the standard Western theories[6] about industrial location which hold that the three key factors in such decisions are proximity to large market demand, cheap production factors, and a favourable political climate. To believe that these are the critical considerations in explaining the political economy of the Chinese "miracle" would show ignorance of Chinese ways. In the case of China, the key variable has been the particularistic bonding of Overseas Chinese to specific communities and kinship group-ings.[7] Nearly all the active investors from Taiwan, Hong Kong and the Overseas Chinese communities of Southeast Asia and elsewhere have personal ties with the coastal regions of the mother country, and that is why their money has flowed to those locations. Officials in interior China are just as desirous of attracting foreign invest-ments as those in coastal China, but hardly any of their former residents went abroad and did well financially, hence the lack of potential entrepreneurs with a natural interest in investing in their communities. ('Factions', p. 51)

Local country and township officials, then, promote investment; and they will act to protect their own personal financial and political stake in those investments as vigorously as those large, inefficient state enter-prises whose officials will do their best to ensure that subsidies continue and that their interests are not forgotten. 'Thus there will be strains between the imperative to have good connections in the higher ranks of the government and the need to champion what has been developed locally' (ibid., p. 52).

Without strong laws or a popular faith, argues Pye, coercion may have to play a key role. If the system remains intact, however, then it can be expected that 'the different interests of the elite will drive the whole structure toward factional competition. If the system is without a new ideological basis, as seems likely, then maybe factions will have to come out into the open and seek popular acceptance' (ibid., p. 53).

What seems to be happening, then, is that, in the absence of ideo-logy, *guanxi* is at once holding China together and providing a means through which personal material interests at local and central level can be pursued. This in turn has meant that the traditional denial of legitimacy to 'interest articulation' is fading away as cadres feel that they must act in those local interests and concerns in which they have a personal stake. The result is an inchoate form of competitive politics. Tensions and strains there may be between local and central government, among different interest groups, and between the need to have good connections in the higher ranks of government and the need to champion local interests, but these strains are common to representative and pluralistic systems of government: 'through a ... complicated process China may be slowly working its way toward a more pluralistic political system and thereby joining the ranks of the modern nation-states' (ibid.).

However, this transition will depend upon subtle, but crucial, alterations in *guanxi* – an extraordinary force that *is* Chinese politics and administration:

> Ultimately, the test of maturity of China as a modernising society will be the ability of the Chinese people to arrive at a shared understanding as to what kinds of *guanxi* behaviour should be seen as honourable, decent qualities of human relations and what practices of *guanxi* should remain shameful and dishonourable. *Trust* in human connections is the very essence of civility, which in turn is the absolutely critical foundation for any well-functioning society and polity. As long as the very mention of *guanxi* is treated by most Chinese as being a black mark on Chinese national character, it will be impossible for them to forthrightly determine which forms of human bonding are legitimate and which are not acceptable. As long as *guanxi* is seen as inherently bad, the entire realm of personal interchanges, with its attendant considerations of reciprocity, will be tainted as questionable, if not shameful. But of course no society can function without forms of trusted exchanges. Therefore, as long as the Chinese continue to class actions as shadowy which should be able to stand the light of day, they will be driven to believe that current conditions are worse than in fact they are. (ibid., pp. 45–6)

We noted earlier that in Pye's argument there appeared to be a contradiction between today's officials in whom neither a legal system nor a moral order has been adequately 'internalised' so as to govern their behaviour, and, on the other hand, the deeply ingrained rules of proper human relationships which still influence Chinese administration and government even today. It would seem that the Chinese do, and do not, have a sense of moral code.

Alongside this contradiction we can now position a second. The Chinese people today, we are told, have been unable, or are unwilling, to distinguish (or to acknowledge any distinction) between those kinds of *guanxi* behaviour that are honourable and decent, and those that are not. This has always been so in China, for the Chinese, we are told, have traditionally denied legitimacy to all forms of *guanxi*, and they have never experienced the loyalty traditions of feudalism which Europe and Japan had with the personal bonding of lord and knight. Just as the affective quality which Europeans and Japanese associate with personal connections is determined by centuries of structuration or chains of cause and effect, so it is with the Chinese reluctance or inability to distinguish between honourable and dishonourable forms of *guanxi*. But if this is so, then how are these arguments to be reconciled with traditional China's moral order and those deeply ingrained rules of proper human relationships which remain effective even today? For, unless Pye is claiming that *guanxi* is somehow an entirely separate category of reciprocity, then does not traditional China's Confucian moral order and today's ingrained rules of proper behaviour and relationships imply that the Chinese then, as now, do have a sense of 'good' and 'bad' personal connections? The Chinese it would seem do, and do not, have a sense of honourable and dishonourable *guanxi*.

To these contradictions we can add a third. On the one hand, we learn that in China *guanxi* has always had a strongly utilitarian and pragmatic rationale, and that is why it was more heavily masked during the ideological era of Maoism, and why it was 'less hidden' following the advent of Deng Xiaoping's regime. But on the other hand, Pye appears to regard that same pragmatic and utilitarian attitude towards *guanxi* as an indication that neither a legal system nor a moral order has been adequately internalised by officials. This constitutes a state of affairs which is both very different to China's golden past (when certain differences between proper and improper conduct were widely recognised and accepted), and also unlike that 'other' modern China where rules for the proper conduct of relationships are deeply ingrained. Again, it would appear that the Chinese do, and do not, have a sense of good and bad personal relationships.

Pye, then, argues that the Chinese, who never experienced a feudalistic tradition of loyalty, have always had a deep sense of shame about *guanxi* (and factions); they have consistently and indiscriminately denied legitimacy to all forms of *guanxi*; and, for these reasons, they have always regarded and treated *guanxi* in a highly utilitarian manner. And yet, Pye also suggests that in traditional China the Chinese had a strong sense of moral order, and that there exists today a deeply ingrained sense of the rules governing proper human relationships.

The arguments may be contradictory, but it is a contradiction that helps explain the paradox: that a sense of shame and hostility should be felt towards *guanxi* and factionalism which in practice constitute the very heart of China's polity. Clearly, if a sense of shame is felt about some action, then there must also be a sense of what is a good and proper action. If it is accepted that the Chinese had a sense of shame about *guanxi*, then they must also have had a sense of what constitutes good and proper relationships. The Chinese do, and do not, have a sense of proper and improper behaviour, and of what makes relationships 'good' or 'bad'; and the Chinese have always suffered from this curious split personality. Moreover, if the Chinese have always had a sense of what constitutes good and bad relationships, then, following Pye's train of thought, the conditions for democracy have long since been present in China, as indeed many writers would agree.

This is not the first time that we have seen paradox descend over China, nor is it the last, for is not paradox the essence of the Inscrutable East? Actions, beliefs, values, and institutions, shrouded in contradiction, cannot quite be grasped; like some mysterious, half-remembered scent, they slip in and out of our conscious mind, evoking emotions and once-forgotten dreams from long ago. But although they elude the Western mind, they are grasped by the cognescenti of the Chinese world.

Paradox is not a fault; it adds lustre to that sense of complexity, subtlety, and (what is to most, though not all, Western minds) elusion. What is of paramount importance is the image of China's cultural difference and morality – an image which, through comparison with what was or should be, may then be used (in the manner of China's scholar-politicians) to condemn, to praise, to explain, to rationalise and to justify.

In the well-worn, comfortable style of the social scientist, Pye's study appeals to common sense, and yet at the same time continues to invoke unspecified cultural forces and chains of cause and effect. On the one hand Pye emphasises the utilitarian and pragmatic nature of *guanxi*; he acknowledges that there are differences between social science and natural science; and he recognises that if China were to find itself held together by personal networks (and his analysis would appear to suggest that this has long been the case), then China would not be the first, or only, example of a polity to be organised in such a way. He also explicitly questions the theme of 'Chinese exceptionalism', for 'it needs to be noted that factionalism is not unique to the Chinese communist party'. Factionalism characterised Russia's Social Democratic Party before the Revolution and the early years of the regimes under Lenin and Stalin; and even the American Communist party was riven with factional divisions. Pye continues:

> There are several reasons for this propensity towards factional strife among Communists. First, the ideology has the character of a religion in which there is the presumption of a single truth that guides the Party line at all times. Therefore, anyone who does not openly support the line must, "objectively speaking", be against the Party and therefore working for the enemy, and hence a subversive element. Second, the tradition of secrecy means that conflicts take place in a sealed atmosphere and consequently they tend to become highly personalised. Differences cannot be aired, diluted, and balanced by other considerations. The focus of action cannot escape considerations of personalities, much as in any small inward-looking community. ('Factions', p. 44)

And by emphasising the need for trust, and for a distinction to be made between honourable and dishonourable forms of *guanxi*, between the decent qualities of human relationships and the shameful, Pye appears to be arguing the case for expedient absolutes.

But on the other hand, Pye invokes culture and history with ease, and we are presented with the image of a culture that is traditional and yet – rather like Chinese scientific thought, China's democratic elements, Chinese orthopraxy, and Chinese cultural meanings – contains within it the seeds of the modern. Factionalism may not be unique to China's Communist Party, but in China the 'phenomenon' of factions has been profoundly influenced by traditional and contemporary Chinese political culture which 'has made the very idea of factions an abomination... Whereas in other countries factions have a normal, even honoured, place in politics, in China there is a general conspiracy either to deny their existence or to denigrate opponents by calling them a faction' (ibid., pp. 44–5).

If factions were brought out into the open, the political system would become more transparent, and 'the country might take a significant step forward to become a stable, pluralistic system' (ibid., p. 45). But this is dreaming the impossible, believes Pye, because the cultural taboo about factions, this obstacle to democracy, is 'far too strong to be easily wished away'.

Guanxi, too, has 'extraordinary powers'. It is *guanxi* that enables China to function in an 'astonishing' fashion without a binding legal system, without the open articulation of interests and without institutions; for it is *guanxi* which structures authority, gives form to administration and politics, and enables Chinese public life to be ordered without being institutionalised. It is to *guanxi* that the Overseas Chinese merchant in deciding to invest in China subordinates matters such as: market demand; the cost of labour, land and capital; and, presumably, currency movements, regulations over safety and conditions, tax differentials, and channels for the circumvention of export quotas. All these considerations are subject to *guanxi*; and it is *guanxi* that explains the 'Chinese miracle'. Personal connections are not unique to China, but, given its 'astonishing' influence and extraordinary powers, including the power to suspend economic imperatives, *guanxi* is clearly something different. It is after all a 'phenomenon' steeped in centuries of Confucian tradition. The essence of this difference is the fact that it *is* manipulative; that it does not possess that affective, idealistic and heroic dimension which 'the Western', or, for that matter, 'the Japanese', 'mind' would expect; and that, to the Chinese, *guanxi* 'has such a vivid quality as to be a very substantive part of physical reality'.

Here again, we see that distinction between 'West' and 'East', and that intimate knowledge which defines the cultural intermediary. Pye recognises that social science is different from natural science and that to judge motivations is no easy matter. Yet Pye is so much a part of the Chinese mind and so aware of the differences between Chinese and Western thinking, that he sees what others do not. He knows the raw earthiness and Chinese politics *because* he is intimate with the culture that *is* China; he knows of its taboos and of the 'general conspiracy' to deny the existence of factions. (And what better phrase is there other than 'general conspiracy' to describe a cultural force?) Part of the problem in understanding the phenomenon of *guanxi* declares Pye, is that 'to the Western mind a bonding tie which is clearly very effective must have a strong emotional base' (ibid., p. 43 nn). But Pye sees the pragmatism, the essential Chineseness of *guanxi*; he perceives its vivid qualities which seizes the Chinese mind. Pye knows that economic imperatives are subordinate to *guanxi* in the mind of the Chinese merchant because the merchant is Chinese, and *guanxi* is Chinese; to think otherwise, he declares sniffily, is to demonstrate 'ignorance of Chinese ways' (ibid., p. 51).

It is, then, with an unequalled view of Chinese ways, that Pye observes: 'We western analysts, with our propensity to emphasise the importance of public policy rhetoric, tried to establish some intellectual order in the confusing relationships by writing about the "reformist" faction being opposed by the "leftists" and/or "conservative faction".' (ibid., p. 48). Pye knows that the rhetoric of policy, and the confusing relationships, are only the shadows cast by China's ruling elite as they manoeuvre to preserve their position; and deeper still within the substance of those forms, he senses the first gentle stirrings of a representative and competitive polity.

Pye's down-to-earth knowledge of China's, unwrought, coarse polity derives from his knowledge of the Chinese mind, Chinese ways and Chinese culture. Pye knows the reality of Chinese political life *because* he knows the Chinese mind, Chinese culture and Chinese tradition. It is no wonder that although Pye allows the significance of expedient absolutes (particularly trust and 'honourable forms' of *guanxi*) to surface, he should then allow them to sink again into the quagmire of culture. It is upon the Chineseness of *guanxi* and the subtle changes in Chinese factionalism that pluralistic, competitive and representative politics must be founded. For it is the strongly utilitarian, pragmatic and manipulative nature of *guanxi* (which, in other countries, is known as 'corruption') that brings stability and cohesion; and it is upon this basis that the open recognition and practice of factionalism will lead to democracy. The lynch-pin of this transition is the willingness to identify and to distinguish between honourable and dishonourable forms of guanxi: trust is enough to foster a pluralistic state; but its absence is enough to drive that state into the arms of the 'Mafia' (ibid., p. 53).

Pye has elevated what is already held in high esteem – the ability to handle and manipulate individuals and complex networks of reciprocity and their soft-framed institutions (including trust). It is a virtue in itself and the measure of social status; it is an ability to be much admired, even more so if the individual is able to achieve particular economic or political aims; but, as was suggested elsewhere,[8] the relationships formed, and the institutions thrown up, are inherently unstable. Pye therefore denies precisely that which is necessary to realise both democracy and, over the long term, a more stable economy and sustained material progress. He repudiates the significance of relationships distanced from the conduct of business, government and bureaucracy such that while personal relationships may allow faster, intuitive, flexible and nuanced behaviour, they do not interfere with, distort or corrupt the operation of institutions and procedures. Trust, if regarded as an expedient absolute, is part of this 'distancing'. But as organisations and their external networks grow in size and complexity, then more than trust is needed. A degree of manipulation there must always be; but without that quality of 'being absolute', the manipulation of relationships becomes unbridled, and institutions and procedures become unstable and very brittle. Without the perception of and treatment of institutions, procedures and values as if absolutes, those institutions will never amount to more than a sham. If an organisation (whether a business company, political party, or the entire polity of a state) is not to degenerate into factional chaos or to be frozen by autarky (the two are closely associated), then individuals, groups and their representatives should agree to bind themselves to the conventions of a shared institution (such as a parliament in the case of political parties), shared symbols, shared values, and shared procedures through which argument and disagreements may be conducted – and all of which must be regarded as expedient absolutes. Open or closed, a faction is a faction.

Pye's argument that the manipulation of relationships, open factionalism and greater trust will lead to pluralism is a skilled rationalisation of Chineseness and the purported difference of China; and it lays out a 'Chinese way' to pluralism and economic progress. It is an argument that, on the one hand, implies that vast cultural forces and chains of cause and effect are at work: the manipulation of reciprocity and its soft framed institutions (including trust, friendship, loyalty) will, for some reason, lead to institutional and individual probity; and open factionalism, we must believe, will lead to a stable and coherent democratic polity in which individuals and organisation agree to subordinate themselves and their interests to abstract values, institutions and procedures. On the other hand, in his deferment to culture, Pye negates democracy, and elevates attitudes and practices that make still more uncertain sustained economic progress over the long term.

The mirror dance: structure versus culture

We have often noted that an appeal to common sense is so often accompanied by the assumption that some kind of force or structure does, in fact, exist: individuals and their independence of thought and action is recognised in word, and yet in the working of analysis individuals are marginalised and made subordinate to those intellectual imaginings. We have also suggested that the search for universals is little different from the search for cultural determinants: both approaches share the same assumption (that there exists some internal or external force or structure) and the willingness to interpret observations in the light of that assumption. Thus, policy cycles *are* China; the act of fabricating Chinese culture *is* Chinese culture. And we have argued that, because they share that same philosophical base, universal or cultural forces and structures are able to pivot as the one is turned in support of the other, usually through providing contrast: universal and cultural determinants are set opposite each other, the one a dancing reflection of the other. Thus reciprocity is not peculiar to China; but its strongly practical and utilitarian nature is; factionalism is not practised only in the Chinese communist party, but its closed nature and the cultural taboo which that quality reflects, are peculiarly Chinese. Indeed, as the case of marketing 'systems' in China examined elsewhere illustrates,[9] it is also quite respectable and quite easy (given their shared philosophical foundation) for universals to find themselves transformed into cultural determinants.

A further example of this mirror dance is Nathan and Tsai's modification and development of Nathan's[10] original factional model which, as Nathan and Tsai point out, has been found useful by scholars 'as a starting point for analysing how China's political elite works'[11] for more than 22 years.[12] One of its problems, however, derives from:

> the fact that it did not succeed in distinguishing between cultural and structural (or institutional) variables in explanation of political behaviour. The model was intended as a structural argument: one about how factional groups' institutional patterns affect their patterns of behaviour. Factions as structures were said to have certain attributes regardless of the culture in which they operate. The argument claimed to identify patterns of behaviour that would be true of factions in any cultural setting. It thus resonated with what later came to be called 'new institutionalist' theory, which explains patterns of political behaviour by reference to opportunities and constraints presented to actors by institutions.
>
> Over the years many readers have remained unpersuaded by the structural claims of the argument. If Chinese factional behaviour is structurally determined, they ask, why does the same behaviour not appear more fully in other systems that are similarly factionalised, say Italy? Why don't other systems where clientelist connections play a major role also become factional, say Massachusetts? Why do Chinese politicians behave in many of the ways that the theory describes even when they are functioning not in factions but in one man's court, in bureaucratic 'fragmented authoritarianism', or in 'informal groups' that do not fit the strict definition of factions?

Why is it that even though the Chinese style of politics remains fairly constant, major shifts occur in ideology and in policy directions contrary to the predictions of the theory? And why does China have such a system in the first place? To many readers, the theory seemed to put more explanatory burden on structure than structure could bear.

Culture was available to share the explanatory burden. Culturalists argued that the behaviour manifested in the factionalist pattern was cultural in genesis. It occurred throughout Chinese history and in all sorts of Chinese arenas, whether or not factions were the dominant form of organisation at the given time and place, and (by implication) not in other cultural systems even when dominated by factions. But this reading had problems of its own. If factionalism is a cultural phenomenon, why does so much of the same behaviour occur in other cultures, say in the US Congress? Why does the theory apply only to the elite level of the Chinese system? Moreover, the culturalist argument runs into the problems of proof and of the emic–ectic distinction. Are Chinese politics substantially different in practice from other systems, or chiefly in self-image? Perhaps Chinese culture is not as distinctive as many Chinese claim. Perhaps it is theoretically fallacious to restate a Chinese self-stereotype in the guise of a social science finding about the differences among cultures.

In short, many scholars agreed that things often happened in China the way the factionalism model described, but felt uncomfortable explaining these patterns in terms of either structure or culture. This quandary relates more broadly to the traditional polarization of cultural and structural approaches in China studies: the respective independent variables are presented as mutually exclusive, yet they are hard to distinguish. And neither cultural nor structural arguments alone seem to carry sufficient explanatory power. ('Factionalism', pp. 158–60)

Nathan and Tsai then set out what they mean by 'structure' and by 'culture':

Throughout the social sciences . . . structure tends to be conceptualised as patterns of incentives outside actors' heads, and culture as attitudes, values, and beliefs inside actors' heads. From an actors' point of view, structure is a situation (or part of it) and culture a set of attitudes (or some of them) that he or she brings to the situation. Structure in this sense is thought to impose the exogenous discipline of means–end rationality on actors, while culture is the source of values that are not determined by structure and are in this sense non- (or pre-) rational.

Like the factionalist model, most variants of new institutionalism intend to be arguments about the behavioural consequences of structures – that is, how institutions *structure* outcomes. Structured explanations based on institutional constraints are seen as being rigorous and theoretically appealing due to their relative transposability across culture. In contrast, cultural explanations appear to be limited to specific cases and often seem unfalsifiable. Most new institutionalists thus avoid using the term 'culture' in their analyses.

None the less, the culture/structure problems persists... Cultural variables enter the argument in the guise of 'historical and contextual factors' either when theorists realise that the norms embedded in institutions do not conform with those expected under a 'hard' rationality assumption, or when they encounter difficulty in accounting for variation among cases. Like earlier behaviouralist analyses, such institutional approaches produce tautological arguments due to their conflaion of culture and structure. For example, Robert Putnam's *Making Democracy Work*, which employs both historical institutionalist and behaviouralist arguments, associates certain institutions (social structures) with political outcomes. He then traces the institutions inductively back to a particular culture and associates the culture with institutional results. It is difficult to identify culture and structure as distinct independent variables because they are *defined* as a mutually-reinforcing pair.

The factionalism model, like new institutionalist frameworks, was intended to be a theory about the 'rules of the game', conceived not as cultural givens, but as consequences of structure. But in a new institutionalist perspective, it is difficult to treat these rules *a priori* as either structurally or culturally generated because rules are themselves institutions, and institutions embody, in their phenomenal existence, both structure and culture. Although certain technological, ecological and geographic realities may create incentive structures that are exogenous to culture, in *political life* most structures are created by actors who are also the bearers of culture. That is, political institutions represent products of human interaction, which itself is culturally conditioned. Certainly this is the case with the scenarios described by the factionalism model. In these situations, structures (such as the rules of the game) are partly derivative of culture, if only because participants are able to understand these rules and accept them as legitimate; and culture in turn is shaped partly by socialisation to existing patterns of incentives – that is, to structures. Hence, struture and culture are not only socially constructed but also mutually constitutive in the Geertzian sense. Most of the criticisms of the factionalism model flow from this failure to clarify the relationship between culture and structure, a failure widely shared in the new institutionalist literature. ('Factionalism', pp. 161–3)

Nathan and Tsai's solution is to tighten up their understanding of factions as institutions (or structures). Following Berger and Luckmann[13] they argue that while human interaction defines both culture and structure, institutions, once created, become an 'objective reality' to actors. 'In other words, once institutions are established, actors manoeuvre within their boundaries. The factionalism model sought to specify how strategies of actors are available or limited for actors located in the particular institutions defined as factions' ('Factionalism', p. 164).

As for culture, Nathan and Tsai write that:

> the attempt to explain Chinese behaviour by a unique Chinese pattern ultimately defeats the purpose of comparative studies, because causal propositions in theories of particular systems are tautological and untestable ... a cultural argument needs to be specified as part of a cross-culturally general theory to be useful in a positivist research programme ... While we suggest an institutional rather than a cultural approach in this essay, we recognise that cultural explanations can be valid for certain purposes. But they need to state how particular cultural attributes or syndromes affect particular behavioural attributes across systems. (ibid., p. 167)

Analyses of China's polity, then, must emphasise institutions (or structures). Although Nathan and Tsai do not rule out cultural influences, the cultural explanation should, logically, be considered only as part of broad comparative analyses. The authors therefore accept the 'mutual constitution' of structure and culture, but they contend that 'once they take shape as everyday, taken-for-granted reality, institutions provide an objective basis for substantially structuring behaviour ... While institutions have historical roots, they can be treated as if there were relatively autonomous at a given point in time in the way they affect the choices of individuals acting in social situations' (ibid., pp. 167–8).

Anxious to demonstrate that their institutional approach is practical and firmly placed in the real world, the authors detail the 'institutional structures' by setting out a typology of political groups and organisations. Two classifications are used: members' bases for associations; and groups' patterns of coordination. These classifiers, argue Nathan and Tsai,

> provide serviceable first cuts for explaining the behaviour of political groups and organisations. If we know *on what basis members associate with another* we can understand something about how highly committed they are, what their goals and interests are, what rewards they require from the leadership, and what sacrifices the leaders can ask from them. This in turn helps us predict whether the group is capable of postponing gratification of its members in pursuit of long-term strategies, whether it can use violence, and whether it can outlast the lives of its members. If we know *what channels of communication* a group uses to coordinate its activities, we can to some extent explain the accuracy, complexity, extensiveness and authoritativeness of its communications, and hence its capability for flexibility, speed and coordination in action.
>
> In this sense, the typology seeks to classify the institutional contexts within which actors formulate strategies of action. It suggests different rules for different games, within each of which actors' incentives for making particular choices are defined in substantial part by the institutional environment. (ibid., p. 170, italics in original)

Four bases of association are identified: kinship, community, agreement and exchange-based participation. These bases are not mutually exclusive but for 'conceptual purposes' the authors 'enforce the boundaries' around them. The patterns of communication are also divided into four types: 'hierarchical', 'segmentary', 'noded dyadic' and 'open network'.

These two classifiers – bases and communication – give rise to four-by-four typology of organisation and groups that might be involved in political activity. In all, 16 types of groups are produced: kinship-hierarchical, kinship-segmentary, kinship-nodal, and kinship-open network; community-hierarchical, community-segmentary, and so on; and each type 'can be expected to behave politically in characteristic ways that are explainable in terms of its institutional form' (ibid., p. 174). For example, type 7 (community-based, noded) appears when individuals turn for cooperation to others with whom they share a tie of some kind, perhaps religion, ethnicity, caste, or place of origin. 'In the West, this is called an "old boy network", in China a "relationship net" (*guanxi wang*). In pre-communist

China, an individual could appeal to another for special treatment on the basis not only of kin ties but on the basis of dialect, home region, attendance at the same school, or service in the same bureaucracy. These practices have been revived in China in recent years' (ibid., p. 177). Types 14 and 15 refer specifically to factions. Type 14 comprises:

> political parties which are long-term coalitions of factions (as defined in Type 15) ... Activists in such parties aim at advancement in office, influence-trading, and financial pay-offs, which are gained from factional participation. The success of the constituent factions is maximized by cooperating with other factions under a party label in order to maintain an electoral and legislative majority and control the government.
>
> *Type 15* (*exchange-based, noded*) consists of factions as described in the original factionalism model. Factions occur in villages, bureaucracies, legislatures, or other settings when a leader mobilizes a set of followers (who may in turn mobilize their own followers) to support him or her on the basis of expected rewards of office, influence or money. Due to their flexibility, factions can engage in a wide variety of tactics. But since they are limited in size and follower commitment, they do not challenge the *status quo*. An isolated corrupt pay-off would also belong to this type, paralleling the old boys network and cooperation among kin as ways for an individual to mobilize influence though personal connections. (ibid., pp. 179–80)

All sixteen types, and the behaviour that is characteristic of each type, are similarly outlined. The typology, argue Nathan and Tsai, 'implies a model of how the two institutional attributes of associational basis and communication pattern yield different kinds of behaviour in different types of groups. The model specifies the links between institutional structure and actors' behaviour in *ceteris paribus* manner' (ibid., p. 180). These links between each of the two classifiers (associational bases and communication patterns) and their respective behavioural characteristics are then set out rather like a series of rules by which institutional forms are translated into certain types of behaviour. Associational bases 'differ in the *types of ends* actors seek when participating in a particular group. No single dimension underlies the four types' (ibid., p. 181). These types of ends vary in a number of ways, not all of which are specified. However, we do learn that types of ends do vary in the degree to which they are psychological or material, self-regarding or group-regarding, consummatory or instrumental, and immediate or long-term.

'Kinship involves roughly equal portions of all these attributes; the mix of attributes in community motivated activity leans toward being psychological, group-regarding, instrumental, and long-term; the mix of attributes in agreement-based activity tends to be relatively material, self-regarding, instrumental, and immediate; the mix in exchange-based activity leans still more heavily to the material, self-regarding, instrumental, and immediate poles' (ibid.). The dimensions underlying the respective patterns of communication are differentiation, tightness, authoritativeness and secrecy. Hierarchical and noded patterns are 'tighter, more authoritative, and more secret than segmentary and network patterns. But the hierarchical and segmentary patterns are more differentiated than the noded and network patterns' (ibid., p. 182).

The authors go on to identify the various types of behaviour produced at group and systems level by the different combinations of bases of association, patterns of communication, and their respective 'dimensions' or rules. Thus, for instance: 'Members are more willing to take risks of personal sacrifice for more psychological, consummatory and long-term goals (regardless of whether they are self-regarding or other-regarding, and public or private). Other things being equal, kinship provides the strongest willingness to take risks, community the second, agreement the third, and exchange the least' (ibid.). In short, a willingness to take risks is strongest in associations based on kinship because in such associations the 'ends' are combined in roughly equal proportions; exchange-based groups are least willing to take risks because in such groups material, self-regarding, instrumental and immediate 'ends' dominate.

Nathan and Tsai's study presents the reader with a statement of assumptions which shape political behaviour. It is, in effect, another *fait accompli* – a declaration of what China *is*. Associational bases and communication patterns produce certain types of groups which exhibit certain types of behaviour in accordance with particular attributes which are inherent in those associations and patterns of communication. Layer upon layer of rules are unrolled, forming an operational *millefeuille*. Some of these rules are specified. There is the rule that choices are defined in substantial part by the institutional environs; and there are the rules that govern the link between the types of associational base and channels of communication, the motivations and organisational abilities of those groups, and the political behaviour of those groups. For example, there is the rule that community-based, hierarchical groups are capable of organising specialised armed force and of conducting elaborate military expeditions; the rule that kinship has roughly equal portions of 'types of ends'; the rule that community-motivated action is more 'psychological' and 'group-regarding'; and the rule that exchange-based groups are least willing to take risks because their 'ends' are predominantly 'material' and 'self-regarding'.

But some of the rules are left unsaid. Why are there four associational bases, four patterns of communications, and why may they be multiplied together to produce 16 types of groups? For if, as Nathan and Tsai argue, the bases of association are not mutually exclusive, then we may assume the same to be true of patterns of communication and of the groups. Therefore, the number of possible gradations between one group and another must be incalculable. This is an inconsistency that the authors seem to acknowledge: toward the end of their study, they write that their 'sketch' does not address 'the problem of mixed cases', for political groups and organisations, especially large ones, are 'structurally diverse'; nor does it achieve 'an adequate sorting of the wide variety of political organisations and groups' ('Factionalism', p. 192). These comments, however, may only represent a nod to academic convention which requires the author to identify unresolved questions and problems and so lead the way into avenues of further research which others may wish to explore. This is a convention which in the natural sciences has a genuine purpose (that of testing and falsification) but which in the social sciences often appears to be either little more than a symbolic display of modesty or a means of avoiding difficult questions. The problems which Nathan and Tsai identify in their model do not prompt them to question the assumptions upon which the creation of types have been made. Rather, they suggest that the solution is to expand the number of typological classifiers (or institutional variables). This they have not done, they say, because it would have taken them still further away from the Chinese case. But arguably, had they done so, then the problems would have been left unresolved, for if the bases of association are not mutually exclusive, then the types of groups could be divided and sub-divided again and again *ad infinitum*.

The question remains unanswered: why are four associational bases, four patterns of communication identified, and why are these multiplied together to produce 16 types? Why not 8 or 32 or 64 or 128 or 256 or, if this is more than a syllogistic exercise, some other number? The *purpose* of specifying the number of bases, communication patterns, and types, it would seem, is to provide a framework through which the causal links between groups and types of political behaviour can be identified; for unless boundaries among the bases, patterns of communication, and the types of group were defined and enforced in practice (as well as conceptually), then clearly the establishment of such links would be impossible. So it would appear that there *are* different types of groups, and that in their unadulterated form they must be mutually exclusive. The authors make this point quite explicitly. A theory that deals with types, they observe, leaves out or distorts many cases; and yet, in the next sentence, we are told that 'no theory can deal successfully with mixed cases until it has dealt successfully with pure ones, since any mixed-pure classification arises from the theory in terms of which cases are classified as pure or mixed' (ibid.). On the one hand, then, we are told that bases, patterns of communication and types are not mutually exclusive. On the other hand we are told that there are different groups.

Moreover, while this typology of groups exists in order to identify and explain particular types of political behaviour that institutions yield (for factions tend to operate in certain ways that can be explained by reference to their institutional form), it would seem that these groups may also be defined by their political behaviour: factions and factional behaviour are synonymous with exchange-based association which possess noded dyadic communications; type 15 (exchange-based, noded) groups 'consist of factions'; factions *are* based on exchange and operate though noded communications (ibid., pp. 180 & 185). A further problem is that the behaviour which is said to define, or to be yielded, by factions would also appear to explain the existence of exchange-based, noded dyadic groups: groups are organised in a particular way *because* of their 'types of ends'. We are told, for instance, that types of ends (such as being self-regarding) underlie the bases (ibid., p. 181), and that *because* of their self-regarding motives for participation, exchange-based groups are less likely to take risks, and so members of factions (which are exchange-based groups) are unwilling to risk violence on behalf of factional goals. We are also told about factions that:

> The personal nature of communications permits flexibility and endurance in factional politics. Although the members seek particularistic gains of personal power, position and wealth, because of their intimate understanding of leaders' strategies they tolerate indirect tactics that bear little obvious relationship to their goals. Group actions are often cloaked in ideological garb, but ideology is flexible and does not restrict factional alliances or policy positions.
>
> Factions are as concerned to protect what they have as to gain more, so they often use defensive strategies. But periodically they initiate offensives to try to take office and power from rival groups.

Unlike lineage systems, factional systems are characterised by shifting alliances dictated by the defensive strategy. While the level of violence is low, the level of ideological disputation, rumour, and personal character assassination is high. A faction continues in existence as long as its leader remains active and the net flow of rewards continues. After the leader's retirement, the faction usually dissolves or splits along vertical cleavage lines of the previous sub-factions.

As long as they deliver the benefits for participating members, political systems dominated by factions tend to be stable. Factions rise and fall in size and influence, but the system as a whole tends to persist rather than to evolve into something else. By defending their power positions against one another, factions prevent the rise of dominant leaders who might supersede the factional system as a whole. The resulting balance of power may be considered systemic. In other words, would-be hegemonies (certain factional leaders) are thwarted from achieving pre-eminence in the system. (ibid., pp. 185–6)

This behaviour, which is yielded by, or which defines, the faction, is also very similar to Nathan and Tsai's explanation of exchange-based associations and noded-dyadic patterns of communication that together make up type 15 groups (factions). Exchange-based participation, write Nathan and Tsai, 'is motivated by the individual's pursuit of relatively tangible and immediate incentives, such as money, goods, office or protection. This includes both short-term, socially disvalued or neutrally valued exchanges such as pay-offs or log-rolling and relatively well-established, persistent, socially valued patterns of exchange such as "clientalism"' (ibid., pp. 171–2). And a noded-dyadic pattern is described as one 'in which communications are transmitted through a network of two-person links, but are disproportionately routed through certain individuals, who thus stand at the foci or nodes of the network. Groups with this communication pattern are likely to have unclear membership boundaries. Yet they are internally differentiated, since the persons standing at the communications nodes have greater power and are perceived as leaders. This is the class to which factions belong' (ibid., p. 173).

Combinations of associational bases and patterns of communication, it would appear, can be explained by the behaviour which they are also said to 'yield': the chains of cause and effect are thus confirmed by teleology. And since bases of association and patterns of communication may be explained by the behaviour which those groups are also said to yield, it would seem logical to assume that certain patterns of behaviour will result in the formation of *only* one type of group, base, and pattern of communication, and that certain patterns of behaviour may be used to identify the existence and operation of a particular institutional form. A particular institutional form yields certain types of behaviour, but certain types of behaviour also produce a particular institutional form. Institutions explain behaviour, and behaviour explains institutions. The rules just *are*; the model just *is*.

Ambiguity

As part of what appears to be an attempt to justify their declaration of *what is*, Nathan and Tsai outline (but only for 'heuristic purposes' ('Factionalism', p. 168)) the theoretical relationships among culture, structure, institutions and behaviour in the following way:

Human Interaction ➤ Culture + Structure ➤ Institutional Form (Groups/Organisations) ➤ Behaviour

They comment:

> Rather than indicating causation, the arrows refer to the constitutive priority among the labels. Hence, the string could be read backwards: behaviour is structured by the institutional form of groups and organisations, which are constituted by culture and structure, which in turn represent products of human interaction. A reaction to this formulation might be that, in reality, a feedback loop exists between structured 'behaviour' and 'human interaction' on the one hand, and 'culture' and 'structure' on the other. Point taken. However, the question of what causes what is different from the question of analytical priority. To ask about the consequences of factions' existence is not to claim that factions – their existence, structure, prevalence or patterns of functioning – are uncaused or unexplainable. It is only to say that factions have consequences as well as causes. To illustrate the explanatory logic of institutions, a focus on institutions is necessary. (ibid., p. 168)

This is a rather curious paragraph. It is claimed that the string refers to constitutive and analytical priorities. It is also acknowledged that the string could be read backwards, that a 'feedback loop' may exist, and that an interest in the consequences of factions does not mean that factions are uncaused or 'unexplainable'. All this would seem to imply that the string *does* refer to a chain of cause and effect, particularly since the factions (number 15 in the typology) are the consequence of a particular combination of associational bases and communication patterns which together yield certain types of political behaviour. The authors are not, in practice, concerned only with the consequences of factions as a way of understanding the explanatory logic of institutions – their openly declared interest. Thus, the theoretical string could be understood to reinforce implicitly the line of cause and effect which appears to stem from, and lead to, factions.

Why, then, is there such ambiguity over the meaning of the string? Why is there a need to play down this chain of cause and effect, and in its stead, emphasise 'constitutive' and 'analytical' priorities? The reason, perhaps, is that if the chain of cause and effect were to be acknowledged openly, this would draw attention to the teleology which, as we have seen, has been used implicitly to strengthen the model, but which invokes a chain of cause and effect running backwards along the string. A charge to which they are clearly sensitive – that the institution which they claim explains behaviour is itself the product of that behaviour – would be confirmed. The authors would, in effect, have provided an explanation for factions that is explicitly cultural.

The authors have not denied that culture may form part of an explanation of factionalism in China; it would be impossible for them to do so given the difficulty they have in distinguishing between institution and culture. However, in their efforts to strengthen an institutional explanation, their *fait accompli*, they have resorted quietly to a teleological explanation. The chains of cause and effect, and therefore the cause of institutions, must therefore remain ambiguous if they are not to give succour to the cultural determinists.

In an attempt to escape from this impasse, Nathan and Tsai emphasise that their analysis is:

> not a brief against cultural explanations as such. But we have shown that certain patterns of belief and action that some analysts treat as cultural can be better explained by reference to organised situations that actors face. Since culture and structure are mutually constituted, institutions can be said to have cultures. A given political action, say an episode of factional manoeuvering, is for the actors at once a decision adopted from within a set of attitudes and a choice taken with an eye to an institutionalised situation. 'Bases for association' are at once attributes of organisations and value commitments that motivate individual action. But culture and structure are analytically

distinguishable. At a given moment, institutions confront their participants in the form of incentives and disincentives, possibilities and impossibilities, and prudential and normative rules. These influence behaviour in addition to, apart from, and in many respects more than, the concurrent influences of culture.

We have not made this case at the most general epistemological level, which would go beyond the scope of this symposium. Rather, we have focused on a sufficiently large example of types of political behaviour in organisations and groups. With regard at least to this set of problems, we have tried to show that an institutional explanation explains more, with fewer variables, across more cases, and in a more monothetic manner than at least the cultural one proposed by Dittmer . . . It might be argued that the institutional approach begs a cultural explanation as much as the cultural approach begs an institutional one. If culture is to some extent produced by institutions, so too institutions are ultimately produced by culture. Explaining the origins of institutions often runs into the culture/structure problem, which continues to challenge the new institutionalism, especially its historical branch.

We hope we have clarified the issue. We do not claim that institutional structure is an 'independent variable' in the ultimate sense. If factions exist, their existence has an explanation. If besides existing they are exceptionally important in the political process, their importance likewise has causes. But culture is not the only one of these explanations and causes. Other include the effect of larger environing institutions (say, bureaucratic or electoral system), economic change, war or other international events, and the micro-logic of historical conjunctures. This is not the place to discuss whether culture is the most powerful of the available explanations for the origins of institutions, but it should be clear that we think culture's potential explanatory role is limited. (ibid., pp. 189–90)

One may question whether they have indeed clarified the issue. Culture is 'conceptualised' as attitudes, values and beliefs inside actors' heads; structure is the patterns of incentives outside actors' heads; structure is a situation; culture is the attitudes which the actor brings to that situation. Clearly, it cannot be argued that values, beliefs, and attitudes learnt by an individual did not exist outside their head. So, Nathan and Tsai, in common with the cultural determinists, invoke 'socialisation'. Nor can it be argued that a situation or institution, or the perception of, or reaction to, that institution or situation, is not influenced by the attitudes, beliefs and values of individuals. Culture and structure are thus 'mutually constituted': structures are created by actors who are bearers of culture; structures are 'products' of human interaction which is culturally conditioned.

Yet, when individuals are faced with institutions and institutional situations (which are shaped by culture), at a given moment in time, at some exact point, in the blink of an eye, institutions and institutional situations 'take the shape as everyday, taken-for-granted reality'; culture and structure become not just 'analytically distinguishable' but an 'objective basis'. At one moment, structure and culture are fused or inextricably entwined; the next moment they suddenly reveal themselves as separate entities as the one precipitates out of the other.

The assertion is useful in that it appears to free the institutional explanation from teleology. Institutions are no longer required to look to the behaviour they yield to explain their own existence. Institutions now have their own 'endogenous logic'; the institutional approach no longer begs the cultural approach. But what is this element or component or catalyst that allows institutions to stand free of culture? The answer, perhaps, is the 'environing institutions' (such as the bureaucratic or electoral system), economic change, war, international events or the 'micro-level of historical conjunctures'. But from where do they come from, these rip-tides of forces that run throughout mankind? How do they operate, and why are they sufficient to produce the regularities demanded by the model across time and space? Unfortunately, this train of thought is quickly cut short by another of those academic platitudes: 'this is not the place to discuss whether culture is the most powerful of the available explanations for the origin of institutions,' although we are left with no doubt that culture's explanatory role is limited. The model, and the idea of these forces, are justification in themselves.

We are left only with the authors' knowledge that these forces exist, with 'environing institutions' and the 'micro-logic of historical conjunctures' and other highly ambiguous jargon, with tangled loops of constitutive and analytical priorities, with a few platitudes, and with the author's statement of 'what is'. But if the idol of origin is invoked, then it must be revealed. If it is not one of these mysterious rip-tides of forces that run throughout mankind throwing up institutions, then it must be culture, for as the writers themselves acknowledge, culture informs structure, structure is to some extent a derivative of it, and presumably structure must have some influence upon the imagined rip-tides of forces. If the authors will not identify these universals and show us how they work, then we must fall back on what they say is not the explanation – culture, for at least they admit culture exists and can be specified. The only alternative is to accept on faith their statement of 'what is': in this case we have only to read their paper and to interpret all we see in its light in order to discover and to know.

There is, for all its twists and turns, a contradiction inherent in the argument which Nathan and Tsai advance – a contradiction which inescapably leads us back to culture; and we must conclude, therefore, that their statement of 'what is', cannot be. Even their language seems to taunt them, for they are clearly sensitive to the sameness of the lexicon, such as 'structuration' and 'socialisation', which they and the cultural determinists use. An institutional theory, they proclaim, includes a dynamic element, an endogenous logic, which the cultural explanation lacks. 'In fact, cultural approaches often fall back on institutions – family, schools, political parties, class structures and so on – to explain the mechanisms that reproduce or transform the culture' ('Factionalism', p. 190).

There is, I have argued in these pages, no confusion between culture and structure. They are one and the same, the idol of origin which goes by many names. 'Universal', 'culture', 'structure', or 'force' refer simply to the preferences and preconceptions of the observer. Nathan and Tsai have chosen to see in their idol not this common malaise but vindication of their assumptions. Such is the power of theory and self-belief.

The mirror dance: culture versus structure

Dittmer[14] makes similar criticisms of Nathan's earlier work[15]:

> Nathan launches a wide-ranging tour through the comparative social science literature to arrive at a universally valid model. He then applies this construct to China – and finds, *mirabile dictu*, that it fits! Recent CCP elite political behaviour is then reconstructed in the light of the model. ('Informal Politics', p. 2)

Dittmer then toughens his criticisms of abstract model building, and lays out the broad aims of his own 'conceptualisation':

> Any new conceptualisation should avoid the problems of excessive modesty and overweening ambition that have plagued earlier definitional efforts. In the former, we are given a purely negative definition of the central term, defining informal politics not in terms of what it is but in terms of what it is not – formal politics. Clearly, it is

important to note the interdependency between formal and informal politics, but informal politics should not be derogated to the status of a residual category, dependent upon the definition of its positive counterpart. The opposite problem is the tendency to strive for prematurely ambitious conceptualisations – to aim at a model of factionalism that is valid throughout the Third World, for example, or even applied to Chinese organisations on the whole – and then to interpolate from these general models to the political situation within the Party Politburo. This sort of abstract model-building is understandable, in view of the paucity of hard empirical evidence about the inner workings of the politburo and other powerful leadership organs. Yet a definition that is valid for a universal or even a comparatively broad range of factional behaviour cannot be expected to capture the *differentia specifica* of the Party Leadership. (ibid., p. 9)

Dittmer's inquiry is restricted to the top 20 to 35 Party officials who make up the elite of China's leadership. Central to his 'conceptualisation' are 'relationships'. Two kinds of relationships are identified: the purpose-rational (those which are a means to an end); and the value-rational (those valued as ends in themselves). The purpose-rational are

typically formed with those colleagues, subordinates and superiors with whom one has routine occupational contacts. These relationships may be mobilised in support of career objectives so long as they are in the collective interests of the organisation of which all are a part; thus we may refer to this ensemble of occupational relationships as one's *formal base*. By mobilizing one's formal base one is able to exert official power which the Chinese refer to as *quanli*. (ibid., p. 10, italics in original)

Value-rational relationships comprise 'an informal "political base" . . . on the basis of which one can exercise informal power, or *shili*. A political base may be measured in terms of its *depth* and *breadth*: a "broad" base consists of a network of cronies located throughout the Party, military, diplomatic, and governmental apparatus, whereas a "deep" base consists of supporters going all the way back to the early generations of the revolutionary leadership, hence having high seniority and elevated positions' (ibid., p. 12, italics in original).

This informal base is put together 'through the incremental accretion of discrete "connections". People have a large but finite number of potential affinities, including kinship, common geographic origin, former

classmates, teachers or students, or common former Field Army affiliation – at least one of which is usually necessary to form a connection
(*guanxi*). A cadre assigned to a new task or post will immediately can-
vass the area for such objective affinities as a priority *sine qua non*
objective, not just wait for them to emerge haphazardly.... An objective base for an affinity does not necessarily create one ... An informal
base must be "cultivated", which involves investing selected potential
affinities with value' (ibid.).

The official power (*quanli*) of the formal base is limited. If removed
from their job or rotated among different posts, the formal base disap-
pears; and in any event it is unlikely that colleagues will risk their own
positions and some to defend one of their number. Informal bases,
however, which are not mobilised for the sake of bureaucratic policy
matters but rather for political reasons and in support of the individual's
own power, therefore have little relevance to policy (ibid., p. 14).

The relationship between formal and informal politics, argues Dittmer,
'is fluid and ambiguous – informal groups are often absorbed into formal
structures, and formal structures in turn operate with a great deal of
informality – but the distinction remains relevant in at least three
respects' (ibid.). However, only the first of these is clearly specified by
Dittmer; the other two are left in rather ambiguous forms.

(i) First, the distinction between formal and informal politics appears
in the recruitment and utilisation of the base members, for there are
'those who are relatively pure cases of informal connections, and those
who have formal credentials' (ibid.). Individuals with informal connections are exclusively dependent upon their patron, and they are more
inclined to exhibit personal loyalty and to indulge in *courtiserie*. Individuals with formal connections are likely to balance their patron's
request against their own bureaucratic interests and their future career.
Bases may also be mixed. In these situations, individuals will behave
like court favourites while their patron remains strong, and build up the
formal power bases on which they must rely once their patron falls.

(ii) The distinction between formal and informal is also relevant in
that it finds expression as the historical dominance of informal politics
where formal politics often provides no more than a façade. 'Informal
politics plays an important part in every organisation at every level, but
the higher the organisation the more important it becomes. At the
highest level, because the tasks to be performed are relatively unstruc-
tured, the area of discretion is large, personal judgement crucial, the
demand for quick decisions is great, and secrecy imperative, informal
politics prevails...

An adept leadership while using informal politics to cobble together a majority within the formal apparatus, will then turn to formal politics for public policy implementation' (ibid., p. 17).

(iii) Finally, the relevance of the distinction between informal and formal politics also appears in the 'norms' of the game. In the highest echelon of the Party, the formal norms include collective leadership and democratic centralism. But while formally members are supposed to be equal (in the sense that each member, including the Chairman, only has one vote), they each preside over a formal hierarchy and may be assumed to have a broad and deep informal base (ibid., p. 19).

'Though the combination of formal and informal power bases renders each member of this elite extremely powerful, there seems to be an intra-elite balancing process, in which the functional division of labour and a rough equality consonant with the formal norm of collective leadership are in constant tension with the need for hierarchy' (ibid.). The need for hierarchy (which is equated with 'order' and opposed to 'chaos') is an informal norm cemented by patron client relationships within the leadership. The normal relationship among the political elite, then, is hierarchical.

The power of each member of China's political elite is, in sum, determined by informal connections (*guanxi*) within the leader; the formal positions which they hold beyond Politburo membership; their formal bases (or credentials); the depth and breadth of their informal bases; and any opportunities which may present themselves (such as the illness of the leader). The Supreme Leader is in a somewhat different, and stronger, position, for he has a public image of flawlessness, the final word on ideology, the freedom to act at any level of the hierarchy (and with any one he chooses) without fear of being charged with factionalism, and privileged access to information within the bureaucracy.

The alignment of the leadership, argues Dittmer, is best understood as the interaction of two axes. One, the extent of agreement, proceeds along a continuum from cleavage to factionalism; the other, the distribution of power, runs along a continuum from hierarchy to collegiality. This gives rise to a 'two-by-two' pattern of alignment. The sharper the cleavage and the more collegiate the distribution of power, the more factionalised the elite; the sharper the cleavage and the more hierarchical the distribution of power, the stronger the hierarchical discipline; the more collegiate the distribution of power and the more solidarity there is, the greater will be the extent of collective leadership; the more hierarchical the distribution of power and the stronger the solidarity, the closer the polity will be to the ideal of 'first among equals'.

Cleavage is most likely when the attention of the Supreme Leader is distracted, or ill, or if there is a pre-mortem or post-mortem struggle for succession; when policies have brought about a situation or problem which could be handled in a number of possible ways, each of which may favour one or other faction; or when the leader delegates such power as may allow him to explore policies and to collect any credit or deflect any blame that may thereby accrue, to test loyalties, to justify or initiate dismissals, and to circumvent procedures.

Dittmer summarises his 'conceptualisation' as follows:

> informal politics can be defined on the basis of a combination of behavioural, structural and cyclical criteria. Behaviourally, informal politics consists of value-rational as opposed to purpose-rational relationships functioning in the service of a personal base. Informal politics tends to be implicit and covert...rather than explicit and public; to be flexible, casual and irregular rather than institutionalised. Structurally, informal politics may be assumed to affect leadership more than routine administration, and high-level leadership more than low-level. This informality is a function of discretionary latitude and is limited to small, closed groups. The structural circumstances most conducive to informal politics are those in which the leadership is beset by a crisis not resolvable through standard operating procedures, permitting the existing hierarchical monopoly to breakdown into a more open competition among elites. Informal politics tends to occur at those times in the political cycle when this type of structural breakdown is most likely to occur – particularly leadership successions, of course, but other national crises as well. ('Informal Politics', p. 33)

The criticisms which Dittmer makes of Nathan and Tsai are no less true of Dittmer's own conceptualisation, for their thinking, and their models, share the same philosophical base despite of the distinction which he, like Nathan and Tsai, makes between cultural determinism and universal structures. Dittmer's analysis is a presentation of the rules which determine how China's polity works. We are told, for example, that there are two types of bases with their own particular characteristics and limitations; that informal bases are mobilised for political reasons in support of an individual's own power; that formal bases are used in support of bureaucratic policies; that there are three important distinctions between informal and formal politics; that individuals with informal connections are more inclined to personal loyalty; that individuals with formal connections will balance their patrons' requests against their own bureaucratic interests; that an adept leadership will turn to formal bases for policy implementation; that a 'hierarchy' is an informal norm, and that democratic centralism is a formal norm; that the perceived stability of the leadership hierarchy determines whether the leadership will be settled through negotiation and compromise or thorough a zero-sum struggle. There are also the rules concerning the power of the Supreme Leader and other members of China's political elite; the rules which govern cleavage; and the rules which determine the interaction of 'power' and 'agreement' and the characteristic pattern of elite alignment thereby produced. Observations are interpreted in the light of this conceptualisation, and this interpretation is regarded as evidence of the model's validity.

But why do these rules apply? Why does China's polity work in the way that the model suggests? In common with Nathan and Tsai, Dittmer must, in his presentation of 'what is', call upon the idol of origins. Unlike Nathan and Tsai, however, Dittmer chooses to be more explicit about the force which holds the model and China together, and so allows both theory and polity to work as he describes. Chinese culture, we are told, is neither individualistic nor group oriented but rather 'relationship based' (ibid., p. 10); and 'Chinese' attributes (such as kinship, classmate and school ties) 'may articulate into vast networks', and may also be defined by 'fixed frames' (such as family, village, and workplace). These attributes and relationships appear to be roughly equivalent to 'informal' and 'formal' bases. Dittmer views this latter distinction as an 'analytical' one, and argues that it is more useful than the former, and rather blurred, distinction between 'extendible' and 'fixed frame' attributes. We also learn that 'the need for hierarchy has deep cultural roots' and that the 'implicit cultural model for China's elite politics is the imperial court system, the role of the emperor being played by what Deng called the Party "core", but which we term the "Supreme Leader"' (ibid., pp. 20 and 19).

The suggestion that the imperial court is a cultural model for China's modern polity chimes with Nathan and Tsai's belief that cultural determinists must constantly fall back upon institutional arguments, though, as we have noted, the importance which Nathan and Tsai attach to institutions simply reinforces the cultural argument. Therein lies the advantage of the cultural determinist. In the absence of universals, and in the presence of the dictates of the scientific approach, whereas the institutionalist must return to culture, the cultural determinist need not specify the First Cause: there can be only culture. Their model, with its variables, rules and hypotheses and chains of cause and effect need not be so tightly delineated, complex, or consistent, for it is known that ultimately everything can be traced back, one way or another, to culture; and all contradictions and inconsistencies can be explained, one way or another, once bathed in its light.

It is with confidence, then, that Dittmer shifts his position as seems necessary. Initially the reader is told that the power of the formal base (*quanli*) is limited, for it can be extinguished by simply rotating or removing individuals from their post; and that it is to their informal bases that leaders (particularly at the highest levels) will look to protect themselves and their own careers. We are also told that in China informal politics has been historically dominant.

But it would also appear true that 'without a formal position an informal base has little leverage; thus normally a factional network can be destroyed simply by removing its leader(s) from the formal positions in the organisational structure that enables it to extend its informal relationships and loyalties' (ibid., p. 17). And it is also true that while informal politics remains more potent in China than in other countries (and is likely to remain so), 'the historical trend is toward political formalisation' (ibid., p. 18). This is especially true since the death of Mao, for the 'overall thrust of development since the advent of political reform (despite such interruptions as Tian'anmen) has been towards increasing formalisation, as measured by the frequency, length and regularity of meeting sessions, and the number of people or procedural stages involved in drafting legislation' (ibid., p. 17). But then again, we are told that the formal rules of the game 'have the best chance of prevailing when they coincide with informal loyalties; when they do not, a clash may occur in which the depth and breadth of one's informal base is likely to be the most decisive factor. Yet even in the event of such a clash, the winning faction will probably (1) use formal-legal norms and organisational levers . . . to augment informal resources prior to the clash, and (2) legitimate victory *post hoc*, via constitutional engineering and the proclamation of new formal norms' (ibid., p. 19). This seems to take the reader back to the original position – that the formal bases depend upon the informal, and that today, as in the past, informal politics is dominant. The shift is reinforced by Dittmer's comment that Deng, who was proficient at manipulating the bureaucracy and 'indifferent' to political reform, tore down many of the reform institutions when he found it expedient to do so (ibid., p. 22).

However, Dittmer shifts his position yet again when describing the power and tactics of the Supreme Leader. A faction opposing him is able to communicate only informally and secretly (and so can reach only a limited number of individuals), and, being an informal group, it is therefore dependent upon a formal organisational structure which serves as a 'trellis' (to use Nathan's term) (ibid., p. 23). By contrast, the Supreme Leader can communicate openly, officially and quickly, and he can 'clip short' the faction's 'trellis' by invoking formal organisational sanctions. The authority of any opposing faction is thereby undermined.

But then we are presented with developments that seem to indicate a move in China towards informal politics – a move which is consistent with the historical dominance of informal politics in China, but which runs against the 'historical trend . . . toward political formalisation' also noted by Dittmer (ibid., pp. 17, 18). As the ideological barriers to the operation of factions breaks down and factional behaviour, though still forbidden, is less clandestine, the contemporary elite factions have 'begun to engage in the active pursuit of policies', and they are doing so as 'policy groups' – an 'emergent operational form' which is 'informally constituted but takes coherent positions on policy issues of central interest to its constituency' (ibid., p. 31). Recruitment to these groups is 'based on patronage rather than issue-orientation, and loyalty to the patron tends in the event of elite cleavage to override bureaucratic interests. This, then, is a half-rationalised (that is policy-oriented but still personalistic) form of factionalism corresponding to the "half-reformed" status of the Chinese political system' (ibid., p. 32). It would now seem that by 'formalisation', Dittmer is referring to informal groups oriented more towards policy than towards individuals.

In view of these swings in position, it is legitimate to ask whether there ever was any distinction between formal and informal politics in Dittmer's mind? After all, as he himself notes, the relationship between formal and informal politics 'is fluid and ambiguous – informal groups are often absorbed into formal structures, and formal structures in turn operate with a great deal of informality' (ibid., p. 14).

Within all this chopping and changing there is also uncertainty regarding the distinction between *guanxi* and purpose-rational and value-rational relationships. Initially we are told that Chinese culture is 'relationship-based (*guanxi benwei*)' and that analytically we may distinguish between two types of relations – the purpose-rational and the value-rational. *Guanxi*, then, refers to two kinds of relationships (ibid., p. 10).

In his description of the assembly of an informal base, Dittmer argues that 'people have a large but finite number of potential affinities, including kinship, common geographic origin, former classmates, teachers or students, or common former Field Army affiliation – at least one of which is necessary to form a "connection" (*guanxi*)' (ibid., p. 12). The term *guanxi* is not mentioned in his initial outline of formal bases, formal power, and purpose-value relationships which are typically formed with those colleagues, subordinates and superiors with whom one has routine occupational contacts. If *guanxi* is explicitly associated with informal relationships and informal bases, then a niggling question arises – does a 'connection' or *guanxi* refer to a 'value-rational' or 'purpose-value' relationship? The ambiguity becomes more pronounced during the discussion on the impact of reform upon informal politics. Dittmer argues that:

> the overall decline in the status of ideology . . . and the increasing importance of purpose-rational relationships seems to have had both an emancipatory and corrosive impact upon *guanxi* – emancipatory because with the relaxation of constraints on lateral communication brought about by the end of class struggle and the spread of the market, contacts of all types are multiplying. At the same time the reform's impact is corrosive in the sense that such connections have become suffused with utilitarian considerations. As a consequence, the dichotomy introduced earlier between value-rational and purpose-rational relationships has tended to break down. A new type of connection has emerged that is more instrumental and less sentimental. (ibid., p. 29)

The argument would seem to imply that *guanxi* is indeed distinct from purpose-rational relationships, and possibly synonymous with value-rational relationships, and that *guanxi* (with its value-rational qualities) has become suffused with the 'purpose-rational'. If we assume that *guanxi* refers to relationships in general – to relationships which are either purpose-rational or value-rational – then we are presented with a tautology: purpose-rational relationships are emancipating, and corroding, both purpose-rational relationships as well as value-rational relationships. Alternatively, the passage cited above might suggest that *guanxi* is closely associated with, but remains distinct from, value-rational relationships, and that it is being affected by purpose-value relationships. Another possible reading is that *guanxi* is an undifferentiated relationship which is now being overwhelmed by utilitarian considerations.

The issue becomes more confused when we are told that: 'The new hybrid *guanxi* . . . is *both* value-rational and purpose-rational . . . the trend is for *guanxi* to become indistinguishable from collegial or other superficially affective business associations' (ibid., p. 30). This argument would seem to reinforce the implied belief that, originally at least, *guanxi* is closer to, or synonymous with, value-rational relationships. Or it may imply that *guanxi is* an undifferentiated relationship which may become suffused either with the purpose-value or with the value-rational, or with both, but which under the influence of the reforms, is being soaked in the purpose-rational.

Confusion is piled upon confusion if we also take into account Dittmer's response to Nathan and Tsai's criticisms of his arguments: 'My own conceptualisation' (writes Dittmer),

> draws a sharp analytical distinction between formal and informal in terms of the "relationships" (*guanxi*) on the basis of which they are formed: formal groups consist of "purpose-value" relations, typically recruited from current bureaucratic subordinates and colleagues, while informal groups consist of "value-rational" relationships, recruited from primordial associates and cronies.[16]

It now appears that all along *guanxi* was, and remains a generic term for relationships which may be either purpose-value or value-rational. But if so, then, as we have already noted, we are left with tautology and contradiction. Purpose-rational relationships are a means to an ends, whereas value-rational relationships are an end in themselves; and yet we are told both purpose-rational and value-rational relationships have their uses in high-level elite politics. Then again we learn that under the reforms, the distinction between purpose-rational and value-rational relationships is breaking down, and a new type of connection that is more instrumental is emerging.

To Nathan and Tsai's criticism that it is difficult, if not impossible, to make a distinction between the purpose-rational and value-rational relationship, Dittmer replies that value 'has nothing to do with morality, but means simply that the relationship has a value transcending the immediate issue at stake'.[17] If instrumental means use that is 'immediate' rather than 'long-term' (a similar position is adopted by Smart[18]), is it being implied that under the Reforms 'use' is judged to have become more 'short-term'. In which case, at what point does use that is immediate or short-term become long-term?

Words, concepts, and arguments may be twisted and turned at will because it is known that the underlying explanation is cultural. Inconsistencies, contradictions, the absence of specified origins, the absence of detailed chains of cause and effect, the reliance on implied forces, and the invocation of recursive phenomena and vestigial beings, are treated as little more than incidental problems: for the First Cause, and the final explanation, is known to culture. Formal and informal bases; formal and informal relationships; formal and informal politics; *guanxi*; value-rational and purpose-rational relationships; relationships that are sentimental and instrumental; and objectives that are long-term, short-term, material and non-material: all these are but wisps of fantasies which (because they are known to be derived from, and so can be explained by, culture) may take on different meaning from one moment to the next as the explanation of any particular event seems to demand. Ultimately, therefore, it is to China's image – an image of difference and morality – that analysis must defer.

As we have come to expect, that difference, that sense of Chineseness, is highlighted by comparison with other cultures. There is, in Dittmers's analysis, the inevitable comparison with 'the West': in China, unlike in most Western countries (where, we are told, formal politics is dominant), informal politics has always held sway, though curiously Dittmer uses several European phrases which convey adequately enough that sense of 'informal' political behaviour in both Europe and China. A Chinese official can be dismissed on grounds of ideological deviation as defined '*ex cathedra* by a Caesero-papist leader'; and the Chinese Communist Party is governed by a *Fuehrerprinzip* in the sense that the Supreme leader has supreme access to the levers of bureaucratic power, the media, and the symbols capable of moving the masses ('Informal Politics', pp. 17 & 20). And was not Deng capable of manipulating the *vox populi*? And did not the Red Guards deem any reference to "sun spots" as evidence of *lese majesté*? (ibid., p. 23).

There are also comparisons to be made between China and Japan:

Ambrose King has postulated that in contradistinction to Japanese relationships, which are based on fixed frames or *ba* (the family, workplace or village) that set a clear boundary and give a common identity to a set of individuals, Chinese relationships are formed on the basis of attributes (such as kinship, classmate, school ties) which are infinitely extendible. Attributes provide a pluralistic basis of identification depending on the specific attribute shared; thus the more attributes a person has, the more relationships one is able to establish. While it is certainly true that Chinese attributes sometimes articulate into vast networks, many Chinese attributes are also defined by fixed frames, such as those within the same family, parochial village, or 'basic work unit'... Perhaps the deciding criterion determining how far attributes extend within a given culture is the amount of social mobility. In any case, the Chinese political scene includes both types of connection, which are not always clearly differentiated. (ibid., p. 10)

Dittmer (like Needham, Solinger, Schram and many others) reaches deep into the uniqueness that is Chinese culture, draws aside the *courtiserie* among China's elite, and therein reveals a moral essence which may well transform China into a society that is pluralistic and democratic, but still very much 'Chinese'. It is true that reform has, in Dittmer's view, negative features. *Guanxi* has become more instrumental, less sentimental: it is a hybrid form which much to the consternation of more traditional types who deplore the adulteration of value-rational relationships with short-term material interests (ibid., p. 30) – is both value-rational and purpose-rational.

> Here, one is using connections cultivated for their intrinsic value as an instrument to achieve other ends, or even cultivate 'connections' with material gain in mind. This is particularly noticeable at the lower levels, where cadres with direct responsibility for managing the economy are constantly offered new opportunities for rent-seeking behaviour. The other tendency is for networks of connections to metastatize throughout society at large... (ibid.)

Here, then, is the unmistakable smell of something rotting. 'Corrosive' (ibid., p. 29), 'adulteration', 'rent-seeking', and 'metastatize': the words convey a sense of corruption, decomposition, deformation, perversion and evil. Something is dishonouring true *guanxi* and its essential Chineseness, or so Dittmer (like Yang, Smart, Solinger, Jacobs and Lau[19]) would have us believe.

And yet, in spite of the growing influence of the market among the elite (who are still insulated by reasonably high salaries and comprehensive benefits) 'material interests have not yet adulterated value-rational relationships in any obvious way' ('Informal Politics', p. 30). More importantly, purpose-rational relationships – the manipulative, instrumental use of relationships – may also have a favourable influence, potentially at least, on China's polity. Such relationships may lead to greater formalisation, and even to pluralism, in a state where 'the diminution in the relative importance of ideology has led leaders to resort to formal-legal rationality as the most potent available means of legitimisation' (ibid., p. 17). The secularisation of Mao Zedong thought, Deng's pragmatic focus on growth at any cost, and 'the attendant dismissal of the spectre of an elite "struggle between two lines" and "people in the Party taking the capitalist road", have reduced the ideological barriers to the operation of factions' (ibid., pp. 30–1). The ebbing of ideology, combined with an easing of disciplinary measures against officials and attempts to legalise their tenure, and to restore popular respect for officialdom, have allowed factional behaviour to become 'somewhat less clandestine'. Elite factions have now begun to pursue and to represent the interests of their constituencies. Indeed, in the wake of Reform, elite coalitions have even begun to move away from 'factions' towards 'policy groups', the next stage being the formal structures and formal alliances which make up a 'bureaucratic' polity.

Of course, few things are certain: informal politics in China, reactionary in its 'power-political implications', tends 'to reinforce traditional hierarchical relationships (including the "cult" of leadership inherited from the empire), and culturally embedded relationships more generally (for instance, time-honoured primordial "connections") at the expense of a rational-legal and meritocratic arrangements' (ibid., p. 33). Surrounded by the unspoken influence of Skinner, of Skinner and Winkler, and of Solinger,[20] Dittmer suggests that future development will depend upon the business cycle. With the reforms, the business cycle appears to have intensified and is now also more tightly aligned with the political cycle. Elite cleavage at the top and bottom of the economic cycle is now clearly visible; but even more important, perhaps, is 'whether the cycle has reached an outer limit, according to which at least one faction within the leadership is prepared to fight "against the current" for a correction' (ibid., p. 33).

Nevertheless the outlook remains generally positive, for is there not within Chinese culture that essential morality? There is a growing institutionalisation of various bureaucratic systems at all but the highest levels; the reliance on explicit rules and procedures is increasing; informal groups, now oriented towards policies designed to enhance bureaucratic interests, are being transformed into professional, vocational, business, and pressure groups – and even, as in the case of the reformists and conservatives, into quasi-parties. As a political form, believes Dittmer, 'informal politics . . . tends to be progressive in terms of policy, as its flexibility facilitates more rapid change by offering short-cuts to standard bureaucratic procedures. This has helped make China an extraordinarily well-led country compared to others in the Third World (albeit not always wisely governed)' (ibid.).

Conclusions

Although cultural and structural explanations of China's polity appear to stand in opposition, the one explanation is but a reflection of the other, for both are founded on the scientific approach. The need to establish origins, chains of cause and effect, or some kind of recursive phenomena (a more sophisticated version of origin, cause and effect) demands the invocation of culture or structure, universals or cultural determinants, and some internal or external force. A fluid, multi-dimensional reality is frozen and then shattered into countless, two-dimensional fragments. The pieces are reconstituted as an awkward framework which is then used to interpret observations and thereby to confirm some pleasing image. The choice between structure or culture, universals or cultural determinant, and internal or external forces which are to be woven into the framework depends upon the preference and judgement of the writer: how plausible is the concept of 'structure' or 'culture' given the nature of the observations to be interpreted, and what is the nature of the image to be propagated? The use of a framework to provide a reasonable and generally consistent interpretation, and the fact that a writer's intuition and perceptivity (though such qualities owe nothing to theory) can be found a sensible place within that interpretation, are taken as evidence that the framework is essentially valid.

Every now and then, among the formal explanations of China's polity, we catch glimpses of the *courtiserie*, the secrecy, the muddled and malicious treachery, the hypocrisy, the ruthless manipulation of emotions and ideas, and the climate of fear and vengeance in which there is no restraint upon the individual's base emotions, save the ambitions of others. But for the most part social scientists are not concerned with these empirical trifles. Their interest is in formal scientific theory – the hallmark of the scholar. They are concerned to identify the larger system, the structures and forces which lie behind the expression of human nature. The social scientist's own perceptivity, common sense, experience and judgement, become part of the rationalisation, or justification, of the theory by which China's polity is to be interpreted.

We have often had occasion to remark that such criticisms of the scientific approach, though they have profound implications for social science, have little relevance to those sentiments which drive and guide analysis and to those intellectualisations of 'what is'. Science, in the tradition of medievalism, exists merely to legitimise, rather than to exert discipline over, beliefs and sentiment. This concourse of emotions and intellectualisms which is called social science parallels the reluctance of those who rule China to treat values, beliefs, ideals and institutions not as expedient absolutes, but as instruments for manipulation in the pursuit of political or economic ambitions. Just as the medieval Chinese state appeals to the stylised representations of its culture, so the social scientist, either directly or (because of their failure to specify universals) indirectly, defers to that culture. The word-play of their intellectualisations is thus brought perilously close to the hard politics of the everyday.

4
Masters of Image: China and the World

Introduction

On numerous occasions in this book I have commented that although perceptivity and threads of facts pleach the study of China, it is not so much the details of the arguments from which China's stylised representations are constructed as the representations themselves that matter, so strong is the hold which a deference to culture is permitted over our thoughts and perceptions. We are, in consequence, presented with images that are, I suspect, even more unrealistic than I have suggested. As we shall see in the remainder of this book, these images not only shape analyses of China's position in the world and its relationships with other countries, but they have also influenced policy advice and practice.

The Chinese way

In an influential series of lectures delivered to the Nobel Peace Institute, Professor Wang Gungwu,[1] a former vice-chancellor of Hong Kong University, argues that China is essentially different, and that China's various perceptions of itself influence both its domestic and foreign policies:

> Both Chinese and foreigners have often asked why China is not a 'normal' country; that is, why is China not a nation state that behaves like most other countries? It seems clumsy in its dealings with other countries, inviting impatience with its seeming intransigence regarding various international issues, for example, its nuclear testing or trade disputes. It is seen alternately as a civilization, an empire, or a potential superpower. At times, the PRC is condemned as the last communist giant. At others there are predictions of disasters

and mainland China is seen as a precarious polity on the verge of crumbling into a group of fragmented and warring states. Or, China is considered as an unstable hybrid, a strange creature with a socialist body, but parts of it dressed in capitalist clothes. There are numerous paradoxes and contradictions, all giving the impression of instability and the capacity to destabilize the region of not the whole world.

These different images, and the questions they beg, are found not only among those outside China, but also among those within it. We can usefully explore these images through descriptions of China that the reflect the different ways the country is perceived by the Chinese themselves ... Currently there are several layers of such perceptions. 'Layers' suggests a chronological sequence, with the present on the top and the past arranged in order below, but, just as historical events surface in our minds, each layer of the past can be conjured up whenever appropriate to any discourse. This is how Chinese people habitually make use of their past and how I intend to treat these layers. This does not imply, however, that any of the perceptions are shared by all Chinese. Not all layers may be found among every group of Chinese, nor do they all coexist in people's consciousness at any one time. Also, as is natural for a large and diverse people, each layer, regardless of its overall importance, could be dominant for some Chinese some of the time. (CW, pp. 19–20)

If China and its actions are to be seen for what they truly are, believes Wang, and if the actions and responses of the outside world are to be helpful and constructive, then China's self-perceptions must be thoroughly understood.

Nationalism

Wang argues that the idea of 'China as a nation' – one of the three key self-perceptions or concepts (the other two being 'historic empire' and 'Chinese civilisation') – encompasses far more than the question of reunification with Taiwan:

The idea of national identity was a powerful discovery at the turn of the century for the intelligentsia who saw the imperial system collapse. For a people who had lived under an empire for two thousand years, it was remarkable how quickly they accepted the idea of a republic, and they have not seemed to want to return to any sort of imperial or monarchical system since 1911. Indeed, these nationalists started with radical political change. Dynastic overthrow was followed by the complete reform of the system of government, including elected national constituent assemblies. When that failed and the country was dominated for a decade by warlords, both the nationalists and the communists who were allied to fight with the warlords agreed that political restructuring was essential.

The first priority was national reunification, seen as political reform or revolution from above. The leaders looked for an alternative to the mainstream Western model, which was seen as an exploitative system that was impoverishing China. Ironically, they looked to the West for an ideology that was more powerful than orthodox capitalism and liberal democracy, something that would help China stand up against the West itself. Some found it in Mussolini's fascism, others in national socialism, and yet others in anarchism, socialism, and communism. In all of these, economic development was subordinated to the political goal of unification and centralized power, And this remained so under both nationalist and communist leaders on the mainland until Deng Xiaoping's reforms after 1978. Only then, for the first time in modern history, was economic reform given the highest priority, an understandable reaction against the Maoist slogan 'Put politics in command'. This emphasis on putting prosperity before further political reform has brought a totally new dimension to China's nation-building process.

The idea of nationalism itself was an inspiration for all Chinese who felt humiliated by the successive military defeats that led to unequal status for Chinese everywhere, to extraterritorial privileges for foreign residents within China, and to the increasing dominance of foreign enterprises on Chinese soil. Nationalism was tied to anti-imperialism and anti-colonialism as the key to almost all of the political struggles of the twentieth century. Both Chiang Kai-shek and Mao Tse-tung were propelled into politics by their nationalistic urges. And, despite the romantic internationalist slogans after the communist victory in 1949, national pride and interests remained in the forefront of the goals of the People's Republic. With the collapse of communist ideology, little now stands in the way of the current leaders' returning to nationalism to seek a stronger mandate for their rule. Simply put, this would mean a return to the quest for wealth and power by the nation state. (ibid., pp. 46–8)

Nationalism and socialism in China, it would seem, are (or were) closely entwined: regardless of the prevailing ideology and irrespective of whether or not it was thought wise to subordinate the economy to

China's polity, it has been the drive for national power, prestige and strength which has motivated China's leaders for at least eighty years. Wang quickly goes on to argue that the idea of a nation state is nevertheless both complex and constrained. Although China 'is more fortunate than most former empires in having a majority – the Han – that numbers more than 90 per cent of its population' (ibid., p. 48), an emphasis upon nationalist sentiments would provoke and exacerbate parallel sentiments among China's minorities. The government in Beijing, he argues,

> seems to be sensitive enough about the danger of wielding such a double-edged weapon not too make too much of the act of nation-building right now . . . Thus, despite the obvious power of nationalism as a unifying force, the Chinese are not really at liberty to beat the nationalist drum. China remains in the ambivalent position of encouraging national pride in becoming a great power while developing the national dimension of minority peoples on its borders. Instead, the focus will, in the long-run, have to be on the development of a larger national culture for an 'imagined community' that could attract the loyalty of all peoples who live in China. (ibid., p. 50)

Running against these concerns, however, is the very great importance which China's leaders attach to national unity – a matter that will continue to be 'of central importance to the Chinese leaders in the country's international relations until it is finally resolved to their satisfaction. If other powers actively seek to prevent China's national unification or, worse, encourage parts of China to secede, such action would become a permanent source of instability in the region. Thus, the Chinese believe they must maintain a strong central government, something their history inclines them to do in any case' (ibid., p. 51).

Historic empire

The idea or self-perception of 'a glorious imperial past', Wang believes, is quite distinct from nationalism. His argument begins with the qualification that the Chinese are no more obsessed with their history than are any other people:

> All countries that have full records of a long and distinguished past are just as fascinated with their own history. When there exists such a vivid, continuous, and concrete record of the activities of various people living in an extensive territory, which the people themselves

recognise as always having had a unified core, it is inevitable that stories of specific successes and failures are regularly invoked. (ibid., p. 52)

He then goes on to emphasise that the oneness of China's historical experience, and the didactic quality of its historical judgements, are unusual:

Inapplicable to Europe, Africa, and other parts of Asia, where kingdoms and empires rose and fell to form different nations, this sustained picture of historical oneness is unique to a continental territory like China. Most of the core lands of North, Central, and South China, where the Han Chinese have always been in the majority, have an unbroken history of two or three thousand years. Others farther north and west have been alternately inside and outside the borders of Chinese empires, but have been regarded as integral parts of the ebb and flow of Chinese history. For example, the fact that many of the more powerful tribal federations, such as the Turks, Mongols, Tibetans, and Jurchen-Manchus, have actually ruled over all or parts of the core lands has established the tradition that they all shared a common heritage with the Han Chinese. That many of these people have also been assimilated into the dominant Han culture over time has confirmed this common heritage. Thus, although China has been divided in the past because of the fall of dynasties or foreign conquest, the driving force behind all governments has always been to reunify the empire. The inclusive rhetoric used in historical writings to represent such a theme of unity in diversity is seen to have sanctified the idea that it is the land that is China, and that all those who rule it, whatever their origins, and all those who live there, become Chinese. (ibid., pp. 52–3)

The problem with this self-perception, argues Wang, is that 'long stretches of the northern and western borders have never been clearly defined. Understandably, in past centuries, there was no concept of boundary demarcation. Nor was there a concept of sovereignty or jurisdiction. The most important factor was the reach of the central government' (ibid., p. 53). The only two exceptions in Chinese history were Korea, which kept itself out of China through a combination of geographical location, self-restraint and diplomatic skills; and Vietnam which struggled for centuries to define its own nationhood and to preserve its lands from Chinese invaders (ibid.).

These exceptions are believed to prove the rule: the way in which influence was exerted and, in consequence, the vagueness of China's borders, were expressions of an empire that had grown naturally, almost organically; very rarely would China ever attempt the conquest of sophisticated, discrete cultures, most especially if they did not present a threat to China. These characteristics of the Chinese empire – its oneness, its continuity, it expanse, the way in which it exerted power and influence, the vagueness of its borders, and its didactic treatment of history – not only make China unique, but speak against adventurism and aggression. The Chinese empire was

unlike that of the Persians, Greeks, or Romans, that of Asoka, Tamerlane, or Babur, or, in more modern times, that of the Ottomans, the British, the French, or tsarist Russia. These were empires by conquest; in recent times, they were by conquest over long distances and even across oceans. They lasted only as long as their military forces were victorious. For most of its two thousand years of 'imperial' history, this was not the case with China. With the exception of the short Mongol period of 90 years, when China was itself part of the world empire of the Mongols, no armies marched out of traditional Middle Kingdom (*Zhongguo*) lands. The Mongol expeditionary bursts far into Eurasia, and across the seas to Japan and Java, were strictly un-Chinese. On the contrary, the successor dynasty of the Ming, which was led by Han Chinese, strongly resisted the Mongol world view. After three decades of exceptional voyages by Admiral Zheng He early in the fifteenth century into the South China Sea and across the Indian Ocean to the shores of East Africa, the Ming emperors insisted on returning to the control of traditional lands and forbade foreign adventures. They saw these voyages as aberrations and turned inward toward their land frontiers. The Ming reaffirmed what had distinguished the Chinese historic empire for more than a thousand years: its self-centredness and its belief in its invulnerability and self-sufficiency. This was reflected in the history of growing complacency and arrogance, and in the empire's adherence to the tributary system that the Chinese rulers had developed internally and then applied in varying degrees beyond China . . .

In all the histories written before the twentieth century, the lessons to be learned from the imperial past were that China was a land power, that adventures outside China were to be avoided, and that Chinese rulers who had been ambitious on the borders usually exhausted the empire's resources and failed to profit from their efforts. Also, there are records of a long list of negative and positive role models for future rulers, from examples of those who had impoverished the empire in pursuit of foreign adventures, to those who defended the sacred lands successfully with minimum effort and cost, to those who used the tributary system skillfully to keep the imperial peace and foreigners in their place. Thus, the lessons of political and institutional history were as important as the celebrations of past imperial glories. (ibid., pp. 53–5)

Not surprisingly, therefore, Wang is critical of those historians in China who, during the first part of this century, allowed themselves to be influenced by their study of Western Empires. 'One of the consequences of this reinterpretation was to cast the tributary system in an unhistorical frame, one that tended to match tributary states with European colonies even though the Chinese had not conquered or governed any of the states outside imperial borders. Perhaps without intending to, they began to depict past Chinese empires as comparable, if not superior, to modern Western ones' (ibid., p. 56). Attempts to equate past events in China with those which occurred in Europe and in other parts of the world amount to little more than gross distortions of history.

After 1949, however, as Mao's sinized version of Marxist-Leninist theory became the dominant framework for the interpretation of China's past, the more traditional and more accurate concept of historic empire and its lessons, was reaffirmed.

For many decades, all Chinese history tended to be written in accordance with the existing borders with the Soviet Union. Meticulous care was taken to avoid controversy about overland boundary disputes, and this practice was extended to include all borders with countries regarded as friendly to China. This might have been done merely for the sake of diplomacy. But it did lead to important results, one of which was to strengthen the sense that the central lands of China were sacred, and that its borders were legitimately (and historically) extended to where they are today. The other was [quite accurately in Wang's view] to play down the function of the tributary system altogether. The former has encouraged the practice of respecting borders of friendly neighbours. The latter also has produced something positive and correct, namely, the reversal of nationalist claims to historic tributary states as former Chinese 'colonies'. (ibid., p. 57)

The Chinese people, the reader is led to believe, have always has been content to remain within their own historically and culturally defined borders. To compare China with an aggressive, adventurist empire of conquest and domination is to distort history.

Chinese civilisation

Wang believes that the concept of civilisation, unlike that of historic empire, is of the greatest importance as a focus of nationalistic sentiments and national loyalty in China:

> the concept of a modern Chinese nation is imperfect and is contingent on China's having a larger national culture for the Han majority and all its ethnic minorities to share and embrace. To that extent, a cultural heritage that is both modern and based on the continuous civilisation that everyone recognises as belonging to China could be the foundation of new national loyalty. Until this century, the Confucianism that supported the imperial system, together with the popular culture based on a mixture of Confucian, Buddhist, and Daoist practices, provided that heritage. But for nearly a century, nationalist and communist revolutionaries have done their utmost to relieve China of that cultural baggage. What, then, is left for those who still see China as the home of Chinese civilization? In so far as the Beijing government acknowledges the validity of Confucian role models and ethics in schools, and permits the revival of some Buddhist and Daoist groups around the country, the heritage is still real. To understand how important this is likely to be, we need to survey the extent of the damage done to Chinese civilization during this century and the kinds of repair being attempted to make this heritage viable again. Is it possible for this heritage to be modernised? If so, how relevant would it be for China's position in international relations? (ibid., pp. 60–1)

The damage caused by both nationalists and communists to 'their proud civilisation' (ibid., p. 61), though unintentional, was consequent upon their attempts to move beyond the selection and adoption of bits of western science and technology and to absorb Western learning defined more broadly. The Chinese, we are told, 'were unable, like the Japanese, to retain the core of their values and institutions while learning what they needed from Western science and engineering. The Chinese felt that they had to redefine their civilisation in order to modernise their country and their ideas. It was thought that their civilisation could be revitalised as modern and progressive if carefully selected bits of western learning could be grafted onto it' (ibid.).

After all, Chinese civilisation had been associated with 'the ruling class of Mandarins who dictated artistic taste and endorsed all forms of orthodoxy, especially those pertaining to government and to religious and ethical systems. That small and privileged class was generally seen as having served the foreign Manchu rulers in the context of Confucian ideals, and, therefore, was highly suspect in the eyes of the nationalists who overthrew the Qing dynasty' (ibid., pp. 61–2).

It was only natural that 'the best minds ... turned to the professions, to the study of science and technology, or to modern economics, business, and management. They were more familiar with Keynes, Mussolini, Henry Ford, Madame Curie, and Einstein and the latest artistic ideas in Europe and the United States than with the unglamorous efforts to keep traditional values alive. Already, the Great Tradition was seen by the best and brightest as more dead than alive' (ibid., p. 62).

Those intellectuals who remained interested in cultural values abandoned the Great Tradition and took up anti-Confucian nationalism, and championed liberal ideals and capitalist practices. Wang describes these intellectuals as 'two-time losers': 'they had lost most of their own cultural bearings', and were regarded by the 'progressive revolutionaries ... as scions of the landlord and new capitalist classes' (ibid.). Many intellectuals emigrated, and those who remained had to submit to the will of Mao who 'saw himself as a bearer, and an arbiter, of all that was great and worth preserving in Chinese civilisation' (ibid., pp. 62–3).

Over the last two decades, however, China's cultural heritage has begun to be restored with the help of scholars and publishers in Hong Kong and Taiwan; and Chinese traditional values – and in particular a belief in the work ethic, education, and loyalty to the family – have begun to resurface, again with the help and example of Chinese in Hong Kong and Taiwan:

Since the 1980s, the more independent minded [Chinese intellectuals] have taken advantage of the relative freedom to resurface and write on controversial subjects such as intellectual freedom, liberal democracy, legitimacy, the rule of law, and human rights. Understandably, most of them were more excited by the fresh ideas from the West than by any return to Chinese traditional values. However, with the loss of faith in communism, and given the tight limits on publishing and the media, there seems to be a spiritual and ideological vacuum, especially among the young. Chinese leaders are worried by the materialism and corruption in the country today and are seeking ways to bring back some of the revolutionary purity of earlier days. All the same, among them are cultural loyalists who now find the atmosphere more congenial and openly advocate that 'Chinese learning' be given back its rightful place in the curriculum before it is too late. How late it is, and how the extensive damage to China's cultural roots can be repaired, will not be known for some time. But it is impressive to see authors, editors, and publishers all around the country, and in collaboration with their counterparts in Hong Kong and Taiwan, busily producing new textbooks, literary and artistic collections, and annotated editions of the classics for students and scholars at all levels. The print and electronic media in all three parts of China have also joined in to a lesser extent, less didactically, but, through entertainment and recreational activities, probably more effectively. The will to revive interest is not in question, and the number of people keen to do the work seems to be growing. It is possible to say that, at least among the Han Chinese, the glorious civilization and the idea of a new nation can coexist. (ibid., pp. 63–4)

This interest in the Great Tradition is much stronger among the common the people than it is among officials. The most notable expression of this popular interest has been the desire to revive respect for family institutions.

This is particularly relevant following the demise of the extended family and the introduction of the one-child policy. This can be seen not only in the new school textbooks, but also in the increasing number of primers and catechisms dedicated to *jiaxun*, or 'family instructions'. These have been significantly revised and modernised, but are still presented along traditional lines. They are popular not only because they embody the deepest levels of cultural consciousness among most Chinese, but also because they express a practical need when other institutions seem to be failing to sustain local communities. This is particularly true on the mainland. The new pressures toward private profit, the inadequacies of the welfare system, the trend toward insecure employment, and the growing threats of falling real incomes for the rural majority leave most people with little choice but to turn again to their families. Fortunately, the cultural heritage within the country concerning the family seems to have remained strong. Furthermore, as a common bond still appreciated by the Chinese in Taiwan and Hong Kong as well as those overseas, this can easily be reinforced through regular contacts wherever family relationships can be established. (ibid., pp. 65–6)

Indeed, so important is the role of Chinese intellectuals in Hong Kong and Taiwan and in other parts of the world, that Wang raises the possibility that without them, and without their attempts both to demonstrate that 'the Great Tradition' is still essential to China, and to inspire fresh confidence among themselves and their successors, then 'there is little chance that much of the civilisation will survive' (ibid., p. 66).

Wang continues:

> But for many Chinese today, it will be enough if certain core values remain strong. Chief among these are respect for education and a meritocracy, including the readiness to upgrade knowledge and acquire the best in science and technology; willingness to work hard and postpone gratification (the importance of combining these first two values with the qualities of thrift and trustworthiness is well recognised in modern business and industry); and, perhaps most of all, loyalty to family networks that most Chinese people still believe is natural and profoundly central not only to the civilization, but also to all areas of practical activity. If all these values could bind the Chinese people together, they would play a key part in fostering a culturally united country. (ibid.)

The question of 'Chinese civilisation' may have implications not only for China's own borders and the Overseas Chinese, but also for China's relations with the rest of the world, provided China can offer something universal to non-Chinese people. In order to do so, however, the Chinese must not only 'produce some defensive walls for the use of the Chinese alone (that is, to strengthen China as a modern nation-state and a great power), but also with a fresh vision of how the values of East and West can work together for all humankind' (ibid., p. 67).

The concept of Chinese civilisation, then, represents a groundswell of sentiments, beliefs, values and institutions which are deeply ingrained in Chinese people, and which are capable of explaining and determining economic success. Chinese civilisation is no mere crude political device: it might inspire both national unity, and a cultural unity that extends far beyond China's borders. Chinese civilisation is a crucial asset in realising economic and wider political influence on the world stage.

Apologia sinica?

Wang is clearly at pains to play down any possibility that China may harbour nationalistic sentiments and imperialist ambitions, and that it might be prepared to use both economic and military strength in any way that is sees fit. On the contrary, the concepts of nationalism, historic empire and Chinese civilisation all demonstrate that, for philosophical as well as sound political reasons, China is very likely to remain as it has always been – a passive entity. Danger would arise only if attempts by outside powers to break China apart were to succeed.

Greater China

Wang is especially sensitive about the term 'Greater China' which he maintains refers, in its most practical and least worrying usage, to Hong Kong, Taiwan and South China. 'But if the concept is extended to include the rest of mainland China, and especially if it includes the ethnic Chinese residing in foreign countries, it does become alarming and needs to be closely scrutinised' (ibid., pp. 16–17). Interestingly, however, he is not concerned with the extension of this term because it may indicate nationalistic or imperialistic ambitions: Greater London, Great Britain or Greater Tokyo alarms no one, and the words 'Great Britain' do not conjure up images of expansion beyond the British Isles, 'although some of my Irish friends might object to the inclusion of any part of the island of Ireland' (ibid., p. 14). Wang objects to the extension of the term 'Greater China' for two other reasons. First, it is an inaccurate description of China's external economic relationships: most areas of China look not to Hong Kong or Taiwan but elsewhere for their external relationships. The economic links between Hong Kong, Taiwan and coastal PRC are 'more apparent than real'. Their interaction cannot be separated from wider international operations. Indeed, all three are dependent upon the world's open markets and 'none of the links have to be specifically Chinese at all' (ibid., p. 16). Secondly, it is a term in which imperialist ambitions can easily be read by politicians and the media in Southeast Asia in order to frighten their own people, destabilise the region, damage China's international relations, and compromise the economic freedom and viability of the Overseas Chinese in their adopted countries. It is even more interesting that Wang should use the term PRC or China to include not only Hong Kong, but also Taiwan – both are a natural and historical part of China, he argues, because they share a common and long-lived cultural heritage:

despite the differences in geography and modern history that have divided China, there is a great depth and breadth in China's continuous cultural heritage. This China has also claimed that, in its undivided manifestation, it could be a country like other countries. It suggests that whenever it can speak and act as one such country, it expects to behave and be treated like other countries. During the twentieth century, all three parts of China have been sharply separated, and at times the people of Taiwan and Hong Kong have been encouraged to behave as if they came from independent countries. In recent years, some of them, together with foreigners, have deliberately and habitually used the name 'China' to apply only to the PRC. Sometimes, of course, this use of 'China' is convenient shorthand, but it would be misleading if it were employed to suggest that Taiwan and Hong Kong are no longer parts of China... there is no question that the PRC, Taiwan, and Hong Kong... have much in common. For example, during the twentieth century, the following have been striking: the speed with which they have changed and seized opportunities; the spirit of defiance they each show when challenged by outsiders; and the propensity of their people to migrate... Thus I use the term 'China' here to include the PRC, Taiwan and Hong Kong. (ibid., pp. 13–14)

The term 'Greater' China, then, cannot be regarded legitimately as imperialistic or threatening because it includes those territories which have always been a natural part of China. It would now seem that 'Greater China' *does* include the whole of the PRC, Hong Kong and Taiwan. Indeed, in an earlier publication, Wang[2] recognises that Greater China can imply a desire for expansionism and a misleading or boastful grandiosity, but he goes on to argue that:

if the emphasis is on the broader picture of cultural China, the term [Greater China] may refer to the traditions of Chinese civilisation and what has transformed them in modern times. In this context, it may be said that Greater China has become Greater because its store of cultural values has been enhanced by modern borrowings, influences and adaptations. As a result, millions of ethnic Chinese now residing abroad might find it possible to identify with it.[3]

On the one hand, then, Wang acknowledges that the term 'Greater China' is alarming if used to describe Hong Kong, Taiwan, and the whole of mainland China, and especially if it were extended still further to include the ethnic Chinese living overseas. And yet he regards Hong Kong and Taiwan as a natural part of the whole of mainland China, and (though he suggests that none of the economic links are specifically 'Chinese'), he argues that 'Greater China' refers to a culture with which Chinese all over the world might be able to identify. This concept of 'China', which appears to be defined as much by its culture as by its borders, is to all intents and purposes synonymous with that extended notion of Greater China which he himself warns against.

This nationalistic concept is strengthened by assigning to 'the Chinese' shared habits and traits that seem more than just conscious expressions of 'culture'. The Chinese 'habitually make use of their past'; they create layers of self-perception which vary in number and emphasis from one group or individuals to the next; and certain traditional, even ancient, values and institutions, such as the family, complex social networks, the work ethic, meritocracy, and education, embody the deepest levels of cultural consciousness among the Chinese. So different are the Chinese that even the term 'diaspora' is, in Wang's view, unacceptable, because the term suggests comparison with the Jews.[4] We know that such values, beliefs, institutions and patterns of behaviour *are* Chinese, and that these characteristics explain, and determine, economic success, because Wang (both in these lectures and in earlier publications[5]) tells us that it is so.

This didacticism is convenient. But if the whole of Wang's analysis is not to dissolve, then we must now accept his implicit assumption that these vital and defining characteristics of the Chinese are culturally determined; and if this culture is definitive and deterministic, then it is not difficult to reach the strong and logical conclusion that the culture itself must be determined racially.

Hardening these cultural-cum-racial divisions is the force of history: 'Chinese' and 'tradition' rest easily together, for Chinese traits and habits are all supremely 'traditional'. China's continuous, unbroken past stretching back over the millennia, is deeply embedded in the Chinese psyche; China has always been propelled by history towards a strong, centralised state; China has rarely, if ever, been aggressive, if only because the Chinese have been too introspective, self-sufficient and complacent; and it is the ebb and flow of Chinese history which determines that the minority groups – Turks, Mongols, Tibetans, Jurchen-Mongols – share a common heritage with the Han (and China is more fortunate than most former empires in having a majority – the Han – that numbers more than 90 per cent of its population).

China is thus defined by its history, and by a remarkably passive, unique and predominantly Han culture, rather than by its boundaries. And yet, fortuitously, China's culture and the ebb and flow of its history determine that its core lands – north, central and south China (where Han culture has an unbroken history of two or three thousand years) – together with all its other lands and minority groups and Taiwan which constitute China today, form a natural, organic entity.

Socialism, Chineseness and the Third World

Wang's rendition of the significance of socialism in China and China's modernisation resounds with similarly nationalistic tones. The term 'socialist market economy,' argues Wang,

> arouses puzzlement and even scorn among Western and other economists and all those interested in economics and politics. It seems self-contradictory, and many have interpreted its use by China as a means of hiding their embarrassment that capitalism is now rampant in the country. It is also thought that the Chinese leaders do not understand modern economics and therefore use the term 'market economy' incorrectly. (CW, p. 20)

Wang, however, believes that China's leaders are determined to make the socialist market work, and that their decision to pursue such a course of action, and to learn from capitalism, was necessitated partly by survival. The Party and the government had little choice but to reform. 'Without it, the country would have faced further economic disasters, threatening everything the party leaders had fought for. Even the collapse of the regime might have resulted' (ibid., p. 22). But Deng's efforts were more positive than that. The reforms did not constitute a rejection of the Revolution; they presupposed that 'the revolution of 1949 and its achievements and failures remain the starting point . . . the injunctions are to learn from the failures and build on the successes' (ibid., p. 39). Deng's 'zeal' to bring modernity to China, and his determination to restore wealth and power to China remained strong.

> I remember the stirring call by one party leader (An Gang, a former editor of *People's Daily*) at an international conference in 1979 that 'socialism should make money', and how that was soon echoed as 'get rich first' throughout the country, with the additional exhortation that socialism should be more successful than capitalism! This was when it was obvious that capitalist Hong Kong and Taiwan, the

'little Chinas', were each producing greater wealth than their big brother.
The leaders who fought in the battlefields still believe that socialism is superior. But . . . they now agree that learning from capitalism conforms to historical necessity. Capitalism is a stage that cannot be skipped on the way to socialism. It is hard, however, to know how many of the younger leaders still believe in this superiority . . . younger party members and intellectuals can now read about what capitalist countries have achieved during the past five decades . . . They can see how all of them have been able to raise the standard of living of the vast majority of their peoples . . . how competitive developments in industrial practices and innovations in financial institutions and managerial methods have made it possible for wealth creation to coexist with the principles of equitable distribution. They can see for themselves that elaborate welfare safety nets for the disadvantaged and disabled have ironically been most developed and successful in these capitalist societies. (ibid., pp. 22–3)

Nevertheless, most writings emanating from the PRC today reflect a loyalty to key Marxist principles, and though capitalism in its modern and mature form is seen as a more benign means to an end, it is still officially regarded as a force that will stand in the way of progress towards socialist ideals.

It is not capitalism in the abstract that is threatening; it is the perception of a market economy, however modified, that will inevitably unleash social forces that have hitherto been under tight control. Every day, there is evidence that some of the worst features of the pre-1949 world have returned: unemployment, corruption, greed, selfishness, immorality, inequality, even dangers of runaway inflation . . .

Thus, the perception of a successful market economy becoming less and less socialist hangs like a cloud over the recent triumphs. Ultimately, if mainland Chinese behave like the Chinese of Taiwan and Hong Kong, their economy could head toward a capitalism that would appeal to the young and ambitious, the newly rich and successful, the natural malcontents and rebels, the exploiters, and the potential traitors. How could the Party then maintain its tight control? Parts of the outside, especially the Western world, anticipate the inevitability of a radical change in the capacity to control everything centrally. Some are already portraying the political reforms of

Taiwan as the necessary next step for the mainland to follow. In supporting the laws and freedoms of Hong Kong, they point to similar democratic reforms as essential to continued progress on the mainland. The Chinese experiences in the two smaller areas are expected to have a profound impact on the mainland.

The achievements of Deng Xiaoping's reforms have created a new volatile environment in which the hopes for ever better economic performance are matched by fears of social turmoil. The next generation of leaders urgently need to reinspire their people to believe that the socialist way to a market economy is the best road to socialism. For the past 15 years, they have enjoined their economists and policy advisers to define that road more clearly and convincingly. These loyal supporters have been asked to map out how to sustain such a socialist market economy without becoming capitalistic like Chinese Taiwan and Hong Kong. They must demonstrate, in addition, why such an economy is different from what social democrats in the West have been content to accept, that is, the various forms of mixed economies in so-called welfare *states*. The time has come for the leaders to stop, if I may use their words, 'taking one step forward and looking around before taking another' and advancing as if they were, using their words again, 'wading across a river by feeling for the rocks under the water' . . . They still seem to be some way from convincing their people that they have found the right formula with which to enhance, and renew faith in, Marxism. But the perception remains that retaining the ideal of the socialist political order is essential to their particular variety of market economy.

Despite the examples of Taiwan and Hong Kong, for most Chinese people, the key to this primary self-perception of the PRC today is the word 'superiority', that is, the superiority of socialism over other systems. The PRC leaders have to believe that the revolution as they see it has not failed. Mistakes have been made, and these are now being rectified through radical reforms. Capitalist methods, where usable, are but the means to an end. To paraphrase an old Chinese saying, 'socialism (now with Chinese characteristics) is the base, and capitalism (without its liberal excesses) is only for application'. Therefore, greater efforts are needed to show that capitalism may be enough for a city like Hong Kong, or a small 'province' like Taiwan, but has no place in a vast country of 1.2 billion people. If the PRC can sustain its successes for another decade or so, it could enshrine the concept of a socialist market economy as the Chinese way for all Chinese, and perhaps for the entire region as well.

> In short, what counts is whether market socialism will take root and produce the wealth that the country needs without political reform. So far, the results have been extraordinary. (ibid., pp. 24–6)

The Chinese leadership, then, see the immorality and dangers inherent in a market economy; they have not rejected Marxist principles; nor is there uncritical praise of post-1949 successes. Corruption, inflation and 'the lack of channels for redress and political dialogue that led to the tragedy in Tian'anmen Square in 1989', while they may tarnish any model for development that the PRC may have to offer, are 'new failures that have yet to be fully addressed' (ibid., p. 40).

Once again we can feel China's inherent morality which frees individuals from the responsibility of their actions. China's leaders have the best interests of the people in mind; they are justifiably suspicious of the market; and even though the tragic 'mistakes' or 'misunderstandings' of Tian'anmen ran out of control because there were no proper channels for dialogue, 'the widely accepted claims' about China's revolutionary successes prior to 1978 may be described with superlatives:

> the destruction of the old landed classes that had supported an inefficient and corrupt system of government is seen as a permanent achievement . . . some of the advances in agriculture, science, and engineering have been widely regarded as outstanding . . . enough food was produced in the countryside, and the famines that had occurred regularly during the previous century were brought to an end . . . But . . . it is probably the unification of China after decades of division under a variety of warlords that is seen by most Chinese as the revolution's greatest achievement. This what saved China from further imperialist advances by Japan and the West. It protected China from bullying by the Soviet Union at its height. It raised the status of China in international affairs, made it a player in the Cold War, and, in particular, earned it the respect of the one country for which most Chinese shared a deep but ambivalent respect, the United States.

All this occurred despite the fact that the unification had not been complete. Hong Kong was deliberately left alone after 1949 as a window to the Western capitalist world. By default, arising from China's lack of air and naval power, and because of US support for Taiwan as well as other distractions on the long frontiers to the north and west, the Beijing government could not cross the Taiwan straits. This unfinished business has probably been as important to the Chinese

leadership as their visions of communism throughout the past half
century. It has always been on their political and military agendas.
(ibid., pp. 40–1)

Nor are the economic advances made since 1978 valued much in
themselves; rather it is what that progress means for unification, and
for China's status, power and influence in the world, that really matters:

What is unfolding today is an intriguing picture of how recent
economic developments may alter Chinese perspectives on the issue
of integration and eventual unification. The prospect of a coming
together of socialist and capitalist ways of achieving progress could
determine the shape and nature of a new universal model. In addition, the possibility of new wealth-making partnerships and ventures
coming out of all three parts of China even before its unification is
a riveting subject for China's neighbours. And it is breathtaking to
imagine the potential for some degree of globalization of trading and
financial organisations centred in the East-Southeast Asian region. If
this were to become a reality, it would transform the international
relations of the world for the next century. (ibid., pp. 41–2)

Wang is playing not only to history, culture and some inherent
morality, but to a sense of destiny. China is not only different from the
outside world: it must strike a path that is obviously different. It is not
enough that the strategy works: it must also be 'Chinese'. The 'Chinese
Way' is to steer away from liberal social democracies and their 'so-called'
welfare states. Wang enjoins the leadership to stop looking back, to stop
feeling their way, and to proclaim 'the socialist market' with strength
and confidence, and to inspire their people with a faith in this Chinese
invention. The rewards which might flow from these successes might
be tremendous: a form of development that is Chinese and yet universal; a form of development that is applicable to the Far East, and to the
Third World; a form of development that would transform East and
Southeast Asia into a breathtaking economic power centred on China,
Hong Kong and Taiwan.

These sentiments are also implicit in Wang's definition of China. If
one believes (as Wang does) that Taiwan is a natural part of China, that
there is a 'Chinese civilisation' which can appeal to millions of Chinese
everywhere, and that the economic success of Overseas Chinese and
that of China has something to do with their Chineseness, then the
success of the particularly Chinese 'socialist market economy' would

seem to lead naturally to the conclusion that an extremely powerful and extensive 'Chinese' trade network is likely to develop across East and Southeast Asia and perhaps beyond. The idea is certainly a common one.[6] But for Wang this economic power is important not in itself, but for the political strength it will bring: international relations would be refocused upon a China defined more by its culture and its own kind of economics and trading networks. This would make reunification with Taiwan little more than a formality, and fulfil China's longing for global status.

Wang acknowledges that China desires global status, yet he also maintains that China only 'hopes' to be a global power, for such power is not an important part of China's self-perception. China is indeed paradoxical, as Wang is careful to point out. China desires greatness and needs influence, not for self-aggrandisement, but for what that power and influence would mean for the world's developing economies – economies which are defined, not by their economic or social conditions, but according to their past. By developing economies Wang is referring to 'most of the former colonies of the West that did not come under communist influence, and those countries that had been under western dominance or some kind of tutelage, in Asia, the Middle East, and Latin America' (CW, p. 29). The oil-rich countries 'do not quite fit the description'; and those economies in East and Southeast Asia which are successfully modernising, learnt from, and are dependent upon, trade with the capitalist West. 'Developing economy' is a status conferred by the past and present actions of 'the West'. China's independence, and difference, thus becomes all the more obvious.

China intentionally distanced itself from its cold war rivals: 'it reached out to the Afro-Asian and Latin American countries as a "fellow-sufferer" of superpower ambitions, and wanted to join them to resist being pawns in that "Great Game"' (ibid., p. 31); and, in the PRC's own perception of itself, 'the emphasis is likely to be on the impact its successes will have on other developing economies of the world. It could give others hope if they remember that China stood with them during the Cold War period and, despite its limited resources and many tragic mistakes, challenged both the United States and the Soviet Union' (ibid., p. 29). China perceives itself to be, and indeed is, the champion of the developing world.

China may be poor, and it still needs to strengthen education and training, to attract external capital and technology, and to win trading and financial concessions. But China's independence, and its leadership qualities, set it apart from the developed and developing countries. The paternalism of this image, and China's pride, are carefully reinforced as its other differences are listed: China is a nuclear power and an economic giant; it is a huge country strategically located near Japan and Russia; it has demonstrated the ability to replicate the latest science and technology and thereby to keep pace with the West and Japan; and the boldness of its experiments in social and economic engineering have no equals.

Human rights

Wang treats his readers to an intellectualised populist manifesto for China's domestic and foreign policy. It is understandable, then, why the subtext of his counsel, though tangled around sentiments designed to appeal to a wider audience in the mature democracies, should amount to a justification of China's actions.

Wang argues that human rights and their protection are universal principles. In China, this principle has been 'thoroughly aired for decades, and is scarcely disputed among civilised peoples' (ibid., p. 67). The point is then repeated: 'For almost a hundred years, democracy has been accepted and desired by the Chinese people as a civilised goal. Human rights, too, as another marker of modern civilisation, have been acknowledged for at least half a century'; 'The debate,' argues Wang, 'is about how these rights should be respected and by what means' (ibid., pp. 67–8). But resolution of the 'how' and the 'means' has been dogged by two problems.

> One pertains to timing. Some have argued that full rights must be implemented immediately, no matter the cost. The other relates to approach. The issue of human rights has not been presented as one of civilisation and morality, but as a diplomatic, commercial and political weapon, and has been presented confrontationally as one between East and West, between inferior Asian values and superior Western values.
>
> This is unfortunate. If human rights and democracy still appear remote and difficult to realise, it is because the Chinese people have failed to create the political and legal structure for the new values to grow among them. On the other hand, insistence upon these values from the outside, and by foreign governments, is bound to be interpreted either as willful ignorance of the immense problems that still exist in the country, or a reflection of the desire of these foreigners to overthrow the present regime no matter what the consequences. Such an approach has also been interpreted as interference in China's

internal affairs or as an attempt by Western politicians to slow down its development. (ibid., p. 67)

Hopefully, democracy and human rights will receive the priority they deserve sooner rather than later. 'But it will be surprising if the form of democracy that eventually emerges and the legal and administrative framework established for the support of human rights will be the same as those that have evolved in a Judaeo-Christian and Graeco-Roman cultural context. That may not, in any case, be as important as having the ideals incorporated in the Chinese way to meet the challenge of the modern civilised world' (ibid., p. 68).

In Wang's view, the tension between China and 'the West' over the question of human rights and democracy is, in part, symptomatic of the West's lack of understanding of China. Detaching MFN provisions from China's human rights performance was the right decision (ibid., p. 72); and much has been learnt on both sides in bilateral negotiations. Even so, expert advisers on both sides 'remain handicapped by political and cultural environments that insist on fighting old wars by new means' and it is it is 'probably true to say that more Chinese understand the West than vice versa' (ibid., pp. 73 & 71).[7] Admittedly, it is extremely difficult to predict events in China, especially when so much depends upon a few dominant personalities and their factional struggles. But the relevant facts about China's potential strength and influence, and its self-image, will help us to anticipate future events (CW, p. 70). China, as we have been told already, never sent armies beyond the 'traditional Middle Kingdom (*Zhongguo*) lands'; it is passive and has always been so; it is essentially moral; it has a complex sense of nationalism and civil-isation; and while many Chinese may hope that China will be a global power, this is not an important part of China's self-perception, nor would the Chinese people stand for national self-aggrandizement at their expense (ibid., p. 72). The heavy irony with which China is com-pared to the colonial powers of Europe, pours scorn and sarcasm over any suggestion that China may prove dangerous.

China's size and location by themselves are powerful reminders of past superiority and possible future threat. China's very existence, however passive and inward-looking, has always aroused interest and concern. What would be new and alarming to the region would be a modernised China finding that it has to behave like the modern great powers of the West. For example, is it likely that China will behave like eighteenth- and nineteenth-century Britain and France in their quest for maritime empires, or like Russia in its overland drive toward the east? Or would China model itself after the intensely aggressive latecomers Germany and Japan, or aspire to some version of the American Manifest Destiny? With all those 'glorious' and recent examples before them, could the Chinese resist the dynamic urges of modern competitive expansion? Could China's neighbours be assured that future regional relations would be based on fraternal cooperation, or, at worst, merely the benign neglect of a patronizing 'big brother'? (ibid., p. 69)

The main responsibility and challenge facing China's leaders is to break down the misunderstanding, fear and prejudice with which the outside world regards China, and then to reveal China as it really is. They must show, and convince, the world 'that the existing structures within the country can cope with the agonies of modernisation'; that China's success will not endanger peaceful relations, that there is no need 'to call for the US cavalry'; and 'that China's failure will harm everybody' (ibid., p. 72).

China's leaders will not find any of this easy: they must constantly manage and compensate for the unpredictable actions and policies which arise partly from US ambitions, and partly from the protectionism, defensiveness and frustrations generated by the relative decline of the West (including its leader, the United States) as it appears to retreat 'from its two-centuries-old dominance' (ibid., p. 86). The Beijing government:

believes that the United States, by its very nature as a superpower, will interfere globally wherever it can. The PRC is forced to deal with the United States at most forums and has to have a global strategy to keep up with US plans and ambitions. It does not have the wherewithal to restrain the United States everywhere, but it can to try to limit interventions in its own region, East and Southeast Asia. Indeed, it must do so if it is to have any credibility as a future power. It can do so by being active in bilateral relations, by encouraging American multi-nationals and financial institutions to invest in China, by opening up for more trade, by being extremely careful in Northeast Asia (especially regarding the two Koreas), where US interests are sensitive and unstable, and by responding as positively as possible to US overtures in regions where China's own interests are minor. Since the tragedy as Tian'anmen Square in 1989, the generally cooperative moves made by the PRC have been extraordinarily successful. Outside

Asia, the Chinese leaders have experienced some anxiety only where US–Russian relations are concerned. But as long as Russia is busy within its own borders, and more preoccupied with its future in Europe than in northern Asia, Sino-American relations need not be affected. (ibid., pp. 70–1)

The tension over human rights and democracy between China and 'the West' is but a sham: an expression of the West's inability or unwillingness to understand China, a weakness that may derive from the defensiveness and frustrations of 'the West' as it retreats from its position of global dominance. The reality is that human rights in China (where, it is stressed, human rights have been debated for more than a century) is a given: the question for China is really how and by what means these universal principles should be implemented. Indeed, China would, and does, claim that it is on course to achieve a political system and society more just and democratic than that found in the West. With time, Wang believes China will evolve its own 'kind' of democracy but even that may not be as important as having 'the ideals incorporated in the Chinese way to meet the challenge of the modern civilised world' (ibid., p. 68).

Wang appears to support these claims to such an extent that the very boldness and Chineseness of the experiments undertaken since 1949 in pursuit of a just and moral society, far more than the realisation of that objective, seem to be justification enough for all those euphemistic 'mistakes', 'misunderstandings', and 'tragedies' which have occurred.

All at once, measured by economic indicators alone, the country could be seen as a supremely successful developing nation. Its performance in social and economic transformation over the past 15 years has been breathtaking. It can now present itself as a 'Newly Industrialising Country'. Only China's size make it ridiculous to call itself another 'Little Tiger'. In fact, there is considerable ambiguity here. In terms of both size and population, China could be compared with developing countries such as India and Brazil. Yet the comparison lacks the one dimension that has aroused controversy within China and among the leaders of the United States, Japan, and China's closest neighbours. India and Brazil are non-communist and practice versions of democracy that are acceptable to the West. Neither toyed with radical social experiments, as the PRC did for decades. Theirs had never been the 'brave new world' of socialist man that Mao Tse-tung tried to lead his people toward. Their minor successes and failures have been mainly incremental. They developed on the margins of capitalism, and, in the case of Brazil, by being dependent on foreign governments as well. Neither had tried the bold leaps into the economic revolution that the PRC did. Neither experimented the dramatic ups and downs that brought, alternately, exhilaration and tragedy to millions of people and ultimately destroyed a whole ruling class, as happened in China. These bold experiments in social and economic engineering really have no equals among the other developing economies. (ibid., pp. 32–3)

The sentiments are almost Tutonic: the wild flights of fancy, the sweeping and bold acts, the grand projects, the massed armies of workers, and the flocks of banners cracking in the wind, signal a leader and a nation that is all the more romantic and great of stature, irrespective of the cost. Attempts to follow, or to sympathise with, 'Western' democratic values, and a failure to make a nation distinct from 'Western' democracies, are almost sneered at. China can feel triumphant, vindicated and justified in the path it has chosen, and in its contempt for those who have not separated themselves from 'the West' because there is no connection between economic success, righteousness, morality and 'Western' democracy.

One lesson stands out. India had its variety of socialism, but rejected the revolutionary communist road in favour of a representative democracy. The Soviet Union under Gorbachev also chose political reform, starting with more democracy in order to support economic change. The PRC claims to have avoided both of these approaches in order to concentrate on using strong central control to reform the economy. The fact that the four NICs in the region, from the 1950s to the 1980s, did not need democracy to be economically successful has given the Chinese much encouragement. The NICs success supports the Chinese position that radical economic reform must precede political change.

Any study of the modernisation process would show that it is a very recent idea to couple democracy with economic growth as part of that process. The imperial powers in Asia and Africa never thought democracy was necessary when they were administering their colonies. Britain and France experimented with democracy only at the final stages of involuntary decolonization. During the late nineteenth and early twentieth centuries, neither Germany nor Japan needed democratic institutions to achieve its own rapid rate of growth. Nor did the new post-colonial nations in the Third World produce any evidence that democracy was necessary for economic development. In many former colonies, democratic institutions did not survive and were never given the chance to prove whether they would have helped or hindered economic development...

...The new kinds of developing economy, like those of South Korea and Taiwan, could be said to have produced models that challenge the idea that democracy is essential for development and should therefore precede it. Instead, their examples show that the people's energies could be channeled toward growth and the production of wealth from the top down, through firm leadership, clear goals, and administrative controls. It is possible for development to success through capitalistic methods without the precondition of liberal democracy. And, if either South Korea or Taiwan is any guide, democracy would *follow* successful development. Why could not Taiwan's form of capitalism and the PRC's form of socialism be brought together? Could not the two combine the free and outward-looking structures of Taiwan and Hong Kong with the strength and size of the PRC to promote China's international position and help to find the Chinese way? (ibid., pp. 33–5)

Wang appears to be suggesting that while 'the Chinese' view development and human rights as issues of morality and civilisation, 'the West' treats these issue as instruments to further its own political and commercial ambitions. If, so far, the Chinese people have been unable to establish democracy and a framework for human rights, it is because they believe that democracy and human rights must wait upon economic progress. Democracy and the observance of human rights will be realised, although the form of democracy and the framework of institutions established to support human rights in China are very unlikely to follow the 'Western' model. In any case, it is more important that these ideals contained within democracy and human rights are 'incorporated' in a way that is 'Chinese'.

The reasoning underlying these elaborate arguments, however, is largely psychological and emotional. First, it is self-evident that human rights are not accepted in China. Unless we are prepared to ignore deliberately the core religious texts of Christianity, Judaism, and Islam, and, for example, the writings of Locke, it is equally clear that outside China the concerns which are now described by the term 'human rights' stretch back over more than one or two centuries, and that these concerns have always been far more than just an issue for debate. Moreover, if one claims acceptance of the primacy of democracy and the universality of human rights – as Wang claims for both himself and China – then how, exactly, does a 'Chinese' democratic principle differ from that of other people? What precisely does a 'form' of democracy mean? What might be peculiar about 'Chinese' legal and administrative frameworks for the support of universal human rights? The acceptance of individual freedom, justice, freedom from arbitrary imprisonment, representative and democratic elections, the presence of a vigilant and vigorous opposition, the removal of politicians from office by people who are not politicians, the distancing of the rule of law from executive command, and the protection of the individual both from the whims and power of those who hold the state's offices and from the mob, would not seem to leave much room for the establishment of institutions, procedures, practices and principles that differ very much except in detail from one country to the next. If Wang is determined to bind democracy and human rights to 'culture', and thereby to deny the expedient absolutes so necessary to the operation of democracy, and if that same determination is also prevalent in China, then the realisation of democracy and the observance of human rights there will indeed remain a vague hope.

Secondly, the belief that human rights and democracy in China 'still appear remote and difficult to realise ... because the Chinese people have failed to create the political and legal structures for the new values to grow among them' (ibid., p. 67) is puzzling. It is difficult to read this statement of belief as anything other than a tautology. The statement also contradicts Wang's view that in China democracy is both accepted and evolving; and it appears to bring into question his belief that there exists a causal link between 'culture' and 'forms' of democracy, for it clearly implies that the creation of democratic procedures, institutions and practices must precede and, presumably, must therefore in some way cause or stimulate democratic values and their infusion into the Chinese way of life. Not only is the statement tautological and contradictory, but it also exhibits a certain naiveté. 'Elements' described as 'democratic' – such as elections or local representation or the decentralisation of power – are not to be equated with democracy, as we argued in Chapter 2; and the imposition of democratic political institutions and supporting values upon individuals who may feel some emotional attachment to these institutions and values, but who see no personal stake in them, and who, in practice, are unwilling to accept them as self-defining and absolute, may well lead only to chaos, or to the formation of powerful groups of special interests founded upon networks of reciprocity and legitimised by the notion of 'democracy'.

Thirdly, Wang chastises 'the West' for tying human rights (which he regards as a universal principle) and democracy (which he describes with more ambiguity as a goal or marker of civilisation) to 'Western' values, and for using those values as a commercial, political and diplomatic weapon. But as we have seen, Wang also gives much status to the cultural explanation; and it is to culture that he ties the emergence of forms of democracy. He even appears to suggest (with characteristic ambiguity) that the emergence of a 'form' of democracy and of a superstructure for the support of human rights in China is not as important as how the ideals contained within these notions are 'incorporated' in the Chinese way. Wang is arguing, then, that democracy and human rights and their associated ideals are desired and accepted by the Chinese people; but he leaves those ideals unspecified, and their incorporation into 'the Chinese way' is believed to be more important than 'Western' democracy or even 'Chinese' forms of democracy. Indeed, it is interesting that Wang should even bother with the notion of a 'Chinese form' of democracy. Many other writers would agree with Harris's belief that China, and many Asian civilisations, have been able to pursue economic growth and interdependency 'without the necessity of being involved in political and social change of a Western liberal kind. This is less critical for those who accept, with Kant, that the process of evolution of an international society does not require the homogenisation of domestic political forms (e.g. democracy), than for those, such as Fukuyama, who believe it does.'[8]

This willingness to defer to culture, as we suggested earlier, denies what is necessary to allow democracy to work. It leaves institutions, values, beliefs, and patterns of behaviour open to manipulation, and, by freeing individuals from absolutes and ultimate responsibility, it represents a justification of, and it further intensifies, the fermentation of personal ambition and the drive for power as an end in itself. It is to this end that relationships, emotions, ideas, desires, beliefs, ideals and almost every conceivable sphere of endeavour – scientific, educational, artistic, economic, social and civic – are 'turned'. To dissemble this seething mire as a stable, long-lived, multi-layered and dripping with concern about human rights and democracy, is, to say the least, disingenuous. The actions of government and Party in China are neither predictable nor benign. Democracy and human rights are neither cultural elements nor are they in China treated as if absolutes. In the hands of the few who live in a claustrophobic and highly introspective world in which attack and defence and the scramble for, and protection of, power is the obsession, who must exert ruthless authority in order to compensate for their own refusal to accept and to subjugate themselves to impartial institutions and expedient absolutes, and for whom there is nothing to give perspective save the firm and clear actions that the outside world may occasionally take, China's governments and the Party are likely to prove unpredictable at best and, at worst, dangerous.

It is equally disingenuous to suggest that democracy and human rights should not be drawn into the political, diplomatic and economic concerns of nations in their dealings with China. Democracy and human rights are not merely convenient material with which to demonstrate school-boy cleverness; nor are they rarefied moral ethers: their treatment as if absolutes is a pragmatic necessity for domestic and international affairs. It could not be otherwise. If those who hold the office of the state are willing to submit to institutions, values, procedures and laws which they accept as if absolute, then the government and the country is far more predictable and its potential for dangerous action much reduced. Wang's beliefs that the people of China desire material progress, that China is historically passive, and that it cannot afford for internal reasons to beat the nationalistic drum, hardly provide a useful framework for assessing China's actions, and they guarantee nothing. If those members of China's political elite who desire power and influence are not subject to constraints imposed by their own people, then they can be restrained only by the actions and raw power of other nations.

By deferring to culture, all values, beliefs, institutions and patterns of behaviour are left open to unbridled manipulation, and thus domestic and international affairs are more likely to be unpredictable and prone to instability. Image and reality seem to merge: this is not a question of orthopraxy versus orthodoxy. (We noted in Chapter 2 that the distinction between practice and belief is unknowable unless we are privileged to know the true intent of the mind with its capacity for deception and self-deception.) It is a question of image and manipulation unconstrained by the notion of expedient absolutes – a notion which is portrayed by Wang as little more than a particularly devious form of moral blackmail and hypocrisy, as a ploy to secure one's own interests at the expense of other people. There is, in the minds of Wang and other writers, much suspicion hanging over the notion of 'democracy' and 'human rights', for are these not concepts manipulated by 'the Other' ('the West') for some ulterior purpose?

Wang's intellectual meandering may come over as being rather vapid, but as a work of propaganda it is masterly. His purpose is to appeal to sentiments, emotions and preconceptions rather than to present a closley reasoned argument. An image of China and Chineseness is constructed which plays most especially to cultural chauvanists outside China, to the acolytes of postmodernism, to sinophilia, and to the Hollywoodesque China of popular imagination, and which consequently is of much political value to China. The image is that of an essentially moral state, battling not only against economic underdevelopment, but against a sinophobic 'West' that is intent on suppressing the Chinese people *because* they are beginning to realise their enormous potential, and because they are doing so without following the Western path.

'Us' and 'them'

Wang's apologia for the absence of democracy in China is accompanied by an attempt to rationalise intensely nationalistic views. He first disconnects 'nation state' from 'empire'. The latter is then transformed into something which is, by comparison with the empires of the western heartland, almost lofty. The Chinese state grew naturally, unforced, and incorporates only that which is, and always has been, essentially Chinese. There is a mystical quality to these claims. In the sacred core lands of North, Central, and South China, the Han Chinese have always been in the majority; people in all other parts of China within its present borders share a common heritage either because those minority groups have actually ruled over all or parts of the core lands or because they have also been assimilated into the dominant Han culture over time. The land as defined by history and by contact with the core people – the Han – is and always has been 'Chinese'. No army ever marched out of these lands; and aggression would, by definition, be 'un-Chinese'.

The distinction which is made between empire and nation, the otherworldly quality with which the word 'empire' is endowed, and the derision with which any suggestion that China has held aggressive intents is treated, appear to be contrivances designed to quell concerns that China may, either now or at some time in the future, constitute a threat to the region. For how, except by dictate, is the concept of empire and its 'oneness' and 'longevity' made separate from civilisation and cultural heritage (particularly if, as Wang argues, Confucianism supported the Imperial system), and from the concept of a nation state?

The image of the organic Chinese state is being used here to create a softer background against which to voice some disturbing sentiments. There is, as we have seen, the causal connection which is drawn between 'Chineseness' and economic success; the curious and didactic objection to the word 'diaspora' being used to describe the Overseas Chinese because it suggests comparison with the Jews; the belief that the Chinese habitually make use of their past and that the Chinese are inclined towards a strong central government by history; the belief that foreigners have attempted to persuade the Taiwanese to behave as if they were not part of China and to use the word China to refer only to Mainland China; the belief that capitalism in China might appeal to the 'natural rebels', 'malcontents' and 'traitors'; and the belief that the Chinese possess a deeper kind of cultural consciousness that stretches beyond China's borders. Indeed, Wang argues that there exists an intimate connection between 'civilisation' and 'nation state', and so also, we may presume, between the idea of nation and its unique and deterministic culture; for is not the concept of a modern Chinese nation imperfect and contingent on a larger national culture for the Han majority and all its ethnic minorities to share and embrace? And could not a cultural heritage that is both modern and based on the con- tinuous civilisation that everyone recognises as belonging to China serve the foundation of a new national loyalty (CW, p. 60)?

This culture, this 'civilisation', this nation, would also produce some 'defensive walls for the use of the Chinese alone (that is to strengthen China as a modern nation-state and great power); it would constitute a 'fresh vision' to show how 'East' and 'West' can work together for 'the rest' of humanity. Among the Han Chinese, apparently, the idea of a civilisation and nation can co-exist, though it would be enough that certain 'core values' remain strong: education and meritocracy; the readi- ness to update knowledge and acquire the best science and technology; the willingness to work hard and postpone gratification, and to com- bine these values with thrift and trustworthiness; and loyalty to family networks which most Chinese people believe is natural and profoundly central, not only to civilisation, but to areas of practical authority.

China *is* Greater China, for China is defined by its history, its culture, its empire, its civilisation: all those people washed by the ebb and flow of this history, this culture, and this civilisation, are a natural part of China; it is a consciousness that percolates beyond its borders and through all Chinese; and it may be relevant to people the world over. The minorities, the Taiwanese, and the Overseas Chinese are an organic part of what China 'is'.

Set against this organic and passive civilisation, this nation, this empire, and this culture, is 'the foreigner'. The foreigner is lavished with obsequious flattery: China never encroached upon those sophistic- ated discrete cultures such as those of Korea and Vietnam, neither of which threatened China, and both of which possessed diplomatic and military abilities sufficient to keep them separate from China; 'the Chinese' have deep but ambivalent respect for the United States; and it may be that the East and the West can work together for 'the rest' of humanity. It is as if China is hoping to establish among a select group of nations an unspoken, mutual recognition of their respective cultures' superiority over the rest of mankind. But if such advances are rejected, then that once-honoured foreigner, is transformed back into a member of 'the Other' (China's antitype), and China, once again, becomes a fellow sufferer with the countries of the Third World. Russia drove eastwards; Germany and Japan were intensely aggressive; it was the Europeans who picked off Southeast Asia; it was the Europeans who never thought that democracy was necessary while they administered their colonies; it was Britain (which today still holds part of Ireland), France, the Netherlands, Portugal and Spain which sought after maritime empires; and unlike the Chinese empire (nation, civilisation, and culture), the empires of Britain, France, Russia, Persia, Greeks, Romans, and those of Asoka, Tamerlan and Babur, were established by conquest, and held together by military force. Today, as throughout the history of their civilisations, the foreigners of the western heartland are expansionist, aggressive, dependent upon brute force and, by implication, uncultured and unsophisticated. Writhing in frustration as their power declines, it is the foreigners who see China as 'clumsy', 'intransigent', 'condemned', 'a hybrid', 'a strange creature', and 'unstable', with its polity lying 'precariously on the edge of chaos', and who, in general, understand the Chinese less than the foreigners are understood by the Chinese.

The connection between culture and economic success, the traits of the Chinese, their deeper levels of cultural consciousness, the wash and backwash of history and culture which emanates from the Han Chinese and sucks other, weaker cultures into the ocean of Chinese civilisation, and the presence of the foreigner, leave the reader with the inference that the Han Chinese are a race apart defined, if not by a genetic code, then by the eons of history. Culture, race, nation, civilisation and empire are merged to such an extent that each term bears the sentiments inherent in every other, and all are Greater China.

Nationalism, Hong Kong, Taiwan and Tibet

The sharp edges of these hard, nationalistic sentiments must eventually cut through the soft mist which surrounds them. The fear that China may become expansionist – a fear which is harboured in the minds of the political leaders in the region, and which has been focused upon the term 'Greater China' – is irrational, believes Wang. But this concern does:

> run parallel to the earlier fears expressed about the Japanese empire, which, having failed to achieve its Greater Asian Co-Prosperity Sphere as a framework for its imperial ambitions, then used its economic power to bring it about. Is this what China might do? Is the idea of an economic Greater China another way of achieving a new economic empire in the region?
>
> If so, it would be a new phenomenon having little to do with the historic dynastic empires of the past. The region has changed beyond recognition. So has the world. There is no return to the past. The new nations of the region may each appear relatively weak, but they have learned the most important lesson of the colonial era. When they were divided, they were easily picked off, one after another, to become bits of other countries' empires. They are unlikely to make that mistake again, and China can hardly fail to see the determination within the region to avoid doing so. Small and large regional groupings, with or without China, will intensify their efforts to bring about peaceful solutions to all potential disputes. If they are successful in ensuring that peace, the concept of empire itself should be discarded. (ibid., pp. 58–9)

What, exactly, is the meaning of this passage? What is the intention of the claim that Japan's economic success after the last war is nothing less than the resumption of its imperial ambitions by other means? Is this an attempt to make Japan – one of the many antitypes created by Wang for China – responsible for concerns about China's possible ambitions? Is Japanese imperialism (as Wang sees it) being presented as another possible justification for any future actions taken by China? And why should the concept of empire be discarded, if other nations (with or without China) are successful in resolving all potential disputes peacefully, if the phrase 'historic empire' in China has never implied aggressive military actions and military conquest, and if 'Greater China' is China as it has always been? Is it being suggested that if other nations are successful in defusing tensions (and presumably manage to rein in Japanese imperialism) then China no longer has need for a concept that may be misconstrued as either offensive or defensive? Or is it being suggested that China should think carefully over any desires it may have to impose a new merchant empire backed by the threat of military force? Is it now up to the outside world to ensure peace?

Then there is that warning issued by Wang to 'other powers' to keep out of Chinese affairs, for were they to prevent China's national unification or to encourage parts of China to secede, such action would become a permanent source of instability (ibid., p. 51). Wang also makes it quite clear that Taiwan, like Hong Kong, is a natural part of China: if Taiwan appears to be separate from China this is only because outsiders have attempted to encourage the Taiwanese and Hong Kong people to behave as if they lived in independent countries, and because some of the Chinese, together with these foreigners, have deliberately and habitually used the term 'China' to refer only to Mainland China (ibid., p. 13). And then there is the warning that reunification remains on China's political and military agenda (ibid., p. 41). To this explosive cocktail, Wang adds the issue of the control over the Spratly Islands which is the most immediately challenging:

It will be most difficult to prevent this political and economic issue from becoming a military one that could spill over beyond the region. The recent flare-up with the Philippines over a few reefs may well remain a purely regional affair, to be resolved between China and members of the ASEAN states. It would, of course, be best if that could be accomplished with a minimum of ill-will. In terms of China as a future global power, however, its approach to the issue will be scrutinised with great care. Which perceptions by China's neighbors will come to the fore?

The territory of a 'historic empire' has been invoked; obviously it is not a matter of civilisational ambit or revolutionary socialist superiority. But this is not a traditional claim; as I have mentioned earlier, there was no concept of clearly demarcated international boundaries in the past. There is nothing in the dynastic records, not even those of the tributary system, to validate China's claims to these islands. In fact, it is a modern claim first made in answer to Western imperialist and colonial practices earlier this century. Thus, it is really a matter of national strategy, or, perhaps equally, one of resources and economic interests. The Spratlys, therefore, remind us that modern great-power and nationalist politics now govern Asia just as much as appeals to history and culture, or to past practices and principles. On the road to global power, China will have to balance its various perceptions of itself and take all of these into account. (ibid., pp. 75–6)

With a line of reasoning infused with sentiments that one might think are clearly understood and supported by Wang, China maintains that it has found historical artifacts on the Islands which prove that the ebb and flow of Chinese civilisation has touched their shores, and that these Islands are part of the organic whole that is China. Perhaps sensing these arguments are unlikely to prove convincing to a more sophisticated international audience, Wang has crafted a different set of rationalisations. The explicit and implicit connections that were once drawn between nation, civilisation, empire and culture are first cut, and the significance of these concepts are downgraded. China's actions in its dispute over the Spratly Islands – a dispute which might easily turn into a general military conflict – has nothing to do with 'empire', 'civilisation' or 'culture'. China's actions in the South China Seas are matters of national strategy, resources, and economic interests. China is no worse that any other nation: nationalist policies govern Asia; and in any case China's actions are merely a response to Western imperialism and colonial practice earlier this century. Is there here, in Wang's twisting and turning, the suggestion that if China should become aggressive, then such actions would be rational and legitimate given the region's history of nationalism and Western colonialism?

Ambiguity also infects Wang's more detailed exposition of the question surrounding Hong Kong, Taiwan and Tibet. The treatment of Hong Kong, writes Wang,

> will mark an early test of China's readiness to play a global role; this is one of the reasons Britain and its allies are pressing hard to ensure that Hong Kong's international position will not be constrained after 1997. It would be easy to underestimate the PRC's hostility to any suggestion that there be any British influence left in the territory, or that China's sovereignty over Hong Kong after 1997 be questioned. To the PRC, Hong Kong should have been a purely internal matter to be resolved between the PRC and the colonial power. But the city's extraordinary importance to Chinese economic reforms since 1978 has given it international clout. If not for the Tian'anmen Square tragedy and the collapse of the Communist bloc in Europe, China could have expected a low-key transition, with Britain, the United States, and Japan assisting in a smooth transfer of sovereignty.

But the international dimension became a much more central issue after 1989. The Hong Kong people, who are used to a considerable amount of freedom, are understandably fearful of losing that freedom. Attention has shifted from economic matters to questions of political rights, press freedom, and the legal system. Increasingly, comparisons are being made with the lack of such protections in the

PRC itself. In their efforts to preserve those protections, Hong Kong people have begun to insist on establishing the principles of universal rights before 1997, and seek to draw international attention to their territory. Chinese officials are increasingly irritated by the widening range of foreign concerns about Hong Kong. To protect the excellent financial and business environment in Hong Kong, the PRC will have to exercise diplomatic skill to persuade outside interests not to interfere. But if the transfer of sovereignty is well handled, it will enhance China's global status. (ibid., pp. 73–4)

The main threat to Hong Kong, it would seem, comes from those outside interests which are being drawn to Hong Kong by attempts there to establish the principle of human rights; and the only protection for Hong Kong will be China's diplomatic skills and its ability to persuade those outside interests not to interfere. Wang's reasoning is logical if set within the context of his other arguments: people in Hong Kong and Taiwan have been encouraged to behave as if they came from independent countries; some of these people in Hong Kong and Taiwan, together with foreigners, have reinforced this sense of independence by deliberately using the word 'China' to exclude Taiwan and Hong Kong; there is widespread and strengthening nationalism in Asia; Japan has successfully managed to pursue its imperial ambitions since the last war through its economic power; the West's imperial history is partly responsible for provoking China's actions in the South China Seas; and there is a well-founded suspicion about the emphasis given by 'the West' to democracy and human rights – ideals which China will eventually incorporate into some new, but as yet un-formed, kind of polity. Over Hong Kong, as over many other issues, China is being forced to compensate for the blinkered and prejudiced attitudes of the world's still powerful, but now declining, nations.

An even more difficult 'test' for China is the pressure from within Taiwan for its independence:

China will have to fiercely defend the principle that this is an entirely internal matter. The mixture of caution and blustering rhetoric has revealed the great tensions underlying this relationship. The United States has supported the leftover regime from a bitter civil war; for over 45 years, the PRC has looked on this as a US thorn in its side. During the latter part of this period, Taiwan's economic success has led to political freedoms that now challenge the fundamental principle that there could be only one China, one nation, and one set of historical roots. This was the principle that gave the Guomind-ang its legitimacy to rule Taiwan after they left the mainland.

Now, however, among some Taiwan people, there are serious ques-tions about the validity of sharing that one civilisation. There are calls for independence; the PRC finds this intolerable, although its actions have been surprisingly restrained so far. It probably has little choice now. But it is not clear whether the mainland government will remain calm if some of [the] excitable Taiwanese take their independence desires much further. What is clear that if the calls develop into action, the threat of war across the straits will be great indeed. (ibid., p. 74)

Wang's stand is partisan but it is clear, at least initially. Taiwan is a natural and indivisible part of China. The Taiwanese who wish their *de facto* independence to be recognised internationally are described as 'excitable'. The regime is regarded as a 'left over', and Wang goes beyond calling successive governments in Taiwan hypocritical with his startling suggestion that democracy in Taiwan challenges the very principle that there could only be one China, one nation, and one set of historical roots – the principles upon which the Guomindang obtained its legitimacy to rule. Democracy has no legitimacy in Taiwan because it offends the 'oneness' of China and its culture. That China has been so restrained over this internal matter, so far, is 'surprising'. But Wang then becomes increasingly ambiguous:

Within the region, Taiwan is diplomatically contained, but trading relations with other countries, including the mainland itself, are growing faster than anyone expected. The biggest challenge would come if Taiwan's position were to gain sympathy as China's power rises. For the rest of the world, the efforts to isolate Taiwan globally are still continuing. It is a manageable problem, but nevertheless one that calls for the greatest vigilance. Taiwan's persistence in not allow-ing itself to be ignored by the rest of the world has frequently put the Beijing leaders on the defensive, and this undermines China's global position somewhat. (ibid., pp. 74–5)

What is being implied here? Is it that the rest of the world is trying to isolate Taiwan from China, or is it that China is trying to isolate Taiwan from the world? For whom, then, is this a manageable problem? And why should China's global position look weak because the Taiwanese are not ignored by the rest of the world? This curious mixture of pique and paranoia seems to indicate considerable immaturity on the part of China's leaders.

On the question of Tibet we again find a similar ambiguity:

> The issue of Tibet . . . requires patience on all sides; it is a long-term problem that will not go away and will call for statesmanship of the highest quality. China has stood firm that this is an internal matter, and international law and UN practice support that position. The challenge today is really neither political nor military. The special quality of Tibet's culture and history, its unique religion, and the loyalty and faith that they arouse have produced a moral authority for Tibet that will continue to bring it considerable sympathy from the rest of the world. China's comparative wealth, its power and influence, or even its legitimacy will not help. Even if conscientious laws, good intentions, and humane administration were to be consistently applied in Tibet, China would still not easily overcome the image of having been the invader. Tibet is the only one among the various autonomous regions and districts along China's lengthy borders where normal methods of control seem to have been adequate to stop secessionist demands. (ibid., p. 75)

The whole issue, continues Wang, 'highlights difficulty with concepts of nation and civilisation . . . Neither [concept] fits the Tibetan story, and the appeal to the idea of historic empire has simply not been convincing enough. As a potential global power, China here faces a real test of its patience and humanity.' Wang appears to be implying that China did not annexe Tibet, and that on the whole, Chinese rule in Tibet has been conscientious and humane – an implication reinforced by his statement that Tibet is only one of several autonomous regions and districts where 'normal' methods of control have been adequate. This begs two questions. What is meant by normal methods of control? And what are the abnormal, or special, methods of control which have been used in the other autonomous regions and districts? If the phrase should have read 'normal methods of control seem to have been inadequate' in Tibet, then we are still left with a sanitized euphemism for ruthless authoritarianism.

The notion that the government needs to act in such ways to stop secessionist demands hardly seems to fit either with Wang's belief that China has grown organically, or with his claim that the principles of democracy and human rights are accepted and debated in China. The treatment of, and attitudes towards, minorities – one of the key tests of democracy and human rights – are as nothing in the face of strategic concerns, the drive for economic, political and military power, and, to that end, the creation and manipulation of China's stylised representations.

Race and culture

There are glaring problems and contradictions present in Wang's lectures to the Nobel Institute. But this does not really matter, for his lectures have much to do with the expression and communication of particular sentiments: all is symbolic, all is image. There is, in English, perhaps no better *apologia sinica*. His use of the terms 'democracy' and 'forms of democracy', for instance, and his discussion of their significance, surpass the phrases and didactic maxims – such as 'democratic centralism', 'democratic dictatorship', 'revolutionary democratic dictatorship', 'peoples' democratic autocracy', 'socialist legalism' and 'national autonomous area are an inalienable part of the PRC' – which emanate from China's own propaganda machinery. Wang's pronouncements are peppered liberally with words such as 'rich heritage', 'cultural heritage', 'continuous cultural heritage', 'traditional', 'historic' and 'oneness', and with references to 'foreigners', 'traitors' and 'loyalty', all of which are used to evoke a sense of destiny for a state, a nation, a culture, a civilisation, a race that is unique, otherworldly and quintessentially 'Chinese'. His lectures do not fall far short of a nationalistic myth, and are didactic in the extreme. Culture, nation, civilisation, empire and race are merged; China is struggling to unify itself because its people are culturally and racially unified; the people exude values and create institutions which explain their economic success; they are a people who put the collective before the individual. Against these people are the 'the foreigners' – a ragtag collection of people whose empires held together only so long as their armies were successful in the battlefield, who were responsible for the collapse of imperial China, who are continuing to do their best to prevent China from rising and taking its rightful place in the world, and who work surreptitiously and dishonestly through traitors, malcontents and rebels. No matter that this caricature will not bear even a cursory reading of European and American history. The logic is not intellectual: it is psychological. The purpose is to create an antitype against which the nationalistic-cum-racial myth can be developed. The images of China and its antitypes justify China's actions whatever they may be. China and its lands have always been as they are; its people, their culture, and their race as they have always been. China's foreign and domestic policies must safeguard the civilisation from the envy and aggression of other powers, and shield it against further humiliation. To survive, China – the nation, the people, the culture, the civilisation, the race – must become a global power.

These are images, and sentiments, that we have seen before. In *Mein Kampf* Hitler preached that Germany had been brought down by a culturally inferior but more brutal people.[9] Germany – the nation, the people, the culture, and the race – were as one; the state was merely a framework for the survival of the race; and Germany's survival depended upon, and was equated with, its military, political and economic ascendancy – a destiny which could not be separated from visiting retribution upon those who had been instrumental in Germany's defeat. No 'social sacrifice' was too great; Germany's rise was the end to which every individual, and all their energies, should be directed and organised, and which excused all actions. The only judge of right and wrong was success. Majority rule was explicitly rejected; parliamentarianism and decay were one and the same. The people enjoyed another 'form' of democracy – 'Germanic democracy': the leader was elected but then exercised unconditional authority; and for this role only the hero, only the individual strong enough to bear the consequences of his actions, was cut out to lead the race. The Aryan race, declared Hitler, was boundlessly honest, creative and culturally superior. But the characteristic he singled out and raised above all the other attributes of the Aryan was *pflichterfüllang* – the willingness of individuals to put their abilities to the service of their community, to renounce or subsume their personal opinion and interests in favour of the group, to sacrifice the self for the good of others; this was the quality of social cohesion. Pitted against the Aryan was the Jew. The Jews were individualistic and fissiparous; they were selfish, egotistical, and deceitful; they regarded commerce as their own special privilege; they took ownership of national production; they created political class divisions between employer and employee; and they organised capitalistic methods of human exploitation. The Jews seemed to overflow with 'enlightenment', 'progress', 'freedom', and 'humanity', and yet, in truth, they were interested only in advancing themselves. Their ultimate objective was to make victorious 'democracy' or, as the Jews understood it, the rule of parliamentarianism.

The similarities between, on the one hand, Aryan and Chinese and, on the other, Jew and foreigner are striking: the Aryan and Chinese cultural-cum-racial virtues of collectivism and selflessness are set against the individualistic, egotistical and selfish Jew and foreigner (most especially 'Westerner'); the oneness of the respective cultures of the Aryan and Chinese is set against the fragmented but invasive Jew and foreigner;

the purity, necessity, and righteousness of all attempts by Germany and China to realise global power are strengthened by comparison with the desire of Jewish anti-hero and envious foreigner to frustrate those legitimate ambitions; forms of democracy other than those which are distinctively 'Germanic' and 'Chinese' are at best irrelevant, and at worst instruments designed by the Jew and foreigner to suppress the German and Chinese people; exception is taken to the use of the term 'diaspora' apparently because it suggests comparison between Jews and Chinese; a pious, almost sentimental, respect is declared for those 'cultures' which are deemed to be strong and distinctive, whereas those people who belong to a 'culture' thought to be weak and moribund are dismissed as the flotsam of Darwinian evolution; and racial distinctions are made between Aryan and coloureds, Chinese and Westerners. 'White Europeans', writes Francis Hsu,

> have exhibited throughout their colourful history a consistant flair for Utopian idealism and for dark nihilism ... Their way is one of extremes: the good are all good and must eliminate the evil; and the evil are, of course, the same and must do likewise. Westerners generously support child and animal protection societies; but many of them also rape and mutilate young girls and vandalize zoos and decimate defenceless animals. The Chinese have, on the other hand, thoughout their cyclical history, shown no comparable tendency towards such extremes. They bore a heavy burden of their ancestors; their Utopia was an unspectacular golden age of the past. The founder of their Taoism was even alleged to have been born of a virgin mother who carried him for eighty years. He was very old at birth, hence he was known as Lao Tzu or Old master. But the Chinese made nothing of the myth, for in their mental scheme of things male and female are complementary, like light and darkness; but not opposed or antagonistic to each other, in which case the prevalence of the one means by definition the destruction of the other. Hence no Chinese leader ever spoke of a war to end all wars, instituted the Inquisition, or even fantasized anything resembling Hitler's final solution ... *Lacking affective relations among humans,* Westerners have been preoccupied with the control of things or privatization of the supernatural for personal fulfilment. The Chinese preference for human relations over gods and things sprang from their kinship system. The system is so tenacious that it simply refuses to go away or greatly alter its intrinsic attributes in the face of revolutionary or colonial or post-colonial cicumstances.[10]

Hsu's westerners, his 'white' Europeans, are not only fanatical and barbarous, traits which, like their colour, are inheritable; they are even missing certain qualities which define humanity. They are, in some respects, therefore, sub-human. That Hitler and his acolytes saw Germany as being 'of the East' makes the thickening atmosphere of irony which surrounds all these comparisons still more piquant.

Above the noise of these crude extremes sound the enharmonics of Dikotter's analysis of racism in China. With final collapse of the imperial system early in the twentieth century, argues Dikotter:

> neo-Confucian knowledge rapidly lost its credibility and authority. Previously imagined as a purposeful whole, a benevolent structure which could not exist independently from ethical forces, 'nature' was now conceptualised as a set of impersonal forces that could be objectively investigated. No longer were physical bodies thought to be linked to the cosmological foundations of the universe: bodies were produced by biological laws inherent in 'nature'. With the decline of conformity to the moral imperatives enshrined in a canon of Confucian texts, a growing number of people believed 'truth' to be encoded in a nature which only science could decipher: identity, ancestry, and meaning were buried deep inside the body. Embryology or genetics could establish differences between population groups, not philology or palaeography. Human biology replaced imperial cosmology as the epistemological foundation for social order.[11]

The racialised folk beliefs and the 'indigenised' notions of race which appeared in China during the late nineteenth and early twentieth centuries, we must believe, were clearly different from their earlier versions. The softer beliefs of a more gentle past had emerged within a state that was essentially moral and saw little difference between nature, ethics, purpose and benevolence. Dikotter's strong criticism of those who would deny the existence of racist thinking in China,[12] or who blame racism in China on Western influence and 'Westernisation', appears to be little more than a foil against which to make seem more balanced, moral and reasonable both his explicit argument that culture should not be equated with racial categories of thought and analysis, and also his implied argument that whilst racial discourse may have thrived thanks to folk models of identities (which were 'reconfigured' by a biological pseudo-science imported from the West during the nineteenth century), China was not a source of racist thinking. Race, contends Dikotter, is situated on the periphery of the Chinese symbolic universe. And though racial prejudice has proved resilient in China's recent history, it is more virulent and widespread in the West where, in certain countries, it has been translated into a characteristic practice with gruesome efficiency.[13] Indeed, if we accept Dikotter's understanding of racial categories of analysis and thought, and if we accept the distinction which he makes between culture and race, then racial categories of thought could *only* have been transmitted from the West from the nineteenth century onwards; for that, after all, is where, and when, the word 'race' first became associated with alleged biological differences among groups of people.[14] Racial categories of thought are *defined*, curiously, by a pseudo-scientific approach to the study of human biology that arose in Europe during the nineteenth century. I say 'curiously' because, as Thompson in his study of Classical Rome clearly demonstrates,[15] neither the prejudice of supposed profound biological differences, or of physical appearance (including colour), or of class, accent, behaviour, education, ideology, religion or personality, nor the institutionalisation, nor belief in the inheritability, of these differences, are confined to the nineteenth century.

The question which arises is this: since profound biological differences are only imagined, then surely the idea of race is no less 'cultural' than other cultural differences? The essential problem, as we have already seen, is that the cultural explanation calls ultimately upon a force which, if not historical, recursive, habitual or environmental, must be genetic; or which, if thought to be historical, environmental or habitual, has become so deeply ingrained that it is now effectively an inherent trait capable of being transmitted from one generation to the next (through 'socialisation' for instance), and of evolving in much the same way as a biological species. Those who choose to look to biological science (including both its reputable and disreputable aspects) to legitimise as best they can their beliefs in the inferiority or superiority of one group in relation to another, follow the same line of reasoning as the culturalist who, in a purely analytical frame of mind, looks to recursive structures or history in order to distinguish one group from another, or to explain, say, the economic success of one group over another; and that line of reasoning is the interpretation of observations in the light of some imagined force, and the use of those interpretations as proof of the existence of their imaginings. Dikotter, in order to explain, has deferred to culture whose progeny may include (among other possible rationalisations) a belief in racial differences. And in his effort to explain, to distance culture from race, to emphasise the criteria by which groups are defined, and to distinguish among those criteria, he leads the reader away from an understanding of racism. What matters is not how the individual or group is defined (physical characteristics, habits, beliefs, practices, values, class or some other feature), but how boundaries – however they are drawn – are enforced; how inferior and superior roles are ascribed, fixed and made inheritable; and so the manner in which an individual is constantly chastised or elevated above another simply for being – or for being perceived to be – a member of a particular group. For it is only when petty tensions, frustrations, narrow minds, disappointments, and the village mentality are thus provided with clear direction, and a clear target, that the individual who is deemed to be different is transformed into a kernel around which common prejudice and these base emotions cluster and there find gratification.

Conclusions

I have argued that there is great weakness in the attempt to distance culture from race. I do not regard this weakness as grounds upon which to justify a comparison of views such as those espoused by Wang with National Socialism. Indeed, I should make it clear that I do not believe, nor have I intended to imply, that Wang or other writers who express similar opinions, are proponents of National Socialism and anti-semitism; nor am I suggesting that China resembles Germany of the 1930s. Nor do I believe that Dikotter has deliberately provided a rationalisation for racist attitudes in China or elsewhere in East Asia. It is not sinology's rationalisation of racism that is noteworthy so much as the manner in which this rationalisation is achieved: effortlessly, as a matter of course, almost as a kind of accepted side-effect which occurs as analysts defer to culture, and even if the intention is to uncover and explain racism. Nor is it the similarity between the caricatured Chinese and Aryan, Jew and foreigner that invites attention. It is more that these images emerge unforced from common values, beliefs, institutions and patterns of behaviour manipulated, interpreted and presented merely in order to define and claim difference, as if there is a common set of characteristics assigned to 'us' and 'them', whoever the 'favoured' and 'unfavoured' groups may be. What is perhaps even more significant and disturbing is that this manipulation derives not from any hidden political agenda, but from very human, very understandable and very common sentiments – intellectual hubris and the survival of the self in one form or another.

In the final paragraph of his lectures, Wang, with the exasperated, but good-natured, air of a mentor whose acolytes are struggling to see the truth he has revealed to them, states:

> For years, I have had to argue with my European friends that Communist China is not the same as communist Russia, and that China is not a 'normal' country, not even a 'normal' communist country. Some have agreed with me by pointing out that the Chinese communists misunderstood both Marx and Lenin and did not have much of a clue regarding what communism was really about. What I have outlined above, I hope, does illustrate how China is different. The way it perceives itself shows how its rich heritage as a civilisation and empire has complicated its claims to be a modern nation; why its unique linkages with Hong Kong, Taiwan, and parts of the diaspora have eased the pains of economic reform; and how it derived socialist ideals from its checkered revolutionary history. Together, these factors have made China an entity of paradoxes. China is all of the above, and yet more than the sum of its parts. It is still divided and incomplete, but it has political weight. It is multi-layered, it is large and extensive, it is modernising, but it is also inclusive and able to use traditional values and networks to reach out for new knowledge, new technology, and new investment. Finally, the transformation of China has been a most painful one, dragging on for more than a century, but the Chinese people have never given up and still seek to be modern and global and quintessentially Chinese. (CW, p. 77)

In a style that draws both from the cold vocabulary of the modern social scientist and from the bombast of state propaganda Wang has recast the myth of the paradoxical, inscrutable East. It is an image which evokes memories of balmy, tropical evenings, and visions of incense-filled temples and of cloud-topped limestone karsts. It is the image of a people who exude romantic promise, who possess a quiet unassuming knowledge which rests upon centuries of experience and wisdom. A mysterious people who are struggling to repair a culture and a civilisation that are not properly understood even by the 'experts' of the outside world. A culture so profound, so perfectly connected to, and so strongly rooted in, its ancient past, that nation and nationhood are made complex and perhaps even unnecessary. A people who, because of their difference, are under constant pressure to demonstrate their passivity and true worth, and to compensate for the inappropriate actions and attitudes of other nations. China's responsibility, as presented by Wang in his counsel, is to exhibit maturity, patience and diplomacy in its dealings with other countries; but it is for the outside world to make due allowances for China's uniqueness and difference, or to take the consequences which might follow if China were to fragment. But this self-regarding picture contains another exhilarating tale. It tells of an ancient and long-lived civilisation; a civilisation that has always inspired in others a desire to learn from its rich knowledge, experience and wisdom; a civilisation that has aroused fear and envy as well as interest; a civilisation that has given much to the world and still has much to offer; a civilisation which, despite all the opposition and invasions mounted against it by a fearful and envious world, is now, once again, on the rise, perhaps to become the greatest power that mankind has ever seen; a civilisation whose past, present and future successes are determined by the traditional values, practices and institutions which define its culture. Wang has created a dual image: one side plays to the outside observers and sycophants; the other to the chauvinist; and both are of great value to China. Wang is not the first, nor is he likely to be the last, sinologist to write himself into China's history by creating yet another version of those stylised representations of China and Chineseness.

And yet it is for this reason that Wang's lectures to the Nobel Institute will draw more praise than criticism, for Wang imitates the age-old practice of China's scholar-politicians – a practice imitated by many sinologists. We noted earlier that Needham viewed the presence of 'a certain amount' of propaganda in Chinese classical texts as the '*défaut* of the civilised civilian *qualité*'; and that to Watson, the very act of fabricating and manipulating Chinese culture defines 'being' Chinese. Unger, too, sees virtue in this image-play:

> The recording and interpretation of history has, for the past two millennia, contained a special significance in China. More than in most other countries, history was and is a mirror through which ethical standards and moral transgressions pertinent to the present day could be viewed. This perspective on history was based in Confucian doctrine, which admonished followers to plumb the past for such lessons. It became a method of commentary about contemporary times that members of the literati class learned how to manipulate, sometimes as a means of flattering the incumbent emperor and government – but sometimes as a stratagem for chastising the imperial court. After all, in a centrally controlled empire it was always safer to

place one's criticisms in a past age that to write directly about the present court. Well aware of this potential for allegory, suspicious emperors and their entourages kept a watchful eye open for subversive intent in the historical treatises of the literati. Repeatedly, purges and persecutions in imperial China were rooted in alleged 'historical' aspersions, real or imagined, against the imperial majesty.[16]

Under the Qing, intellectual and cultural debates may have been no more than a plaything in the hands of imperial power;[17] but in communist China, the power-mongers were even more determined both to shape the messages contained in works of history in ways favourable to official policy lines, and to un-pick any dissent or opposition that might be woven into historical allegory. 'They were particularly determined because the traditional desire to police historical references had been reinforced and overlain by a newer, important credo. This of course was the Leninist/Stalinist doctrine, which argued the revolutionary need for an all-powerful Party to push forward Communist social values and attitudes by controlling and re-shaping both intellectual discourse and public sentiment. Given the importance of images of history in shaping both intellectual and popular thought in China, special attention was to be focused on ensuring that the proper line was followed by historians.'[18]

Unger, and the other contributors to *Using the Past*, recognise and detail a vast repertoire of plays, stories and artistic techniques which are manipulated in order to create or support particular images. The form of these images, and the very act of their construction and manipulation, are an expression of mind-sets and practices so deeply ancient that even unwanted images have survived attempts by the state to eradicate them. Try as they might, the Communist authorities 'were never entirely able to dictate the ways in which the Chinese people turned to history for lessons and for political analogies. As but one example, when interviewing respondents from China in the mid-1970s, I could not help but notice how frequently interviewees' discussions of current politics turned toward historical analogy – and almost always within the terms of the *traditional* genres of political allegory. Interviewees were apt to refer to Mao's unpopular wife Jiang Qing and Mao's closet followers, for instance, in phrases that conjured up the stereotypically scheming inner-court courtiers and imperial consorts – who so often in the histories and operas had illegitimately taken advantage of an aging emperor's dotage to usurp power. Playing upon such feelings, within months of Mao's death in 1976 and the coup against the 'gang of four', the official mass media itself was similarly dressing up contemporary politics in the clothes of the past. The just-widowed Jiang Qing was presented to the Chinese people as the modern counterpart to the Empress Lu, one of the great villains of popular lore, who had usurped power in the Han dynasty.'[19]

The flickering images with which the analyst is surrounded are thought to follow every movement of the corporate so closely, that the images themselves are taken to be the reality in which true meaning is to be found. To understand the image-play of this ersatz world is to know China's polity. It is they, today's Figurists, who are able to decipher this symbolic language and to know its meaning; it is they who can lead us beyond even those historical allegories with which the controversies of the present are discussed, and reveal to us the 'sincere debate among professional historians over long-standing issues such as the nature of Chinese society, the periodisation of China's political evolution, and the role of the individual in history. Western historians of China might question the scholarly quality of these analyses, which by trying to make China's past relevant to contemporary political issues produced inevitable distortions of historical reality. But this should not denigrate a controversy whose major themes have attracted Chinese intellectuals throughout this century and still remain central to the Marxist historicism dominating contemporary historiographical analysis and debate.'[20]

The images, their construction, and their manipulation, are no less the expression of genuine scholarly debate than they are a reflection of the corporate world, or so we are asked to believe. Even the very act of using history is itself transformed into an image of Chineseness. An image within an image! What could be more subtle and complex? What could be more oriental? Few other practices are likely to be as worthy of the connoisseur's attention. Why, then, should not those who see true meaning and intent contained within Chinese analyses of China's history, and who are therefore so conversant with the fine art of being Chinese, also practice that art? Why should not the *cognoscenti* present the world in the style and voice of China's own scholar-politicians? More important than questions about the scholarly quality of analyses of China's history, believes Sullivan, is 'whether this articulation of different historiographical views has had any real impact on the political reform process.'[21] Why should not the analyses of Needham or Wang be praised as much for their political value as for their acuity of perception, though they make little distinction between propaganda, image, perception, apperception, fact, fiction and predetermined interpretation?

What does it matter that in China thought should be restricted by the petty concerns of political ambition?

Perhaps a more cogent justification of the collage of images re-fashioned or created anew by the *cognoscenti* of the Chinese world is that they do go to the heart of what China is and always has been – a highly politicised state in which political-cum-social power is an end in itself to which all values, beliefs, institutions, relationships, emotions, patterns of behaviour and energies are turned. I am not suggesting that the very acts of manipulating and fabricating are in themselves indicative of Chineseness, nor that the images created and manipulated are mirrors or allegories of true events. Rather, I am arguing that in those analyses we see, in detail, how ideas, values, beliefs, institutions – and analyses of them – are manipulated, turned and directed at will in order to support and adapt old images or to fashion new ones. It is from this manipulation that we may thereby gain an unspoken sense of how China works.

But there is something disturbing about this refined and complex *rifacimentos*. The apperceptions of China's leaders and their subjects, and the images of China which have been taken up, imitated, and elaborated upon by the outside world, are easily confused with what China *is*. This confusion, when combined with a belief in the inherent and unique distinctiveness of China and Chineseness, is potentially dangerous. If policies towards China were determined or strongly conditioned by the belief that China's culture and history are profoundly different, and if it were thought that more accurate predictions of, and more effective responses to, the actions of China's government are predicated upon a deeper understanding, and deferential treatment, of that difference, then China's government would in effect be given free rein to manipulate its own stylised representations of China and Chineseness. Responses made in China's image would merely confirm, rationalise and justify any action which the Chinese government might wish to take, whether or not those actions offended the interests of other peoples in the Far East and beyond.

And indeed, it would appear that analyses which defer to China's stylised representations, and from which is spun policy advice on how to handle China in international affairs, are even now exerting their influence upon the actions of the outside world. As if parodying the eighteenth century Figurists, today's democratic nations in pursuit of their policy of 'constructive engagement' seem prepared to give considerable benefit of the doubt to the actions and attitudes of China's elite. So sophisticated, subtle, irresistible and compelling is the policy thought to be that any challenge to it, and any suggestion that a much firmer and clearer stance towards China should be adopted, is described as a belligerent and hawkish display of ignorance. The policy's allure derives in part from its ability to encompass and reconcile three prevalent but apparently different beliefs about China's role and its future development. There is, to begin with, the belief that the US and China share parallel interests in equilibrium in Asia. We are told that China wants the US to help it balance its relations with Japan, Russia and India; and that the US wants China to cooperate with it in maintaining that balance, in reaching a peaceful solution to the Taiwan question, in managing nuclear proliferation and the transfer of other weapons technology, and in maintaining peace on the Korean peninsula. Secondly, there is the belief that China is fundamentally different: that within this ancient, complex and passive state, lie the seeds of an entirely new and better (though as yet unknown) kind of polity and society, the development of which is destined not to follow the 'Western' path. And thirdly, there is the belief that this ancient state, once lured deep into the international economy, will find itself with no choice but to move inexorably towards a more liberal political system and eventually to full, mass representative democracy, gently guided by the US and Europe.

These beliefs find an easy consensus in the policy of constructive engagement because it plays to an image of China which those beliefs share. It is the image of a factionalised political, military and merchant elite rive by different views, ambitions and perceptions set atop a sophisticated, ancient, profoundly moral, generally stable, passive, cohesive society with democratic strains running throughout its long history – a society that is peculiarly Chinese. For all its divisions and tensions, China constitutes a sound, rational, long-lived and unique entity which, like all complex and large states, has legitimate and wide-ranging security interests. The watchword must be 'dialogue'; and there must be no suspicion of containment. China must therefore be given plenty of latitude when inevitable misunderstandings arise; and it is the more favourable interpretations of China's behaviour and motives which should be the first to receive attention from open minds.

And there, in its dependency on the mantras of culture and universals, lies the essential fallacy of constructive engagement. By playing to culture, and to the expectations which derive from a belief in the forces of modernisation and democratisation, the most valuable set of ready-made thought-formulae with which to legitimise actions and ambitions is handed to China's military, political and merchant elites, and to interest groups, commercial or otherwise, within America and Europe. Furthermore, while the deferment to culture celebrates relativity and denies expedient absolutes, the deferment to universals breeds a false certainty which is likely to shatter if events prove unpredictable, throwing analysis, explanation and advice back upon culture with added vigour.

The deferment to culture; the faith in the spells being worked by the deep forces and structures of modernisation and democratisation, and the subtlety of constructive engagement: with beliefs like these dominant within British and American governments and among their advisers and experts in things Chinese, who in China will want to promote values, institutions, procedures, patterns of behaviour and attitudes which are not only associated with the mass representative democracies of 'the West", but are even regarded by many sinologists and other academics (including those who teach at centres at centres of learning in Europe and America attended by China's own policy advisers) as a product of 'western' culture and 'western' perceptions? The authority and reputation of an institution become shallow things once transferred to the views of the individual scholar. But they still retain substance enough to weigh thought down with prejudice. If China's politicians, administrators, merchants and military can manipulate to their own political and material advantage the atmosphere of reason, the Rolls-Royce serenity, and the sense of balanced argument which surrounds that deference to culture, to universals, and thus to those images of China which inform the policy of constructive engagement, then why should they worry about a slavish adherence to impartiality, political freedom, justice, and the probity of institutions and individuals?

The freedom given to the invocation of all manner of cultural, historical, economic and political forces as a means of providing explanations and justifications for China's actions now and in the future are such that one might think that administrators, governments and their advisers in Europe and America are determined to shape policy around China's images rather than around China's actions. One could even be forgiven for thinking that many commentators are happy to give China so much latitude because they are more concerned to demonstrate the validity of their own knowledge and perspicacity than they are to consider the implications which might attend their advice if subsequently they should find that all along they have been supine before China's image. The more democratic governments and their advisers twist and turn with China as it plays to its own stylised representations and to those constructed for it by the *cognoscenti* of things Chinese; and the more the representatives of the democratic states appear to question the absolute quality of their own beliefs, values, institutions and behaviour, then the more the Chinese leadership will view democracy as a thin, tawdry cloth best suited to 'the West's' *demi-monde*.

* * * * *

The relative stability and predictability which expedient absolutes bring to the conduct and expansion of trade might suggest that an easy association exists between, on the one hand, trade, democracy, humanitarianism and human rights, and, on the other, technical, scientific and material progress. This impression is strengthened by the practical importance of trade and profit to the sustained creation of material wealth; and by the argument that those who would defer to culture (with all its attendant cultural, historical, economic, religious and mystical forces) in order to maintain their own power and status are likely to demand the suppression or marginalisation of any idea or method of thought which is held to challenge or question 'The Culture'. And clearly, the ease with which an association can be made between trade, democracy and scientific progress could be taken to suggest that the policy of constructive engagement will bring profound and welcome change in China.

Even its most ardent supporters, however, recognise that the policy of constructive engagement may not work. The primary justification for the continuation of this policy, therefore, is that a more hostile and confrontational attitude towards China might generate the very risks and dangers that the outside world is trying to avoid. Since the US and its allies have a strategic and economic head-start on China, they should enjoy the luxury of observing Chinese modernisation before adopting a more assertive posture. The policy is certainly a luxury for today; but what does it hold for tomorrow? Those who advocate the policy of constructive engagement may find that while they are playing their too-subtle game, China's intriguing, ambitious and unpredictable courtiers look on with amusement as they transform China into a strong economic and military power for their own benefit. It is not inconceivable that China's bureaucratic, merchant, political and military elites view with considerable cynicism those governments and merchants of the democratic states who are willing to suspend the most basic values and practices upon which the character of their own societies rest, merely in order to do business with China. If it should also appear that these democratic representatives have fallen under the mesmeric influence of China's stylised representations, then China's mercurial intriguants may well feel vindicated in their own belief that democratic states are fundamentally shallow and hypocritical. What greater encouragement to, and what stronger confirmation of, the righteousness of 'being Chinese' and of China's subsequent actions could there be?

Alternatively it may be that China will fall apart as the practice of trade bubbles through China's society, as people turn away from the oppressive weight of Chineseness and towards the outside world, as the state sector continues to weaken, as a sense of national economy begins to dissolve, as mounting debt is followed by threat of fiscal collapse, as unemployment grows, and as China comes up against even sharper competition from the countries of the West Pacific Rim. Faced with their power and wealth slipping away, China's political, military and merchant elites might conclude that a revival of Maoist fantasies or virulent nationalistic sentiments would best serve their interests. But what if they failed to hold China together? The policy of constructive engagement might then realise its intentions, though by a far more circuitous route. The suggestion that fragmentation would de-stabilise the entire region might only reflect a belief that China's disintegration is inconceivable and would only mean chaos. This fear, however, may have been over-played. If China were to fragment, and if its parts were to be drawn closer to Northeast Asia, Central Asia, South Asia and Southeast Asia, then its people, released from their marioteers and from the dictates of a fabricated culture, might find themselves poised on the edge of a new renaissance. Genuine political change, the rise of human-itarianism, a broadening of outlooks and attitudes, and a less haphazard evolution of experimental and creative thought and action, may be far more likely once the state whose very unity defines 'The Culture' and 'The Civilisation' has gone.

Clearly there are many possibilities. But there is one constant: that only democracy within the area that we now call China will bring the necessary long-term stability and predictability so vital to the interests of the region and the world. Whether or not China survives as a single entity, clear and extremely firm parameters should be set within which China as it now is, or may become, must shape itself. Regardless of threats or warnings either from China, or from special commercial inter-ests within democratic states, or from the *cognoscenti* of the Chinese world, unequivocal and open support should be given to Taiwan and to any country upon which China might attempt to impose its will through economic, political, diplomatic or military blustering and brinkman-ship. Human rights and progress towards democracy in China should be firmly linked to, and given precedence over, trade and investment, for these are issues which touch upon the interests of America, Europe and Asia and thus range far beyond the semantics, pride, chauvinism, sycophancy, and intellectual hubris which attend China's stylised representations.

Conclusions

There is nothing new in criticism of our understandings of China. Many of today's interpretations are built upon the ruins of past icons, torn down because they were seen as expressions of Europhilia. The images then borrowed or adapted from China, or created anew, have in their turn been criticised as unrealistic, politically biased in favour of China, and protected by the personalistic networks which inveigle academics, the civil service and government, and by a 'bamboo curtain' which, until the late 1970s, made the confirmation or refutation of interpretations all but impossible. These criticisms have been acknolwedged on occasions but, as Shambaugh's eulogistic volume on Chinese studies in America makes clear, they seem to carry little weight.[1] Segal lays the blame for the pusillanimous attitude of the outside world towards China squarely at the feet of weak-minded business leaders, short-sighted governments, and paranoiac officials at the Pentagon, most of whom take China (which is, after all, only a mediocre power) far too seriously.[2] It is Segal who realises the truth that China matters less than 'most of the West thinks'; and it is Segal who understands the true significance of 'constrainment', who knows with certainty that those who advocate either 'containment' or 'engagement' mutually exclude the other's point of view and thereby create a 'foolish and puerile' dichotomy. Of his own statements that Taiwan's independence and the claims of ASEAN states to the South China Seas need not be defended (though he concedes that it seems more necessary to defend the right to settle such disputes peacefully), Segal makes no mention. Of his own declaration that China is on the way to 'enlightenment' propelled by the overwhelming forces of modernisation and democratisation, and of his appeal to Fukuyama's Trust (which may also be read as a cultural explanation of economic success) in support of that declaration, he has nothing to say. Of sinology and its batteries of cultural and universal forces, and of its influence upon the evolution and strengthening of China's images, he is silent.

But the aura of steely confidence and authority surrounding the analysis of the Chinese world is already being worn thin, though more so by events outside China. Running through the criticisms levelled in this book against the study of things Chinese are two themes which I believe are indicative of shifts in attitude towards academe, the social sciences and notions of culture, which are perhaps more widely held than students of the Chinese world may appreciate, and which, for this reason, will prove difficult to ignore.

The first theme concerns the nature of social science. Although I might, perhaps, have given the contrary impression at times, my objections have not been the political and moral sentiments of any particular writer. The beliefs, the affections and loyalties, and, above all, the personality and experience of each individual writer can rarely be insulated from analysis, nor should they be. These influences carry with them strengths and weakness, preconceptions and open-mindedness, prejudice and perceptivity. The problem lies fundamentally with the interpretation of observations in the light of theories which depend upon explicit or implicit assumptions about the existence and operation of laws, forces and recursive structures, and which thereby prefigure conclusions. This pretend science, medieval in its nature, provides a set of techniques which, like a badge, may be attached to any specific analysis, endowing it with an air of professionalism. Beliefs, faith, preconceptions and prejudice are then easily legitmised. It makes respectable the most convoluted apologies for China's actions, the confusion of history with story-telling and mysticism, and the selective use or dismissal of the significance which other people's actions, beliefs, values, thought, behaviour and institutions may hold for an understanding of China. The versatility of this science even allows a search for universal principles to be pressed into the service of China's peculiarity – the prime doctrine of much sinology. Inevitably, it seems, the discovery of those tools which enable the existence and operation of universals to be identified, leaves even those writers who are concerned about the ease with which Chinese culture is presented as unique and deterministic with little choice but to delineate, by default, the exact ways in which that culture is distinctive, determines outcomes, and interacts with universal principles. It is as if the scenery is being painted against which the details of different characters may be highlighted and elaborated upon. There is no need, no reason, and no support or praise to be had, in challenging the philosophy underlying the search for laws, forces and recursive structures – universal or cultural.

This medieval science and its use to prefigure the interpretation of observations, and to construct and support images of China, is the proper subject of criticism. One may never demonstrate that the experiences and perceptions of others, and their opinions, beliefs, and assumptions about China, are 'right' or 'wrong'. But free observations from their scientific pretensions, and China's stylised representations may at least be revealed for what they are – ornate but gimcrack sentinels of expedient analysis and expedient policies. Strip away that science, and we begin to see (as I have argued elsewhere[3]) that values, beliefs, institutions, relationships and patterns of behaviour are multi-dimensional expressions of multi-dimensional individuals, and that their redirection, or 'turning', reveals striking similarities among people who might otherwise seem very different. These similarities, it must be assumed, derive not from laws, forces or structures, but from reasoned thought and action in the light of the realities of what we are (our commonality of being) and of our circumstances.

It follows, I believe, that similarities are indicated even by the very act of 'turning' values, beliefs, institutions, relationships and patterns of behaviour in order to create differences, by the very desire and willingness to defer to culture, and by the manipulation of its stylised representations in economic, social and political life. For if individuals are to fulfil whatever ambitions they may harbour, and if others are to be cajoled, persuaded, organised, inspired, or coerced, then an appeal to 'culture' with its retinue of forces and structures whether internal, external, historical, genetic, mystical or religious, is of considerable psychological and practical value. Indeed, it is precisely the fluid, uncertain, and random nature of this existence, the seeming absence of external or internal forces, and the ease, therefore, with which values, beliefs, institutions, relationships and patterns of behaviour can be turned and pressed into the service of personal ambition, that makes so apparent the superficiality and weakness of image, and the need for expedient absolutes.

Contained within my strictures of China's images, and of the method of their creation, is another implied criticism of theory in the social sciences. I argue that the treatment of values, institutions, procedures, beliefs and patterns of behaviour (such as human rights, justice, fair play, individual autonomy, and the principles of the rule of law and democracy) *as if* absolute, is an attitude vital to the operation of the mature democracies. Within these societies, this attitude, which has become such a natural part of everyday thought and practice, has been drawn into academic analyses and there reified. Values, institutions, procedures, beliefs and patterns of behaviour are treated not *as if* absolute: they are transposed into pure absolutes; they have been made incarnate within social science, for they are thought of and treated in analysis as *facts* – as phenomena, forces, or recursive structures which, though created by individuals, nevertheless exist independently of those individuals. Even those writers who claim that all 'cultures' are different, that each can be compared and analysed only relative to one another, and that no 'truth' exists (for truth is a 'western' construct), have merely transformed the respective values, beliefs, institutions, practices and patterns of behaviour of each notional 'culture' into the pure absolutes of recursive structures; and they have declared the dogma of cultural relativity as the only truth. We thus find ourselves in a curious wonderland: where those who see a world of uncertain, unpredictable and fluid circumstances and events (which are but expressions of our own actions and decisions), attempt to bring stability and predictability to their lives through their treatment of values, institutions, procedures beliefs and patterns of behaviour as if absolute; while those who see a world ordered *in fact* by recursive structures and forces (cultural or universal or both), leave society open to the incoherence, disorder, whimsy and intolerance brought about through the manipulation practised by those who claim to perceive and understand better than others the structures and forces to which they demand we should all defer.

This determination to defer to culture rather than to values, beliefs and institutions held to be universal and treated as if absolute represents the second theme running through my criticms of the study of China. Those who defer to Chinese culture (or, indeed, any culture whether national, regional, local, 'village', or institutional), turn their back on attitudes and understandings which, though seemingly abstract, take on very real and concrete expression, and which have nothing to do with 'being western' unless 'being western' is to be a-cultural. If it is believed that rights are inherent in all individuals, and apply equally to all, and that justice and fair play are universal sentiments, and that neither these rights or sentiments or the principle of the rule of law and democracy are bound or determined by culture, and if we act upon those beliefs, then the interpretation of values, rights, institutions, patterns of behaviour, conventions, limits of authority, and the determination of what is acceptable and unacceptable, must be subject to debate, to advocacy, to argument, to a gulf-stream of criticism, to the test of trial and error, to examination, and to considered change. There is no one who may claim with legitimacy to know what is or should not be, for there is no one who may claim with legitimacy to be capable enough, or to have the right, to judge who is above, or who is below, what is held to be common to all, or to enforce or to impose those interpretations.

The idea, then, that individualism may be posted as an opposite to communitarianism is just as false as it is a useful rationalisation for deferring to culture. What greater expression of communitarianism is there than to regard as the ideal the independence and autonomy of all individuals in whom rights are inherent and to whom justice and fair play are applied equally? What greater protection is there against turning the notions and sentiments of 'the collective', 'the community' and 'society' in support of the petty ordinariness of totalitarianism, than the protection of the individual from the majority? The notion that affection, love, kindness, warmth and altruism stand in opposition to autonomy and individualism is no less a baseless justification for deferring to culture. Where are emotions and relationships more likely to be manipulated than in circumstances of uncertainty and inequality (political and material), where those in authority manipulate values, beliefs, institutions, patterns of behaviour, relationships, emotions and individuals to achieve their ends, and upon whose actions there is no restraint except the political ambitions of others? And in what better circumstances may relationships and emotions (such as love, affection, warmth, hate or perfidy) come to be seen as something good or bad in their own right, than in those where the individual is protected from the arbitrary or thoughtless actions of others, where prevails the rule of law, an atmosphere of fairness, reason, tolerance, stability, predictability and the probity of polity and economy, and where relationships and emotions are distanced from the operation of institutions and procedures? In what better circumstances may humanitarianism find both the means and encouragement for expression?

There is no suggestion here of perfection; there is no utopia. Transforming into practice the belief that rights, justice, fair play, individualism and individual autonomy, the principle of the rule of law and democracy are universal and apply equally to all, depends upon fine judgement and action. At what point do formal rules, each of which when taken on their own may seem sensible, come together into a web of unnecessary restrictions and tangled contradictions open to ridicule? At what point does the concept of a single unitary society become so powerful that we see all problems and solutions in its terms, and then find that our formal rules and policies have drawn society and economy together so closely as to make incarnate our once-imagined unitary system? At what point do we decide to end the search for the impossible perfection of a unitary economy to whose technical operation our every action must be made accountable, and in its stead trust to common reason and convention, and in this way allow ourselves the freedom which a contentment with imperfection brings ? But then again, at what point do we say that our common reason and conventions have become so judgemental, so infused with self-righteous opinion, morality and an ambitious desire to embrace and unify, that formal regulation is needed to protect those individuals whose actions and behaviour offend only the sensitivities of the majority?

And yet, for all these hard and often impossibly fine judgements, if it is believed that rights, justice, fair play, individual autonomy, and the principles of democracy and the rule of law apply to all individuals equally, and if that belief is held with genuine intent and acted upon, then there is less opportunity for the manipulation of individuals and their subordination to the political ambitions of others. In that belief and intent lies the most sure protection of the state against its decent into creeping political autarky.

It might be countered that this statement of values and beliefs are no less cultural; that to act upon them is no less a deferment to culture, and that those who propagate such a view are no less guilty of setting themselves up as arbiters of their culture. Are not beliefs in universal rights, in the principles of the rule of law and democracy, and in a sense of justice and fair play, cultural attributes regardless of the most intense protestation to the contrary?

In response to these objections, three strands of the argument pursued above should be reiterated. First, it is the fact that individuals *believe* rights, justice, fair play, individual autonomy, and the principles of the the rule of law and democracy to be universal and absolute rather than 'cultural', and the fact that they act upon that belief, which allows those values and principles to work in practice. It is the *belief* in these expedient absolutes which allows an atmosphere of reason and toler- ance and debate. Second, the notions of culture, cultural differences, cultural determination, and the intellectual foundations of these con- cepts are, for reasons already set out, open to considerable doubt. To make judgements about the validity or likely progress of the rule of law or democracy in the light of these concepts is highly questionable. Third, if ideas and beliefs such as equality of persons, individualism, universal rights, balanced justice, fair play were to be regarded as 'cultural', then what more effective ready-made legitimacy could be supplied to those in authority who might wish to claim that such ideas amount to a kind of imperialism and have no place in their culture, and who might wish to defer to their 'culture' in order to find whatever rationalisation they may like to support that claim.

My contention, then, is that notions of human rights, equality of persons, individualism, the rule of law, and democracy must be treated as expedient absolutes if the reasonable and fair-minded relationships among groups and individuals which those notions are intended to ensure are to be realised in practice. Deferring to culture works against that aim. And to claim that these expedient absolutes are determined by (or, in their turn, determine) culture, while claiming to support, and to sympathise with, notions of human rights, equality of persons, individualism, the rule of law and democracy, is contradictory. Deferring to culture, in practice or intellectually, is an exercise in word-play; it exhibits a willingness to subordinate argument and thought to Chineseness (or to any particular 'culture'), to narrow fashionable and superficial intellectual concerns about the possibility that one may be charged with Eurocentrism. Deferring to culture is an abrogation of reason, fairness, justice and democracy, for the only absolutes which this practice recognises are those of culture, moral relativism and Chineseness – concepts which leave everything open to unrestrained manipulation. Polity, economy, society and every individual are thus made subject to those who are expert in things Chinese, to those with the authority to determine what is, and what is not, Chinese culture.

The criticisms which I direct here against China's images, and against the techniques of their construction, may at times appear rather sharp, and should therefore expect to meet with intense counter-criticism. At best, some might say, my arguments will appear to have been formed around 'western' values and beliefs without any consideration, knowledge or understanding of China and Chinese culture. From the Chinese perspective, some may argue, China's images, its stylised representations, were, and are, real and absolute. To understand the Chinese, we must be sensitive to their cultural assumptions; we must be equipped with both the imagination and the intellectual capacity to put ourselves in the place of the Chinese and to see the world from their point of view. To the Chinese, China *was* the centre of the universe; China *was* more advanced scientifically, technically, intellectually, morally, and in its organizational capabilities, than were other cultures; China *still* possesses the seeds of a new science, a new morality; China *does* represent a new kind of politics, a new world view, a new kind of economics, and a new and better kind of society, though it is still in its inchoate form; China and its culture *are* very different. Unless one accepts this perspective, it is not possible to understand China or the Chinese correctly. There are no images to be manipulated.

To this rigid doctrine there can be no response: the truth has been stated and that's the end of it. The distinction between dream and reality is transformed into an irrelevancy. Image becomes fact; and the only existence we are permitted is the waking-dream of the expert, the cultural intermediary. And though we may think we are able to understand and interpret the world around us by virtue of our knowledge of that culture, it is we ourselves who serve the desires of another.

No doubt, too, I may be accused of slaying dragons, of taking liberties, of self-indulgence and of heresy-hunting. But then any criticism of the terms of reference for analysis is likely to be taken as an attempt to undermine or even to ridicule all that has been constructed around those terms of reference. Perhaps the emphasis which I have placed upon conscious manipulation will also offend theoretical purists who see utilitarian reductionism as an intellectually facile explanation, or as an expression of ethnocentrism. But then such charges, as I have already suggested, are based upon arbitrary rules of 'scientific' analysis which merely replace conscious human decision (regarded by many analysts as something second-rate) with unspecified forces and structures capable of shaping human societies and of determining the actions of individuals. It may also be that many images of China have already begun to fade and crumble. The opening of China, the rise of commerce, and shifts in attitude outside China towards academe, social science and notions of 'culture' will make difficult the survival of stylised representations of China. Yet this attrition is likely to occur only slowly. The Chineseness of China and its people is of enormous political and psychological value to the Chinese state. And there are at least two good reasons why, both inside and outside China, academics, journalists, novelists, travel writers, and film-makers should continue to propagate and defend China's stylised representations: not only do China's images serve as a convenient short-hand in which a numinous atmosphere of profound difference is easily communicated; they are also the symbols, the bearings, of the cultural intermediary's heraldic college. Gernet,[4] with no mention of the work of Mair and others, continues to repeat the canon of China's historical mythography: it is quite clear to all who have been in contact with the Chinese world, he writes, 'that it is quite different from the one in which we ourselves have been moulded and that it remains so today. Its fundamental traditions ... are different from those of the Indian world, of Islam, of the Christian world of the West (in any case, the civilisations whose domains stop short of the fearsome barrier of the Himalayas have had numerous and frequent contacts with each other)'.[5] China does not know the notion of property in the strict sense of the term; she does not like the idea of the absolute, the distinction between mind and matter; she prefers notions action-at-a-distance and the idea of order as an organic totality. But it is Gernet who is able to appreciate these profound differences and to communicate them to all those other civilisations which are defined quite simply by not being Chinese. Two more recent books (one by Waley-Cohen, the other by her mentor Spence[6]) which detail Imperial China's contact with, and knowledge of, the outside world, have been eulogised by Barrett,[7] another doyen of the Chinese world, as yet more evidence of the moral sophistication, moral superiority, and open-mindedness of Chinese society. These noble qualities are highlighted, yet again, by 'the West', and more especially by the British: a rag-bag of muddle-headed, racist, class-ridden, closed-minded, linguistically incompetent, ignorant and often barbarous people; a people whose collective mind, though rife with fatuous stereotypes of China, is mysteriously impregnated with a fascination and readiness for things Chinese. The air is still thick with the pungent, hubristic scent of Needham's High Scholarship and High Morality, and the curious dissatisfaction with anything that is not of the East. So heavy that lingering scent, and so bitter its taste, that Barrett can see in British society today only an ignorance of things Chinese; yet from out of that dark, small-minded and incompetent morass a few points of bright light still shine; and for these few cultural intermediaries we must be truly thankful.

On both intellectual and policy grounds, then, there is a very strong case for questioning many current ideas, beliefs and understandings about the Chinese state. China is now too important for mystification. Either directly or through their influence upon actions, policies and attitudes towards China, these images may reinforce the beliefs that China's leadership and many of their people have about themselves and about the legitimacy of their actions. It is partly for these reasons – both intellectual and practical – that the arguments put forward in this book, and the criticisms levelled here at those who stand in China's image are, I believe, constructive.

But there is another reason why such criticisms should be made: the ways in which we think about China, and our criticisms of those ideas, may reflect, or influence, the way in which we think about our own societies, both past and present. The tensions which faced Imperial China were essentially no different to those which have faced any complex society. Trade at times did flourish and took on far greater significance than would be acknowledged openly. And though it may have been sneered at publicly, if its practice satisfied the tastes or desires of the elite, or if it were thought to hold for them some political or social advantage, then trade would be permitted. But as the practice of trade spread, as the acceptance of its wealth values[8](or sense of worth) widened, as it brought material wealth to all manner of people, so it began to intrude too brashly upon accepted values, social mores and behavioural nuances, and to upset expectations about who should or should not be in a position to obtain material riches. Trade demanded the redirection of existing values, beliefs, institutions and practices, revealed their other dimensions, and threw doubt on the larger social and political visage which they had once comprised. Thus did trade begin to question the means and symbols of social order, power, status and self-worth. Sensitivity and hostility to such changes were only aggravated by external contact which, as many have argued, stimulated trade in the first instance. The transmission of ideas, practices, views, attitudes and goods, invited comparisons and contrast, and provoked questions about the significance and validity of China's images. The response in China was to turn inwards. The maintenance of power and its symbols, the fulfilment of ambition and worth, and the individual's political and social status, were seen to lie ultimately with a deference to culture rather than with trade, profit and secularisation. These same tensions are as true of China today. As the reins are loosened, and as wider values, beliefs, forms of exchange, institutions and patterns of behaviour are redirected towards its practice, trade is being accompanied (as in the past) by a proliferation of markets, merchants associations, and alliances between state and business; by a shift in wealth values; by the swelling ranks of the *parvenu*; by the 'turning' of reciprocity; by the gradual distancing of emotions and relationships from the conduct of professional life within political institutions and economic organisations; by an acceptance of inequality and individual autonomy; and by a questioning, and realignment, of political interests and loyalties. In these ways, as the practice of trade is permitted greater scope, as relationships, attitudes, institutions and beliefs are adjusted to facilitate, or to question, the pursuit of profit and material wealth, trade appears to colour more deeply the lives of every individual; and Chinese society, no less than any other which desires material progress, must come to terms with two sets of choices.

The first set of choices facing government, administrators and people is either to continue with their deference to culture, and to permit the fiat of their exclusive and judgemental conventions of social behaviour, values, attitudes and beliefs to dominate over political and professional life; or to accept that institutions, procedures, values, beliefs and patterns of behaviour should be treated *as if* absolute. These 'expedient absolutes', and such benefits or obligations as they may confer, if held to be universal and to apply equally to all individuals, are, for this reason, less vulnerable to manipulation and personal ambition, more open to critical debate and to considered change, and thus bring greater predictability and stability to human affairs.

The second set of choices concerns the extent to which society is perceived as an aggregate whole; and thus the extent to which individuals as members of that 'whole' may be coerced and directed with fierce prejudice, and may have imposed upon them such policies and criteria of excellence and perfection of governance, administration and morality as its leaders may see fit by virtue of their self-proclaimed insight, understanding, vision, and good intentions, and by virtue of their position as representatives of that 'oneness'. Set against this is the view of society as a loose collection of individuals for whom government and administration acts to weigh and balance the interests of individuals, groups, minorities and majorities, and to protect individuals from the overbearing sanctity of the mass. In this conception of society, policies are shaped less by the 'visions' or 'plans' of governments and by their attempts to engineer what they believe should be, than by individuals as they pursue interests, desires, fulfilment, and a sense of worth, each according to their own values and beliefs; by the practical and psychological need for expedient absolutes; and by common humanitarianism. Society, then, is not thought of as a 'whole' which may be understood by reference to theoretical and conceptual allegories, and which should therefore be engineered and shaped by the seer. Rather, the purpose of governance and administration is understood to be the management of expedient absolutes and their evolution as the beliefs, interests, and values of individuals, and their sense of self-worth and fulfilment, change or appear to change in meaning as the wider context alters; and to manage that evolution without centralising power and authority to the extent that the concept of the 'whole' is made incarnate.

And so, as government and individuals in China come to terms with these choices, as they decide how far they will look to image, rather than to substance, and how far they will treat institutions and personal relationships more as if absolutes than as material for their own personal advantage, we are seeing replayed tensions that we find also in our own societies. We might bear it in mind, then, that our assessments and judgements about the choices made in China and, most especially, our acceptance and elaboration of China's images, may tell us as much about ourselves and the changing fashions and problems in our own societies as they do about China.

Notes

Introduction

1 I use Chinese terms as little as possible, but some are widely used in English-language literature. Readers will find that I have used different forms of transliteration for these terms, and also for Chinese names, though for each term, or name, I use the same form of transliteration throughout.

Chapter 1   China and the Western Heartland

1 Naveh, J. (1982) *Early History of the Alphabet: an introduction to the West Semitic epigraphy and palaeography*, Magnes Press, Jerusalem; E.J. Brill, Leiden.
2 Allchin, B. and Allchin, R. (1982) *The Rise of Civilization in India and Pakistan*, Cambridge University Press, Cambridge; Possehl, G.L. (1979) *Ancient Cities of the Indus*, New Dehli; Possehl, G.L. (ed.) (1982) *Harappan Civilization: a contemporary perspective*, American Institute of Indian Studies.
3 Allchin and Allchin, *The Rise*.
4 Marshall, Sir J. (1931) *Mohenjo-daro and the Indus Civilization*, 3 volumes, London; Vats, M.S. (1941) *Excavations at Harappa*, 2 volumes, Dehli; Parpola, S. (1973) *Materials for the Study of the Indus Script*, Helsinki.
5 Littauer, M.A. and Crouwel, J.H. (1979) *Wheeled Vehicles and Ridden Animals in the Ancient Near East*, Handbuch der Orientalisk, ed. B. Spuler, vii.2.b.1, Leiden.
6 Boyce, M. (1987) 'Priests, cattle and men', in *Bulletin of the School of Oriental and African Studies*, 50, pp. 508–26.
7 Fitzgerald, C.P. (1966) *A Concise History of East Asia*, Pelican, London.
8 Cable, M. (1934) 'The bazaars of Tangut and the trade–routes of Dzungaria', *Geographical Journal*, 84, pp. 17–32.
9 Ibid., p. 24.
10 Ibid., p. 24.
11 Ibid., p. 29.
12 It is also here, on the Oxus, that a fine example of a Greek gymnasium, dating from around the second or third centuries BC is to be found. Veuve, S. (1987) *Fouilles d'Aï Khanoum.VI. Le gymnase: architecture, céramique, sculpture*, Diffusion De Boccard, Paris.
13 See: Robinson, K. (1980) *A Critical Study of Chu Tsai-yü's Contribution to the Theory of Equal Temperament in Chinese Music*, Franz Steiner Verlag, Weisbaden.
14 Aizawa, M., Natori, T., Wakisaka, A. and Konoeda, Y. (eds) (1986) *Proceedings of the Third Asia and Oceania Histocompatibility Workshop Conference*, Sapporo; Tsuji, K., Aizawa, M. and Sasazuki, T. (eds) (1992) *HLA 1991: proceedings of the eleventh international histocompatibility workshop and conference*, Oxford. Cited in Dudbridge, G. (1996) *China's Vernacular Cultures*, Clarendon Press, Oxford.

15 Eberhard, W. (1957) 'The formation of Chinese civilization according to socio-anthropological analysis', *Sociology*, 7, pp. 97–112; (1950) *A History of China*, Routledge and Kegan Paul, London.

16 Sjoberg, G. (1960) *The Pre-Industrial City*, Collier-Macmillan, London, p. 45.

17 *Cf.* Reid, A. (ed.) (1996) *Sojourners and Settlers: histories of Southeast Asia and the Chinese*, Allen and Unwin, St Leonards.

18 Goitein, S.D. (1967) *A Mediterranean Society* (5 volumes), London.

19 Tregear, M. (1995) *Chinese Art*, Thames and Hudson, London.

20 Ibid.

21 Cook, C. (1997) 'Wealth and the Western Zhou', *Bulletin of the School of Oriental and African Studies*, 60, pp. 253–94; Chang, K.C. (1983) *Art, Myth, and Ritual: the path to political authority in ancient China*, Harvard University Press, Cambridge, Mass.

22 Gombrich, E.H. (1991) *The Story of Art*, Phaidon Press, Oxford (15th edn), p. 112.

23 Ch'en, K. (1964) *Buddhism in China: a historical survey*, Princeton University Press, Princeton.

24 Weinstein, S. (1987) *Buddhism Under the T'ang*, Cambridge University Press, Cambridge.

25 Wechsler, H.J. (1985) *Offerings of Jade and Silk*, Yale University Press, New Haven and London.

26 Meskill, J. (1982) *Academies in Ming China: a historical essay*, the Association for Asian Studies, University of Arizona Press, Tucson.

27 Tregear, *Chinese Art*.

28 Meskill, *Academies in Ming China*.

29 Reardon-Anderson, J. (1991) *The Study of Change: chemistry in China, 1940–1949*, Cambridge University Press, Cambridge.

30 Cook, 'Wealth and Western Zhou'; Kryukov, V. (1995) 'Symbols of power and communication in pre-Confucian China (on the anthropology of the *de*): preliminary assumptions', *Bulletin of the School of Oriental and African Studies*, 58, pp. 314–33.

31 Allan, S. (1981) 'Sons of suns: myth and totemism in early China', *Bulletin of the School of Oriental and African Studies*, 44, pp. 290–326.

32 Franke, W. (1972) *The Reform and Abolition of the Traditional Chinese Examination System*, Harvard East Asian Monographs, 10, Harvard University Press, Cambridge, Mass.

33 Qian wen-yuan (1985) *The Great Inertia: scientific stagnation in traditional China*, Croom Helm, London.

34 Cullen, C. (1990) 'The science/technology interface in seventeenth-century China: Song Yingxing on *qi* and the *wu xing*', in *Bulletin of the School of Oriental and African Studies*, 53, pp. 295–318; p. 297.

35 *Shi Ji (Records of a Historian)*, translated in Needham, J. (1959) *Science and Civilization in China*, volume 3, Cambridge University Press, Cambridge, p. 625. Cited in Qian, *The Great Inertia*, p. 75.

36 Lones, T.E. (1912) *Aristotle's Researches in Natural Science*, London.

37 See note 35.

38 Ho Peng Yoke (1991) 'Chinese science: the traditional Chinese view', *Bulletin of the School of Oriental and African Studies*, 54, pp. 506–19.

39 Cullen, 'The science/technology interface', p. 315.

40   Gernet, J. (1985) 'Introduction', in Schram, S.R. (ed.) *The Scope of State Power in China*, School of Oriental and African Studies, and the Chinese University of Hong Kong, Hong Kong, pp. xxvii–xxxiv, p. xxxiii.

41   Needham, J. (1979) *The Grand Titration*, Allen and Unwin, London, p. 201. Hereafter cited in the text as 'GT'.

42   For a discussion on the authenticity of Polo's travels and of the account of his travels, see Jackson, P. (1998) 'Marco Polo and his "travels"', *Bulletin of the School of Oriental and African Studies*, 61, pp. 82–101.

43   Fisher, C.A. (1970) 'Containing China? Part One: the antecedents of containment', *The Geographical Journal*, 136, pp. 534–56; p. 546.

44   Ibid., p. 547.

45   Ibid., p. 548.

46   Witek, J.W. (1982) *Controversial Ideas in China and in Europe: a biography of Jean-François Foucquet, S.J., 1665–1741*, Bibliotheca Instituti Historici S.I., vol. 43, Institutum Historicum S.I., Rome.

47   Fisher, 'Containing China?', pp. 548–9.

48   Fitzgerald, *Concise History of East Asia*, pp. 112–13.

49   Full text cited in Whyte, Sir F. (1927) *China and Foreign Powers*, Oxford University Press, Oxford. Extract cited in Toynbee, A. (1949) *Civilization on Trial*, Oxford University Press, Oxford. For a slightly different translation of part of this text, see: Fisher, 'Containing China?', p. 549.

50   Cranmer-Byng, J.L. (ed.) (1962) *An Embassy to China – Lord Macartney's Journal*, London, cited in Fisher, 'Containing China?', p. 550.

51   Fisher, 'Containing China?'. See also Rabe, V.H. (1978) *The Home Base of the American China Mission, 1880–1920*, London, Harvard University Press.

52   Fisher, 'Containing China?', p. 554.

53   Wittfogel , K., *Oriental Despotism*, London.

54   Fitzgerald, *Concise History of East Asia*, p. 35. See also Gernet, J. (1997) *A History of Chinese Civilization*, Cambridge University Press, Cambridge, pp. 32–3.

55   Ibid., pp. 56–7 and p. 82.

56   Needham, J. (1962) *Science and Civilization in China*, vol. 4, Cambridge University Press, Cambridge, p. 1. Hereafter cited in the text as 'SCC' with volume number.

57   Qian, *The Great Inertia*, p. 27.

58   Ronan, C.A. and Needham, J. (1981) *The Shorter Science and Civilization in China*, vol. 2, Cambridge University Press, Cambridge, p. 17.

59   Ibid., p. 87.

60   Ronan and Needham, *The Shorter Science*, pp. 85–7.

61   Mukerji, Radhakamund (1912) *Indian Shipping: a history of the sea-borne trade and maritime activity of the Indians from the earliest times*, Longmans Green, Bombay and Calcutta.

62   Elvin, M. (1972) 'The high-level equilibrium trap: the causes of the decline of invention in the traditional Chinese textile industries', in Willmott, W.E. (ed.) *Economic Organisation in Chinese Society*, SMC Publishing, Taipei, pp. 137–72 (hereafter cited in the text as 'HET'); Elvin, M. (1973) *Patterns of the Chinese Past*, London.

63   Bullock, A. (1955) *Men, Chance and History*, The Essex Hall Lecture, 1955, Lindsey Press, London , pp. 20–1.

64 Crombie, A.C. (1959) 'The significance of medieval discussions of scientific method for the scientific revolution', in Marshall Clagett (ed.) *Critical problems in the History of Science*, Madison Wisconsin, p. 79; de Solla Price, D.J. (1961) *Science Since Babylon*, New Haven, Conn.; Gillispie, C.C. (1960) *The Edge of Objectivity: an essay in the history of scientific ideas*, Princeton University Press, Princeton; Toynbee, A.J. (1935–9) *A Study of History*, 6 vols, London; Watts, A. (1958) *Nature, Man and Woman*, London; Northrop, F.S.C. (1946) *The Meeting of East and West: an enqiry concerning human understanding*, New York.

Chapter 2   Deferring to Culture

1 Watson, J.L. (1993) 'Rites or beliefs? The construction of a unified culture in late imperial China', in Dittmer, L. and Kim, S.S. (eds) *China's Quest for National Unity*, Cornell University Press, Ithaca, pp. 80–103; hereafter cited in the text as 'Rites'.
2 Ibid. See also: Schwartz, B.I. (1985) *The World of Thought in Ancient China*, Harvard University Press, Cambridge, Mass.
3 Needham, J. (1956) *Science and Civilization in China*, vol. 2, Cambridge University Press, Cambridge, Mass., p. 281.
4 Northrop, F.S.C. (1946) 'The contemplatory emphases of eastern intuitive and western scientific philosophy', in C.A. Moore (ed.) *Philosophy – East and West*, Princeton University Press, Princeton, pp. 168–234.
5 Lau, S.K. (1978) 'From traditional familism to utilitarianist familism: the metamorphosis of familial ethos among the Hong Kong Chinese', *Occasional Paper, No. 78*, Social Research Centre, Chinese University of Hong Kong; (1982) *Society and Politics in Hong Kong*, Chinese University of Hong Kong, Hong Kong.
6 Yang, M.M.H. (1989) 'The gift economy and state power in China', *Comparative Studies in Society and History*, 31, p. 25–54; Redding, S.G. (1980) 'Cognition as an aspect of culture and its relation to management processes: an exploratory view of the Chinese case', *The Journal of Management Studies*, 17, pp. 127–48; Mackie, J.A.C. (1992) 'Overseas Chinese entrepreneurship', *Asian-Pacific Economic Literature*, 6, pp. 41–64; Myers, R. (1989) 'Confucianism and economic development in mainland China, Hong Kong and Taiwan', in Chung-hua Institute for Economic Research, Taipei, Conference Series 13.
7 Wilson, R.W. (1993) 'Change and continuity in Chinese cultural identity: the filial ideal and the transformation of an ethic', in Dittmer, L. and Kim, S.S. (eds) *China's Quest for National Identity*, Cornell University Press, Ithaca, pp. 104–24; hereafter cited in the text as 'Change'.
8 Unger, R.M. (1976) *Law in Modern Society: toward a criticism of social theory*, Free Press, New York; Lyons, D. (1984) *Ethics and the Rule of Law*, Cambridge University Press, Cambridge.
9 'Change', pp. 114–15. See also: Nathan, A.J. (1986) 'Sources of Chinese rights thinking', in Edwards, R.R., Henkin, L. and Nathan, A.J. *Human Rights in Contemporary China*, Columbia University Press, New York.
10 Schram, S.R. (1985) 'Decentralisation in a unitary state: theory and practice, 1940–1984', in Schram, S.R. (ed.) *The Scope of State Power in China*, School of

Oriental and African Studies and Chinese University of Hong Kong, Hong Kong, pp. 81–126: p. 83; hereafter cited in the text as 'Decentralisation'.

11 Schurmann, F. (1966) *Ideology and Organisation in Communist China*, University of California Press, Berkeley; Harding, H. (1981) *Organising China: the problem of bureaucracy, 1949–1976*, Stanford University Press, Stanford.

12 'Decentralisation', p. 122; Schram, S.R. (1984) *Ideology and Policy in China Since the Third Plenum, 1978–1984*, Contemporary China Institute, School of Oriental and African Studies, London.

13 Cited in Kent, A. (1993) *Between Freedom and Subsistence: China and human rights*, Oxford University Press, Hong Kong, p. 51.

14 Meissner, W. (1990) *Philosophy and Politics in China*, trans. R. Mann, Stanford University Press, Stanford.

15 Pye, L. (1972) *China: an introduction*, Little, Brown and Company, Boston.

16 Ibid.

Chapter 3   Reciprocity and Factions

1 Solinger, D.J. (1984) *Chinese Business Under Socialism: the politics of domestic commerce in contemporary China'*, University of California Press, London, pp. 30–1; hereafter cited in the text as 'CBS'.

2 Such as: Chang, Parris (1975) *Power and Policy in China*, Pennsylvania State University Press, University Park; Schurmann, F. (1966) *Ideology and Organisation in Communist China*, University of California Press, Berkeley; Lowenthal, R. (1970) 'Development vs Utopia in communist policy', in Johnson, C. (ed.) *Change in Communist Systems*, Stanford University Press, Stamnford, pp. 33–116.

3 Perkins, D.H. (1966) *Market Control and Planning in Communist China*, Harvard University Press, Cambridge, Mass.; Bernstein, T.P. (1969) 'Cadre and peasant behaviour under conditions of insecurity and deprivation', in Barnett, A.D. (ed.) *Chinese Communist Politics in Action*, University of Washington Press, Seattle, pp. 365–99; Shue, V. (1976) 'Reorganising rural trade: unified purchase and socialist transformation', *Modern China*, 2, pp. 104–34.

4 Pye, L. (1995) 'Factions and the politics of *guanxi*: paradoxes in Chinese administrative behaviour', *The China Journal*, 34, pp. 35–54: p. 40; hereafter cited in the text as 'Factions'.

5 Dewey, A. (1962) *Peasant Marketing in Java*, Free Press, Glencoe, Ill.

6 Such as those advocated by: Krugman, P. (1991) *Geography and Trade*, MIT Press, Cambridge, Mass.; and, Pearce, D. (1989) *The MIT Dictionary of Modern Economics*, MIT Press, Cambridge, Mass.

7 Cf. Wang Gungwu (1995) *The Chinese Way: China's position in international relations*, Norwegian Nobel Institute Lecture Series, Scandinavian University Press, Oslo; (1993) 'Greater China and the Overseas Chinese', *The China Quarterly*, 136, pp. 926–48. But see also Chapter 4 and Hodder, R. (1996) *Merchant Princes of the East: cultural delusions, economic success and the Overseas Chinese in Southeast Asia*, John Wiley and Sons, Chichester, for a critique on Wang's view on the signifiance of Chinese culture in understanding China's economy and polity.

8 Hodder, *Merchant Princes*.

9 Hodder, R. (1993) *The Creation of Wealth in China: domestic trade and material progress in a communist state*, Belhaven/John Wiley and Sons, London.

10   Nathan, A.J. (1973) 'A factionalism model for CCP politics', *The China Quarterly*, 53, pp. 33–66.

11   Nathan, A.J., and Tsai, K.S. (1995) 'Factionalism: a new institutionalist restatement', *The China Journal*, 34, pp. 157–92, p. 157; hereafter cited in the text as 'Factionalism'.

12   The model has found general acceptance, write Nathan and Tsai, and has served as the core for a wide range of research. This research includes works such as: Tang Tsou (1976) 'Prolegomenon to the study of informal groups in CCP politics', *The China Quarterly*, 65, pp. 98–114.; Jacobs, B. (1979) 'A preliminary model of particularistic ties in Chinese political alliances: *kan-ch'ing* and *kuan-hsi* in a rural Taiwanese township', *The China Quarterly*, 78, pp. 236–73; Oi, J. (1985) 'Communism and clientelism: rural politics', *World Politics*, 37, pp. 238–66; Tang Tsou (1986) *The Cultural Revolution and Postmao Reform: a historical perspective*, University of Chicago Press, Chicago; Walder, A. (1986) *Communist Neo-Traditionalism, Work, and Authority in Chinese Industry*, University of California Press, Berkeley; Oi, J. (1986) *State and Peasant in Contemporary China: the political economy of village government*, University of California Press, Berkeley; Bosco, J. (1992) 'Taiwan factions: *guanxi*, patronage and the state in local politics', *Ethnology*, 31, pp. 157–83.

13   Berger, P. and Luckmann, T. (1966) *The Social Construction of Reality*, Doubleday, New York.

14   Dittmer, L. (1995a) 'Chinese informal politics', *The China Journal*, 34, pp. 1–34; hereafter cited in the text as 'Informal Politics'.

15   Nathan, 'A factionalism model'.

16   Dittmer, L. (1995b) 'Informal politics reconsidered', *The China Journal*, 34, pp. 193–205, p. 198.

17   Ibid., p. 199.

18   Smart, A. (1993) 'Gifts, bribes and *guanxi*: a reconsideration of Bourdieu's social capital', *Cultural Anthropology*, 8, pp. 388–408. For a critique of Smart's views, see Hodder, *Merchant Princes*.

19   Yang, M.M.H. (1989) 'The gift economy and state power in China', *Comparative Studies in Society and History*, 31, pp. 25–54; Yang, M.M.H. (1994) *Gifts, Favours and Banquets: the art of social relationships in China*, Cornell University Press, Ithaca; Smart, 'Gifts'; Solinger, *Chinese Business Under Socialism*; Solinger, D.J. (1992) 'Urban entrepreneurs and the state: the merger of state and society', in Rosenbaum, A.L. (ed.) *State and Society in China: the consequences of reform*, Westview Press, Boulder, Colo., pp. 121–42; Lau, S.K. (1978) 'From traditional familism to utilitarianistic familism: the metamorphosis of familial ethos among the Hong Kong Chinese', *Occasional Paper No. 78*, Social Research Centre, Chinese University of Hong Kong; Lau, S.K. (1982) *Society and Politics in Hong Kong*, Chinese University of Hong Kong, Hong Kong; Jacobs, 'A preliminary model'; Jacobs, B. (1980) *Local Politics in a Rural Chinese Cultural Setting: a field study of Mazu Township, Taiwan*, Australian National University, Canberra; Jacobs, B. (1982) 'The concept of *guanxi* and local politics in a rural Chinese cultural setting', in Greenblatt, S.L., Wilson, R.W. and Wilson, A.A. (eds) *Social Interaction in Chinese Society*, Praeger, New York, pp. 209–36. For a critique of the views of Yang, Smart, Jacobs, Lau, and other writers on this question of the 'Chineseness' of social relationships, see Hodder, *Merchant Princes*.

20 Skinner, G.W. (1971) 'Chinese peasants and the closed community: an open and shut case', *Comparative Studies in Society and History*, 13, pp. 270–81; Skinner, G.W. and Winckler, E.A. (1969) 'Compliance succession in Rural Communist China: a cyclical theory', in Etzioni, A. (ed.) *A Sociological Reader on Complex Organisation*, Holt, Rinehart and Winston, New York (2nd edn), pp. 410–38; Solinger, *Chinese Business Under Socialism*.

Chapter 4   Masters of Image

1   Wang Gungwu (1995) *The Chinese Way: China's position in international relations*, Norwegian Nobel Institute Lecture Series, Scandinavian University Press, Oslo; hereafter cited in the text as 'CW'.
2   Wang Gungwu (1993) 'Greater China and the Overseas Chinese', *The China Quarterly*, 136, pp. 926–948.
3   Ibid., p. 926.
4   Ibid., p. 927.
5   Wang Gungwu (1988) 'The study of Chinese identities in Southeast Asia', in Cushman, J. and Wang Gungwu (eds) *Changing Identities of the Southeast Asia Chinese Since World War II*, Hong Kong University, Hong Kong, pp. 1–21; Wang Guangwu, 'Greater China'; Wang Gungwu (1991) *China and the Chinese Overseas*, Times Academic Press, Singapore; Wang Gungwu (1981) *Community and Nations: essays on Southeast Asia and the Chinese*, Heinemann for Asia Studies Association of Australia, Singapore; Wang Gungwu (1958) 'The nanhai trade: a study of the early history of Chinese trade in the South China Sea', *Journal of the Malayan Branch of the Royal Asiatic Society*, 31 (2), Kuala Lumpur. For a critique of Wang's views on the relationship between 'Chineseness' and economic success, see: Hodder, R. (1996) *Merchant Princes of the East: cultural delusions, economic success and the Overseas Chinese in Southeast Asia*, John Wiley and Sons, Chichester.
6   See for instance: Yahuda, M. (1993) 'The foreign relations of Greater China', *The China Quarterly*, 136, pp. 687–710; Sung, Yun-wing (1992) 'Non-institutional economic integration via cultural affinity: the case of mainland China, Taiwan and Hong Kong', *Occasional Paper No.13*, Hong Kong Institute of Asia-Pacific Studies, Chinese University of Hong Kong; Weidenbaum, M. (1992) 'The changing pattern of the world economy – the shifting role of business and government', *Wei Lun Lecture Series IV*, Chinese University Bulletin, Supplement 28, pp. 20–9; Kotkin, J. (1993) *Tribes: how race, religion and identity determine success in the new global economy*, Random House, New York.
7   CW, p. 71. Cf. Yanhuda, M. (1997) 'How much has China learned about interdependence?', in Goodman, D.S.G. and Segal, G. (eds) *China Rising: nationalism and interdependence*, Routledge, London, pp. 6–26 .
8   Harris, S. (1997) 'China's role in the WTO and APEC', in ibid., pp. 134–55, p. 152.
9   Hitler, A. (1982) *Mein Kampf*, trans. R. Manheim, intro. by D.C. Watt, Hutchinson, London.
10 Hsu, Francis, L.K. (1982) Foreword to David Y.H. Wu's *The Chinese in Papua New Guinea: 1880–1980*, Chinese University of Hong Kong, Hong Kong, pp. xi–xvi: pp. xv–xvi, my italics.

11 Dikotter, F. (ed.) (1997) *The Construction of Racial Identities in China and Japan: historical and contemporary perspectives*, Hurst and Co., London, p. 18.
12 See for instance, Stafford, C. (1993) 'The discourse of race in modern China', *Man*, 28, p. 609.
13 Dikotter, F. (1997), *op. cit.*
14 Ibid., p. 3.
15 Thompson, L.A. (1989) *Romans and Blacks*, Routledge, London.
16 Unger, J. (ed.) (1993) *Using the Past to Serve the Present*, M.E. Sharpe, New York, p. 1.
17 Sullivan, L.R. (1993) 'The controversy over "Feudal Despotism"', in Unger, ibid., pp. 174–204, p. 193.
18 Unger, *Using the Past*, p. 2.
19 Ibid., pp. 3–4.
20 Sullivan, 'The Controversy', p. 202.
21 Ibid.

Conclusions

1 Shambaugh, D. (ed.) (1993) *American Studies of Contemporary China*, Woodrow Wilson Center Press, M.E. Sharpe, New York.
2 Segal, G. (1999) 'Does China matter?', *Foreign Affairs*, Sept./Oct., pp. 24–36, and his earlier statements (1997) in 'Enlightening China?', in D.S.G. Goodman and G. Segal (eds), *China Rising: nationalism and interdependence*, Routledge, London, pp. 172–91.
3 Hodder, R. (1993) *Merchant Princes of the East: cultural delusions, economic success and the Overseas Chinese in Southeast Asia*, John Wiley and Sons, Chichester.
4 Gernet, J. (1997) *A History of Chinese Civilization*, Cambridge University Press, Cambridge.
5 Ibid., pp. 31–2.
6 Waley-Cohen, J. (1999) *The Sextants of Beijing: global currents in Chinese history*, W.W. Norton, New York; Spence, J. (1999) *The Great Chan's Continent: China in Western minds*, Allen Lane, London.
7 Barrett, T.H. (1999) 'Under eastern eyes', *The Independent, Weekend Review*, May 15, p. 12.
8 Hodder, R. (1993) *The Creation of Wealth in China: domestic trade and material progress in a communist state*, Belhaven/John Wiley, London.

Bibliography

Aizawa, M., Natori, T., Wakisaka, A. and Konoeda, Y. (eds), *Proceedings of the Third Asia and Oceania Histocompatibility Workshop Conference* (Sapporo: Hokkaido University Press, 1986).

Allan, S. 'Sons of suns: myth and totemism in early China', *Bulletin of the School of Oriental and African Studies*, 44, 1981, 290–326.

Allchin, B. and Allchin, R. *The Rise of Civilization in India and Pakistan* (Cambridge: Cambridge University Press, 1982).

Barber, E.W. *The Mummies of Urumchi* (London: Macmillan, 1999).

Barnett, A.D. (ed.) *Chinese Communist Politics in Action* (Seattle: University of Washington Press, 1969).

Barrett, T.H. 'Under eastern eyes', *The Independent, Weekend Review*, 15 May 1999.

Berger, P. and Luckmann, T. *The Social Construction of Reality* (New York: Doubleday, 1966).

Bernstein, T.P. 'Cadre and peasant behaviour under conditions of insecurity and deprivation', in Barnett (ed.), 1969, 365–99.

Bosco, J. 'Taiwan factions: guanxi, patronage and the state in local politics', *Ethnology*, 31, 1992, 157–83.

Boyce, M. 'Priests, cattle and men', *Bulletin of the School of Oriental and African Studies*, 1987, 1, 508–26.

Braginsky, V.I. 'Rediscovering the "oriental" in the Orient and Europe', *Bulletin of the School of Oriental and African Studies*, 60, 1997, 511–32.

Bullock, A. *Men, Chance and History*, The Essex Hall Lecture (London: Lindsey Press, 1955).

Chang, K.C. *Art, Myth and Ritual: the path to political authority in ancient China* (Cambridge, Mass: Harvard University Press, 1983).

Chang, Parris. *Power and Policy in China* (Philadelphia: Pennsylvania State University Press, 1975).

Ch'en, K. *Buddhism in China: a historical survey* (Princeton: Princeton University Press, 1964).

Clagett, M. (ed.) *Critical Problems in the History of Science* (Madison: University of Wisconsin Press, 1959).

Cook, C. 'Wealth and the Western Zhou', *Bulletin of the School of Oriental and African Studies*, 60, 1997, 253–94.

Cranmer-Byng, J.L. (ed.) *An Embassy to China – Lord Macartney's Journal* (London: Longmans, 1962).

Crombie, A.C. 'The significance of medieval discussions of scientific method for the scientific revolution' in Clagett (ed.), 1959.

Cullen, C. 'The science/technology interface in seventeenth-century China: Song Yingxing on *qi* and the *wu xing*', *Bulletin of the School of Oriental and African Studies*, 53, 1990, 295–318.

Cushman, J. and Wang Gungwu (eds) *Changing Identities of the Southeast Asia Chinese Since World War II* (Hong Kong: Hong Kong University Press, 1988).

Dewey, A. *Peasant Marketing in Java* (Glencoe, Ill.: Free Press, 1962).

Dikotter, F. *The Discourse of Race in Modern China* (London: Hurst, 1992).

Dikotter, F. (ed.) *The Construction of Racial Identities in China and Japan: historical and contemporary perspectives* (London: Hurst, 1997).

Dittmer, L. 'Chinese informal politics', *The China Journal*, 34, 1995, 1–34.

Dittmer, L. 'Informal politics reconsidered', *The China Journal*, 34, 1995, 193–205.

Dittmer, L. and Kim, S.S. (eds) *China's Quest for National Unity* (Ithaca: Cornell University Press, 1993).

Dudbridge, G. *China's Vernacular Cultures* (Oxford: Clarendon, 1996).

Eberhard, W. 'The formation of Chinese civilization according to socio-anthropological analysis', *Sociology*, 7, 1957, 97–112.

Eberhard, W. *A History of China* (London: Routledge, 1950).

Edwards, R.R., Henkin, L. and Nathan, A.J. *Human Rights in Contemporary China* (New York: Columbia University Press, 1986).

Elvin, M. 'The high-level equilibrium trap: the causes of the decline of invention in the traditional Chinese textile industries', in Willmott (ed.), 1972, 137–72.

Elvin, M. *Patterns of the Chinese Past* (London: Methuen, 1973).

Etzioni, A. (ed.) *A Sociological Reader on Complex Organization* (New York: Holt, Rinehart and Winston, 1969).

Fisher, C.A. 'Containing China? Part One; the antecedents of containment', *The Geographical Journal*, 136, 1970, 534–56.

Fitzgerald, C.P. *A Concise History of East Asia* (Harmondsworth: Pelican, 1966).

Franke, W. *The Reform and Abolition of the Traditional Chinese Examination System* (Cambridge, Mass.: Harvard University Press, 1972).

Gernet, J. 'Introduction', in Schram (ed.), 1985, xxvii–xxxiv.

Gillispie, C.C. *The Edge of Objectivity: an essay on the history of scientific ideas* (Princeton: Princeton University Press, 1960).

Goitein, S.D. *A Mediterranean Society*, 5 volumes (Cambridge: Cambridge University Press, 1967).

Gombrich, E.H. *The Story of Art* (Oxford: Phaidon, 1991, 15th edn).

Goodman, D.S.G. and Segal, G. (eds) *China Rising: Nationalism and Interdependence* (London: Routledge, 1997).

Greenblatt, S.L., Wilson, R.W., and Wilson, A.A. (eds) *Social Interaction in Chinese Society* (New York: Praeger, 1982).

Harding, H. *Organizing China: the problem of bureaucracy, 1949–1976* (Stanford: Stanford University Press, 1981).

Harris, S. 'China's role in the WTO and APEC', in Goodman and Segal (eds), 1997, 134–55.

Ho Peng Yoke, 'Chinese science: the traditional Chinese view', *Bulletin of the School of Oriental and African Studies*, 54, 1991, 506–19.

Hodder, R.N.W. *The Creation of Wealth in China: domestic trade and material progress in a communist state* (London: Belhaven/Wiley, 1993).

Hodder, R.N.W. 'China and the world: perception and analysis', *The Pacific Review*, 12, 1999, 61–77.

Hodder, R.N.W. *Merchant Princes of the East: cultural delusions, economic success and the Overseas Chinese in Southeast Asia* (Chichester: Wiley, 1996).

Hsu, F.L.K. Foreword to David Y.H.Wu's *The Chinese in Papua New Guinea: 1880–1980*, Hong Kong, 1982, xi–xvi.

Jackson, P. 'Marco Polo and his "travels"', *Bulletin of the School of Oriental and African Studies*, 61, 1998, 82–101.

Jacobs, B. 'A preliminary model of particularistic ties in Chinese political alliances: *kan-ch'ing* and *kuan-hsi* in a rural Taiwanese township', *The China Quarterly*, 78, 1979, 236–73.

Jacobs, B. *Local Politics in a Rural Chinese Cultural Setting: a field study of Mazu Township, Taiwan* (Canberra: Australian National University, 1980).

Jacobs, B. 'The concept of *guanxi* and local politics in a rural Chinese cultural setting', in Greenblatt et al. (eds), 1982, 209–36.

Johnson, C. (ed.) *Change in Communist Systems* (Stanford: Stanford University Press, 1970).

Kent, A. *Between Freedom and Subsistence: China and Human Rights* (Hong Kong: Oxford University Press, 1993).

Kotkin, J. *Tribes: How Race, Religion and Identity Determine Success in the New Global Economy* (New York: Random House, 1993).

Krugman, P. *Geography and Trade* (Cambridge, Mass.: MIT Press, 1991).

Kryukov, V. 'Symbols of power and communication in pre-Confucian China (on the anthropology of the *de*): preliminary assumptions', *Bulletin of the School of Oriental and African Studies*, 58, 1995, 314–33.

Lau, S.K. 'From traditional familism to utilitarianistic familism: the metamorphosis of familial ethos among the Hong Kong Chinese', *Occasional Paper, No. 78*, Social Research Centre, The Chinese University of Hong Kong, 1978.

Lau, S.K. *Society and Politics in Hong Kong* (Hong Kong: Chinese University Press, 1982).

Littauer, M.A. and Crouwel, J.H. *Wheeled Vehicles and Ridden Animals in the Ancient Near East*, (1979) in Spuler, vii.1.2.b.1.

Lones, T.E. *Aristotle's Researches in Natural Science* (London: West, Newman & Co., 1912).

Lowenthal, R. 'Development vs Utopia in communist policy', in Johnson, 1970, 33–116.

Lyons, D. *Ethics and the Rule of Law* (Cambridge: Cambridge University Press, 1984).

Mackie, J.A.C. 'Overseas Chinese entrepreneurship', *Asian-Pacific Economic Literature*, 6, 1992, 41–64.

Mair, V.H. 'Mummies of the Tarim Basin', *Archaeology*, 48, 1995, 28–35.

Marshall, Sir John. *Mohenjo-daro and the Indus Civilization*, 3 volumes (London: A. Probsthair, 1931).

Meissner, W. *Philosophy and Politics in China*, trans. R. Mann (Stanford: Stanford University Press, 1990).

Meskill, J. *Academies in Ming China: a historical essay* (Tucson: University of Arizona Press, 1982).

Moore, C.A. (ed.) *Philosophy – East and West* (Princeton: Princeton University Press, 1946).

Mukerji, Radhakamund. *Indian Shipping: a history of the sea-borne trade and maritime activity of the Indians from the earliest times* (Bombay: Longmans Green, 1912).

Myers, R. 'Confucianism and economic development in mainland China, Hong Kong and Taiwan', Chung-hua Institute for Economic Research, Taipei, Conference Series 13, 1989.

Nathan, A.J. 'A factionalism model for CCP politics', *The China Quarterly*, 53, 33–66, 1973.

Nathan, A.J. 'Sources of Chinese rights thinking', in Edwards, Henkin and Nathan, 1986.

Nathan, A.J. and Tsai, K.S. 'Factionalism: a new institutionalist restatement', *The China Journal*, 34, 1995, 157–92.

Naveh, J. *Early History of the Alphabet: an Introduction to the West Semitic Epigraphy and Palaeography* (Leiden: Brill, 1982).

Needham, J. *Science and Civilization in China*, 5 volumes (Cambridge: Cambridge University Press, 1956–79).

Needham, J. *The Grand Titration* (London: Allen and Unwin, 1979).

Northrop, F.S.C. *The Meeting of East and West: an enquiry concerning human understanding* (New York: Macmillan, 1946).

Northrop, F.S.C. 'The contemplatory emphases of eastern intuitive and western scientific philosophy', in Moore, 1946, 168–234.

Oi, J. 'Communism and clientelism: rural politics', *World Politics*, 37, 1985, 238–66.

Oi, J. *State and Peasant in Contemporary China: the political economy of village government* (Berkeley: University of California Press, 1986).

Parpola, S. *Materials for the Study of the Indus Script* (Helsinki: 1973).

Pearce, D. *The MIT Dictionary of Modern Economics* (Cambridge, Mass.: MIT Press, 1989).

Perkins, D.H. *Market Control and Planning in Communist China* (Cambridge, Mass.: Harvard University Press, 1966).

Possehl. G.L. *Ancient Cities of the Indus* (Durham, NC: Carolina Academic Press, 1979).

Possehl, G.L. (ed.) *Harappan Civilization: a Contemporary Perspective* (New Delhi: American Institute of Indian Studies, 1982).

Pye, L. *China: an introduction* (Boston: Little Brown, 1972).

Pye, L. 'Factions and the politics of guanxi: paradoxes in Chinese administrative behaviour', *The China Journal*, 34, 35–54.

Qian wen-yuan *The Great Inertia: scientific stagnation in traditional China* (London: Croom Helm, 1985).

Rabe, V.H. *The Home Base of the American China Mission, 1880–1920* (London: Harvard University Press, 1978).

Reardon-Anderson, J. *The Study of Change: Chemistry in China, 1940–1949* (Cambridge: Cambridge University Press, 1991).

Redding, S.G. 'Cognition as an aspect of culture and its relation to management processes: an exploratory view of the Chinese case', *The Journal of Management Studies*, 17, 127–48, 1980.

Reid, A. (ed.) *Sojourners and Srettlers: histories of Southeast Asia and the Chinese* (London: Allen and Unwin, 1996).

Robinson, K. *A Critical Study of Chu Tsai-yu's Contribution to the Theory of Equal Temperament in Chinese Music* (Weisbaden: Steiner, 1980).

Ronan, C.A. and Needham. J. *The Shorter Science and Civilization in China*, 2 volumes (Cambridge: Cambridge University Press, 1981).

Rosenbaum, A.L. (ed.) *State and Society in China: the consequences of reform* (Boulder: Westview, 1992).

Schurmann, F. *Ideology and Organization in Communist China* (Berkeley: University of California Press, 1966).

Schram, S.R. (ed.) *The Scope of State Power in China* (London: SOAS, 1985).

Schram, S.R. 'Decentralization in a unitary state: theory and practice, 1940–1984', in Schram, S.R. (ed.), 1985, 81–126.

Schram, S.R. *Ideology and Policy in China Since the Third Plenum, 1978–1984*, Contemporary China Institute, School of Oriental and African Studies, 1984.

Schwartz, B.I. *The World of Thought in Ancient China* (Cambridge, Mass.: Harvard University Press, 1985).

Shambaugh, D. (ed.) *American Studies of Contemporary China* (New York: Woodrow Wilson Center Press, 1993).

Shi Ji (Records of a Historian), trans. in Needham, J. *Science and Civilization in China*, volume 3 (Cambridge: Cambridge University Press, 1959).

Shue, V. 'Reorganizing rural trade: unified purchase and socialist transformation', *Modern China*, 2, 104–34.

Sjoberg, G. *The Pre-Industrial City* (London: Collier-Macmillan, 1960).

Skinner, G.W. 'Chinese peasants and the closed community: an open and shut case', *Comparative Studies in Society and History*, 13, 1971, 270–81.

Skinner, G.W. and Winckler, E.A. 'Compliance succession in rural Communist China: a cyclical theory', in Etzioni (ed.), 1969, 410–38.

Smart, A. 'Gifts, bribes and guanxi: a reconsideration of Bourdieu's social capital', *Cultural Anthropology*, 8, 1993, 388–408.

Solinger, D.J. *Chinese Business Under Socialism: the politics of domestic commerce in contemporary China* (London: University of California Press, 1984).

Solinger, D.J. 'Urban entrepreneurs and the state: the merger of state and society', in Rosenbaum (1992), 121–42.

Solla Price, D.J. de, *Science Since Babylon* (New Haven: Yale University Press, 1961).

Spence, J. *The Great Chan's Continent: China in Western Minds* (London: Allen and Unwin, 1999).

Spuler, B. (ed.) *Handbuch der Orientalisk* (Leiden: E.J. Brill, 1979).

Stafford, C. 'The discourse of race in modern China', *Man*, 28, 1989.

Sung, Yun-wing, 'Non-institutional economic integration via cultural affinity: the case of mainland China, Taiwan and Hong Kong', *Occasional Paper No. 13*, Hong Kong Institute of Asia-Pacific Studies.

Tang Tsou, 'Prolegomenon to the study of informal groups in CCP politics', *The China Quarterly*, 65, 1976, 98–114.

Tang Tsou, *The Cultural Revolution and Post-Mao Reform: a historical perspective* (Chicago: University of Chicago Press, 1986).

Thompson, L.A. *Romans and Blacks* (London: Routledge, 1989).

Toynbee, A. *A Study of History* (London: Oxford University Press, 1934–61).

Toynbee, A. *Civilization on Trial* (Oxford: Oxford University Press, 1949).

Tregear, M. *Chinese Art* (London: Thames and Hudson, 1995).

Tsuji, K., Aizawa, M. and Sasazuki, T. (eds) *HLA 1991: Proceedings of the Eleventh International Histocompatibility Workshop and Conference* (Oxford: Oxford University Press, 1992).

Unger, R.M. *Law in Modern Society: toward a criticism of social theory* (New York: Free Press, 1976).

Vats, M.S. *Excavations at Harappa*, 2 volumes (Delhi: 1941).

Veuve, S. *Fouilles d'Ai Khanoum.V1. Le gymnase: architecture, c[eac]ramique, sculpture* (Paris: Diffusion De Boccard, 1987).

Walder, A. *Communist Neo-Traditionalism, Work, and Authority in Chinese Industry* (Berkeley: University of California Press, 1986).

Waley-Cohen, J. *The Sextants of Beijing: global currents in Chinese history* (New York: Norton, 1999).

Wang Gungwu, *The Chinese Way: China's Position in International Relations*, Norwegian Nobel Institute Lecture Series, Scandinavian University Press, Oslo, 1995.

Wang Gungwu, 'Greater China and the Overseas Chinese', *The China Quarterly*, 136, 1993, 926–48.

Wang Gungwu, 'The study of Chinese identities in Southeast Asia', in Cushman and Wang (eds), 1988, 1–21.

Wang Gungwu, *Community and Nations: essays on Southeast Asia and the Chinese* (Singapore: Heinemann, 1981).

Wang Gungwu, 'The nanhai trade: a study of the early history of Chinese trade in the South China Sea', *Journal of the Malayan Branch of the Royal Asiatic Society*, 31(2), 1958.

Watson, J.L. 'Rites or beliefs? The construction of a unified culture in late imperial China', in Dittmer and Kim, 1993, 80–103.

Watts, A. *Nature, Man and Woman* (New York: Pantheon, 1958).

Wechsler, H.J. *Offerings of Jade and Silk* (New Haven: Yale University Press, 1985).

Weidenbaum, M. 'The changing pattern of the world economy – the shifting role of business and government', *Wei Lun Lecture Series IV*, Supplement 28, 20–9.

Weinstein, S. *Buddhism Under the T'ang* (Cambridge: Cambridge University Press, 1987).

Whyte, F. *China and Foreign Powers* (London: Oxford University Press, 1927).

Willmott, W.E. (ed.) *Economic Organization in Chinese Society* (Taipei: SMC Publishing, 1972).

Wilson, R.W. 'Change and continuity in Chinese cultural identity: the filial ideal and the transformation of an ethic', in Dittmer and Kim (eds), 1993.

Witek, J.W. 'Controversial ideas in China and Europe: a biography of Jean-François Foucquet, SJ, 1665–1741', *Bibliotheca Instituti Historici S.I.*, vol. 43, Rome.

Wittfogel, K. *Oriental Despotism* (New Haven: Yale University Press, 1957).

Yahuda, M. 'The foreign relations of Greater China', *The China Quarterly*, 136, 1993, 687–710.

Yahuda, M. 'How much has China learned about interdependence?', in Goodman and Segals (eds), 1997, 6–26.

Yang, M.M.H. 'The gift economy and state power in China', *Comparative Studies in Society and History*, 31, 1989, 25–54.

Yang, M.M.H. *Gifts, Favours and Banquets: the art of social relationships in China* (Ithaca: Cornell University Press, 1994).

Index

Af
M.